15th Century

17th Century

16th Cent...

...9th Century

AS THE FALCON
HER BELLS

AS THE FALCON
HER BELLS

Phillip Glasier

Lycopodium (club moss)

E. P. DUTTON & CO., INC.

NEW YORK

Contents

The author would like to thank . . .

John B. Fleming, R.S.W., M.S.I.A., who did the drawings for the end-papers, the title-page and the chapter-headings, and who went to a lot of trouble doing so.

All those people who, having had a camera thrust at them, lugged it around the hill and took photographs that the author could not take himself.

Also the Hon. Mrs Rodd, W. Angus, P. Jacklin, *Today*, Fox Photos, M.G.M. and others.

And everyone who gave advice, encouragement and assistance throughout.

Introduction

In all the practical spheres of life in which I operate I am an amateur; I am acutely conscious of this, and as a result of it I am abnormally sensitive to what is 'bogus' in the self-presentation of others. It has given me particular pleasure to be asked to write an introduction to this book, not because its author is a friend, nor because of any personal preoccupation with falconry, but because it is that extreme rarity, a book by a master craftsman about his craft. That were value enough were the work no more than a treatise, but this is Phillip Glasier's own story, showing how from boyhood his attitude to life was shaped by a passionate involvement with all living creatures around him, and its circumstances conditioned by his enduring devotion to falconry. This is one of the least 'bogus' books I have ever read; I have found it absorbing, often extremely funny, and magnificently unpretentious. In these pages I hope the reader may share some of the pleasure I have had in their author's company.

GAVIN MAXWELL

'As the ox hath his bow, sir, the horse his curb, and the falcon her bells, so man hath his desires.'
As You Like It, Act III, Scene iii

1 * As the Falcon Her Bells

Who can tell the precise moment he falls in love? Surely it is a thing that grows, sometimes springing up mushroom-like overnight, or imperceptibly like full bloom from bud.

It is nearly forty years since I saw my first falcon, and now I cannot remember when it became my ambition to own, and train one myself.

For a long time they have been an integral part of my life, bringing me joy and sorrow, excitement and disappointment. The sight of a falcon never fails to quicken my senses and to give me a certain feeling of affinity with them.

Outside the window, under the apple trees on the lawn, sits one now. At the moment she is tied by her leash to a block of neatly turned wood. She has had her morning bath and is sitting, wings and tail spread, letting the sun, as it filters through the leaves, dry her feathers. Soon she will preen herself, not out of vanity, but so that, when she is flown presently, her plumage will be in readiness.

I have had her for some fifteen months, taking her myself from her cliff-ledge eyrie in the north of Scotland. She was then about a month old and not quite able to fly. I have manned her and trained her and attended as best I know to her wants, and in her turn she has rewarded me.

She has finished preening now, and sits on her block waiting patiently, her long wings crossed, a bloom on her back like that on an untouched plum. Each primary overlaps its fellow in a perfection of streamlining that no man-made thing can ever equal.

Her dark eyes take in every movement, from the pointers on the lawn, yawning aloud their boredom, to a wild buzzard wheeling high up over the distant larch wood. Her flank feathers puffed out, one yellow foot drawn up underneath, even in so static a position she is a pleasure to look at.

But it is later on, when I fly her free of all encumbrances except for her jesses – the leather straps round her legs – and bells, that there comes the full appreciation of her power and beauty.

Strapping on my lure-bag and taking glove and hood, all tools of my trade as a professional falconer, I go to pick her up. The pointers, their boredom vanished, show their excitement by bounding towards me. The falcon too knows what is in the wind, jumps eagerly to my outstretched glove and lets me hood her.

Away on the hill we go quietly about our business. Leash and swivel are removed from the falcon's jesses, and the dogs need no encouragement to range over the heather in search of the grouse that live in this open, almost treeless, moorland.

We skirt the edge of the lochan, bright and blue as a new pair of jeans, and, as we climb slowly up to the height of land past the ruins of some crofts, the older dog comes suddenly on a point.

There is no need for haste. She will stay there, if necessary, for half an hour or more, her mouth open slightly, sucking in the scent of whatever is in front of her. Her tail quivers, though, and tells me that either a blue-hare or one of the few surviving rabbits is not far off. If she were pointing grouse her tail would be still. Neither of these would interest the falcon, so the young dog is called to heel lest she give chase in youthful exuberance, and the old dog is sent in to flush. Sure enough, up gets a blue-hare and goes off uphill in that curious hop, skip and jump that is its natural gait. It stops on the skyline, sitting up on its hind legs to get a better look at us, and, deciding that discretion is the better part of valour, disappears over the top.

The two dogs continue their quartering of the ground, both, I am pleased to see, ignoring the hare's scent.

We reach the outcrop of rock on the top, add another stone to the cairn there, and pause for a spell to get our breath back.

In the distance the Firth sparkles in the sun and the hills beyond are clear and sharp-cut against the sky. The tide is nearly full and will be washing the seals off the sandbanks where they have been basking, and bringing in with it the fish for them to hunt.

A raven croaks his way along the tops, searching for possible food, a dead sheep if he is lucky, or perhaps only the scanty remains of a hen-harrier's kill.

Often I have been asked what it is that appeals to me in these dull, monotonous, empty tracts of land. To me, though, they are none of these things. There is wild life everywhere, and if only people would bother to use their eyes they would find more colour and beauty in the lichens on the rocks than in the holiday camps to which they flock. Perhaps it is just as well that they do not bother, or the hill would look like Brighton beach on a bank holiday.

The dogs are pointing again, one backing the other, honouring its partner as it should. The wind is too slight today to make any difference to the falcon which way the grouse are flushed, so once we have got within a hundred yards or so of the dogs I unhood her and cast her off.

In spite of the sudden change from the darkness of her hood to the glare of full sunlight, she is able to adjust her sight at once. Watch her swing round, gaining height at each circle she completes, making full use of the unseen air currents. Against the sky she looks black, her wings shaped like a full-drawn bow. She has learned from experience that she must go high and when she has reached her pitch she glides, wings outstretched, her wingtips bending and whipping with the pressure, her head turned to look down at the dogs two or three hundred feet below her.

She doesn't hang in the air hovering like a mousing kestrel, but turns easily in tight rings, waiting for me to send the dogs in to flush the grouse. She cannot see them at all, for they are hidden in the heather somewhere upwind of the pointers, but she knows as well as I do that they are there.

Watch very closely now, for this is the moment that all of us, falcon, dogs and falconer, have worked and waited for.

As the dogs go in at command the grouse spring like magic from the heather, where, a moment before, there was no sign of them. Coloured, but for the silvery undersides of their wings, like the heather and lichens among which they live, they speed away across the moor, flying low, following the contours.

In level flight they are nearly as fast as the falcon, and it would take her a mile or more to overhaul them. But from her pitch she has the advantage.

She sees them and turns suddenly, with effortless grace, stooping earthwards. Her wings nearly closed, she hurtles down, the gap between falcon and grouse closing with astonishing rapidity.

If you are close enough to hear it, the wind tears through her pinions, making a rushing sound so curious that once heard it is rarely forgotten. Her bells, pushed against her legs, cannot ring, but you can hear the air whining through the slots in them.

The grouse she has chosen is an old cock, full of the guile and cunning that life in such surroundings has given him and his kind. To my way of thinking he is far craftier than the hoodie crow or the raven, who have fewer enemies on the hill.

Doubtless he has met peregrines before and knows exactly what he must do, for, at the vital moment, he drops suddenly, diving into some long heather that he knew from the start was waiting to give him safety, and for which he has been making as fast as his wings could carry him. The falcon, a split second before she seems bound to destroy herself against the ground, shoots over his refuge and throws up without a wing beat, nearly to her original height. As she climbs she turns her head and looks down over her back. Regaining her pitch once more, she waits on.

She has shown us what we wanted to see, her powers of flight full stretched. Her failure to kill is unimportant, for there are other grouse and other days.

'As the ox hath his bow, sir, the horse his curb, and the falcon her bells, so man hath his desires.'

For me there is an added pleasure, for nothing but the training she has received at my hands stops her from returning to the wild if she is so inclined. Without any assistance from man or dog she could now fend for herself. But her training, and – though many may scoff at this – also a certain affection for me, will bring her back. If this last were not so, then why should she come, at times from out of sight over the hill, and sit beside me, with no lure being shown to entice her?

2 * Introduction to 'Unk'

I still retain a few hazy memories of the house in Wimbledon where I was born: my mother taking a swarm of bees in the garden while we, told to stay indoors out of harm's way, watched from the french windows, our noses pressed against the panes, fogging them with our breath; a droopy-eared, floppy-legged, errant blood-hound, that strayed one day into our drive; the spider-tree on the Common, its roots spreading out from the trunk, daylight show-ing beneath them, for the feet of countless children had scuffed away the earth in clambering around it and made it look like the legs of a spider.

One very vivid recollection: standing by the old horse-pond watching a red squirrel starting to cross the road. A heavy lorry came rumbling towards it, and I suppose that the noise and vibration frightened it, causing it to stop and hesitate for an instant. It ran, turning back to safety just too late.

Why this scene should remain so clear to me I don't know. Possibly I shared its fear and was willing it to escape, in the same way that one rises from one's seat to urge on the horse of one's choice. Moments of fear tend to linger in the memory when lesser emotions are forgotten.

The house we lived in is pulled down now, the grey squirrel has taken the place of the red, and the spider-tree has gone too. Only the old horse-pond is still there, but now no horses splash their way into it, stop to drink, and heave their rumbling cart out at the far side to continue their journey. The local Council with its over-tidy mind has eradicated the track leading to it and implanted a concrete kerb along the roadside so high that a horse would have difficulty in pulling a cart over such an obstacle. The trace-horse that stood by his post at the bottom of Putney Hill, in readiness to help his kind pull their heavy loads to the top, has gone too.

Shortly after my mother's death, when I was about five, my father, with my sister and myself, moved from our house in Wimbledon to Kent. My father, though kind and generous in many ways, was a stern disciplinarian and a firm believer in children being seen and not heard; not seen much either, for my sister, several years older than myself, and I were both made to keep severely to our allotted quarters at the back of the house. To use the front stairs was a terrible crime.

On Sundays, for the good of our souls, escorted by our governess, we would walk some three miles to church and back. It wasn't so much the long, weary walk towards a boring, yawn-stifling, sit-still-and-keep-quiet, hour-long service that riled me so. It was the sight of my father, on those rare occasions when he attended church, as he passed us in the car, sitting in state, driven by my stepmother.

When this occurred I spent the whole of the service wondering whether we would be allowed to drive home in comfort or have to toil back on foot, to be passed once more by the car. It certainly kept us fit but I doubt if it did our souls much good.

Apart from playing golf and shooting occasionally, my father had few hobbies. He rarely used his hands; to mend a fuse was quite beyond him and, although he always held a current driving-licence, I can recall his driving only once. My stepmother being unwell, he drove himself to Knole, where he was agent, and hit the main gate. I don't think he ever drove again.

As his office was in London and his work took him around the country to see the various estates he managed, he was away a good deal of the time. On Sundays, as a treat, we would have lunch in the dining-room instead of in our schoolroom. It never seemed much of a treat to me but such an ordeal that I was only too glad when it came to an end and we were dismissed.

At Christmas-time he would relax discipline, the house would be filled with guests, and we would join in the gaiety. Large crates of Christmas fare would arrive from London and we were allowed to assist in unpacking them. The sideboard in the panelled dining-room would be filled with little silver dishes of sweets and chocolates, boxes of crystallized fruits, jars of ginger, bottles of Carlsbad plums, and various other delicacies, including a large pineapple. We always had a sweepstake on the number of its leaves.

On Christmas night friends and relatives would arrive, among them my step-uncle, Captain Charles Knight, and after dinner by candle-light at the gleaming mahogany table, we would all troop into the drawing-room and cluster round the piano to sing. On Boxing night we would have dinner at my uncle's house and play charades afterwards.

In one of these charades my uncle appeared dressed as the fairy queen complete with magic wand. We laughed so much it hurt, and every time we managed to stop he would wave his wand and endeavour to make his seventeen stone look as fairy-like as possible. This set us all roaring again, and his moustache made it seem even funnier.

In the same charade, Robert, one of my cousins, excelled himself by taking a swig of liquid furniture-polish from a bottle which he thought held water.

Once the festivities were over, discipline was resumed, and as I grew up I somewhat naturally spent more and more time at my uncle's house. My father and I had little in common and being somewhat of a rebel I found my uncle's easy-going ways, as well as his interests, far more to my liking. He lived, like us, a few miles out of Sevenoaks, and his home was only some five minutes' walk from our house. Here I was introduced to my first trained falcon.

My uncle had always been interested in birds and was a keen photographer. During the First World War he had joined the Royal West Kent Regiment and was for a time a sniper, for he was an excellent rifle shot. As 'Sniper Knight' he used the ruins of an old barn for a firing-post, and the efforts of some swallows to rear a family there led him to photograph them, for their reluctance to leave their old home in spite of the frequent shelling seemed to him worth recording.

What amazed him even more was hearing a golden oriole singing in an oak wood in no-man's-land, and in his excitement he temporarily forgot the war and photographed its nest.

'In that he did, on the day and date stated, contrary to King's Rules and Regulations and to the prejudice of good order and military discipline, leave his post and unnecessarily endanger his life, in order to photograph a bird's nest, sir'; that would have been a charge far more noteworthy than the one against the Finn being drunk in command of a reindeer and sledge.

Later on he was commissioned and, after being gassed, went to the United States as a captain in the Honourable Artillery Company, in charge of a demonstration drill team. There his parade-ground voice, which used to terrify me so much, later on, stood him in good stead.

After the war he worked for a while for a tobacconist in the City, a job which he detested intensely. Finding a ready sale for his photographs and articles on birds, he bought an old Newman-Sinclair cine-camera and made his first film, 'Wild Life in the Tree-tops'. He lectured with this film and with lantern slides to schools and similar bodies, and wrote his first book on the subject.

Falconry was his main hobby, and there was invariably a falcon or hawk of some sort to be seen in his garden. In fact on Armistice Day itself he had rescued, and later on trained, a kestrel winged by a shooting-party.

He kept other birds too, among them a raven that delighted in tweaking the dog's tail when it was asleep and could bark exactly like the dog too, and a tame shelduckling that would come running across the lawn when one called 'Puddley, Puddley, Puddley' to it.

Why Unk, as I called him, put up with me, I cannot imagine, for he never 'suffered fools gladly', and I must have been a damned nuisance to him at first. I tagged after him like a puppy trying hard not to do the wrong thing, and wagging my metaphorical tail if I won any praise.

For a long time praise rarely came my way, for he was extremely critical and never hesitated to quote his grandfather's favourite expression, 'I don't mind ignorance but I cannot stand crass stupidity.'

For him I was quite prepared to go through fire and water if need be, and my bare legs certainly suffered in his cause when I waded through the stingiest of nettle-beds and the scratchiest of bramble patches in order to push out a rabbit for one of his hawks to fly at.

Going with him on these hawking expeditions soon became my greatest delight, and in due course he taught me how to train both hawks and falcons.

His methods were basically much the same as those used when falconry started some four thousand years ago. For in spite of all our modern inventions it has changed comparatively little over the centuries. When or where the first hawk was trained will never be known, but presents of falcons were made to the princes of the H'ia dynasty in China in 2000 B.C. There is a bas relief of a falconer in the ruined city of Khorsabad dated about 1700 B.C.; presumably falconry spread westwards through India, Arabia and Persia. Indeed a somewhat violent Persian king is said to have become 'a better and a wiser sovereign' by training and observing the good qualities of a falcon.

I learnt from Unk that the falcons must never be kept in cages or they would break their flight feathers and so become useless for flying. Instead they must be kept tied by a leash, each to its own perch, set in the lawn on fine days or under shelter when the weather is bad.

Short strips of leather called jesses were attached, one to each leg, and these were connected to the leash by a swivel in order to prevent them twisting. On each leg they wore a small brass bell, obtained either from Holland or India. The sound of these bells carried a long way and helped one to find a hawk that was out of sight in cover.

Falcons were hooded when travelling or when another was being flown, in order to curb their restive nature. The hood also helped in training them, stopping them from becoming frightened at strange sights. Hence the word 'hoodwinked', for the falcon is fooled into thinking it is night and so keeps quiet.

The hawks, on the other hand, were rarely hooded, for their entirely different temperament did not require it. Though nervous and moody at times, they soon got used to the rattle and bustle of everyday life and became very tame. They were sprinters, rarely flying more than two or three hundred yards at a time, their short wings enabling them to follow closely every twist and turn of their prey, even in the thick woodland where the long-winged falcons would have been quite useless.

Their dash-and-grab methods were very exciting to watch, but they lacked the dramatic dive from a height of the falcons, which had first to climb above their quarry and beat it in the air before

B

they could put in those breath-taking stoops that have so delighted and thrilled mankind. It is this high flying and spectacular stooping that made falconry not only a means of providing food for the larder, but a sport.

Although we could exercise the falcons in Montreal Park just across the road from Unk's house, we had to take them to more open country than the wooded area that surrounded us locally in order to fly them successfully at wild quarry: rooks, crows and the like.

We would load up the ancient Austin, the falcons sitting on a specially contrived perch in the dicky, and go along the Pilgrim's Way or down to the marshes around the Hundred of Hoo or the Isle of Grain. Sometimes on to Sheppey, where we would have a drink at lunch-time at the World's End pub. It certainly seemed like the world's end then, for it stood on the bank of the Swale at the far end of the island, with nothing but flat marshland stretching for some miles all around it. Sheep and cattle and the occasional farm-hand were about the only living things there apart from the wild birds.

On our way to these places we would stop at Ightham or Cobham and buy our lunch: a new loaf, cheese and butter, and a cucumber. This Unk would eat as one does a banana, after first giving me a share.

If we had four or five flights at rooks we were well satisfied, and I soon learnt that the object of the sport was to see the falcons fly; for, compared with shooting, they kill very little and the day's pleasure is not measured by the size of the bag.

There is more enjoyment from it too, because you see birds and animals that the noise of a gun would have scared off long before.

In 1924, when the Pageant of Empire was produced at Wembley Stadium, my uncle, dressed in the costume of Henry VIII's time, gave a display of falconry in the arena. He used both peregrines and merlins, flying them loose and stooping them to the lure in front of huge audiences; and, although there were one or two occasions when he thought he might lose one, they all behaved properly and flew as though the thousands of onlookers did not exist. When this was first proposed one of the greatest authorities on falconry considered it would be impossible to expect the falcons to do more than fly a few yards.

I was taken to see one of these performances, and both merlins and falcons went up higher than the roof of the vast stadium and put on a magnificent show. But very few of the audience can have realized what an achievement this was.

From April to August the hawks were not flown but left to moult, and then we concentrated on finding nests and other suitable material for my uncle's films. Down at Baker's Farm, at Allhallows, we would hunt through the Norrard wood, where there was a large heronry. Here shelduck nested under the brambles among the bluebells, instead of in their more normal sites down rabbit-holes or in hollow trees.

Below the Norrard, in the marshes, there were plover, snipe, redshank and other birds. Baker, who not only farmed the land but also acted as gamekeeper, used to keep a freshly-cut hazel stick by the gate at the entrance to the wood. Any trespassers going that way could never resist taking the stick, and if it had gone then he knew someone was there without permission.

Mallard too nested there, and sometimes we would find them sharing a nest with a shelduck. A hen pheasant once joined in too, and there was an Easter jumble of eggs of different sizes and colours; we wondered if they took it in turns to keep the eggs warm.

Unk was unsurpassed at tree-climbing and was rarely forced to admit defeat. Hand- and toe-holds seemed to sprout in the most useful places as he climbed, and the filmiest of branches would support his by no means inconsiderable weight.

I did my feeble best and, going up an ivy-clad willow one day, I found a mallard's nest some twenty-odd feet from the ground. I wondered how the ducklings would get down safely, for they leave the nest within a day of hatching, long before they have grown any feathers to fly with. But they are so light that they fall like thistledown and rarely hurt themselves.

We never seemed to have a day without finding something of new interest: baby moles all pink and wrinkled, or a young stoat, its thick scruff like the hogged mane of a horse; a moorhen, caught unawares in one of the fleets that drained the marsh, would dive, swimming under water, looking quite silvery with the air bubbles clinging to it; a Dartford warbler's nest in a gorse bush; all this sort of thing Unk showed me and so aroused my thirst for knowledge and made these expeditions full of enjoyment.

I learnt how to use both still and movie cameras and assisted in the building of hides from which to film the birds and animals we had found.

Unk's success with his film 'Wild Life in the Tree-tops' provided both incentive and money for his next venture, which was to film golden eagles in Scotland, a thing he had long dreamt of doing. At first everything went wrong and it seemed he was never going to succeed. Eggs in one eagle's eyrie turned out to be addled and never hatched. In another eyrie the birds deserted, and on top of all these disappointments came the General Strike.

During one of the periods of waiting for better news, Unk filmed the nest of a golden-crested wren, for he thought that, as this was the smallest British bird, it would make a good contrast to the golden eagles. My cousin Robert and I both helped, and, while Unk was filming in the hide, Robert and I walked down to a near-by lake to see if we could find anything else of interest.

Suddenly I heard him yelp and saw him run up the hill, where he sat down and pulled off one of his gum-boots. Joining him, I asked what was wrong and was told he had put his foot in a wasps' nest. The wasps had, of course, objected and chased him up the hill and stung him. What greatly amused us, though, was that he had pulled off the wrong boot, for when he removed the second one, there was the wasp in a very bad state of repair.

In spite of all these setbacks, Unk finally succeeded in making an extremely good film of the golden eagles. When it was finished it was shown at the Polytechnic Theatre in Regent Street, where it broke all previous records by running for fifteen weeks.

On his return from Scotland he brought back with him a young eagle to train. This bird was a female, called Grampian; she would have been shot by the keepers if he had not taken her, as they considered that the two old parent birds were killing quite enough grouse and they did not want the young bird doing the same.

With a wing-spread of over six feet she was a magnificent bird, but she was so heavy to carry that Unk had to have a special wooden support made for his arm.

He trained her in much the same way as the hawks and she got tame very quickly and duly learnt to fly to the lure, but she had a dangerous habit of snatching with her feet, and, as an eagle's grip is extremely powerful, Unk decided that he would wear a fencing mask as a precaution.

When he left this off one day, because he thought it would look rather cowardly in the slow-motion pictures being taken of her in flight, she seized the opportunity and caught him by the face. This necessitated three stitches, and he had a hole in one ear as well. He was very annoyed, not because of the damage from the eagle, but because the camera operator had gone to his assistance. 'Why didn't the silly fool go on shooting?' he said. 'He missed filming a real scoop, an eagle attacking a man.'

What did worry him, however, was the thought that Grampian might attack someone else, a lady in a fur coat or a child with a teddy bear; so he decided to let her go back to the wild, in a part of Scotland where she would be unmolested.

I once saw a goshawk, a considerably less powerful bird than an eagle, grab its owner's hand with one foot. As the other foot was still holding his gloved hand, he was as good as handcuffed, and completely unable to do anything to free himself. It required all my strength to pull out the two strongest talons, the back and inner ones, in order to release him.

Very few hawks do this sort of thing unless they have been handled incorrectly, but eagles, especially females, do seem rather prone to it.

The following year Unk heard that the Duke of Sutherland had presented two young eagles to the London Zoo and he got permission to have one of them. He chose the female, but Grampian II was as bad as her namesake and so was soon exchanged for her brother.

He proved far more tractable than his sister and became known as Mr Ramshaw, for my uncle's small daughter Jean thought he looked like a friend of that name. Mr Ramshaw became famous and went all over the world with Unk on expeditions and lecture-tours and lived for thirty-one years.

In the next film Unk made he decided that 'just birds' was not good enough, and he endeavoured to avoid boring his audiences by filming a day's hawking in the time of Henry VIII. Henry was a very keen falconer, and the course of history might well have been changed had not one of his falconers saved him from a somewhat muddy end. As the alliterative story goes, Henry, while hawking at Hitchin in Herts, attempted to jump a ditch and, when his pole broke under the strain, fell head first in the mud.

My father got permission for us to use parts of Knole as a suitable setting. Relatives and friends, together with their dogs and horses, were all press-ganged into helping; for Unk was extremely good at turning to good use anyone or anything that might further his plans.

My cousin, Esmond Knight, then at the start of his stage and film career, was roped in to play the hero, and his actress wife, Frances Clare, agreed to join the cast as one of the court ladies.

Our old dog Pip, an animal of uncertain ancestry, was added to the somewhat motley collection of canine extras.

As the old programme puts it 'the main characters were supported by a cast of native gipsies and country cousins'.

I was given the role of cadge-boy and, dressed in costume, with the tops of my gumboots turned down to look like riding-boots, I carried the cadge. This is a light wooden frame on which a number of falcons can be carried in the field. This had to be done very carefully, for there were two stuffed hawks among the live ones, in order to make up the numbers suitable for a royal hawking-party, and these stuffed ones were liable to fall over and remain in a state of levitation if I jolted the cadge.

A great many British sovereigns have shown their interest in falconry. In A.D. 750 King Ethelbald sent to Archbishop Boniface of Mayence for some falcons to catch cranes. Alfred the Great, Edward III, James IV of Scotland, Elizabeth and James I were all noted for their enjoyment of the sport.

Harold is depicted in the Bayeux tapestry carrying a hawk. The Empress Catherine II of Russia flew merlins, but history relates that Peter the Great was too 'busily engaged in occupations of a very different kind' to take much interest in falconry.

We filmed one week-end when the cast was free of its more normal occupations, and, when all were dressed in costume and assembled, it was quite an impressive gathering.

Unk produced, directed and filmed, and once again his parade-ground voice came in useful, making a film director's megaphone quite unnecessary. Of course, with the majority of the cast complete amateurs, plenty of things went wrong; some of the riders had never been on a horse before, and some of the horses objected to having on their backs anyone holding a falcon. The dogs did their best to steal the show by disagreeing at a tenderly romantic moment.

With very few retakes, and by judicious cutting and editing, the finished film ran smoothly and showed none of these troubles.

But Unk was still not satisfied that the film would be lively enough for non-bird-minded members of the audience, and decided to add a further diversion. This consisted of a burlesque, set in Dickens's time, of an eagle carrying off the squire's daughter to its eyrie on a vast cliff overlooking the village, where the annual fair was in progress.

Dickens costumes were used simply because there was a Dickens fête about to take place locally, and Unk saw that he could fit it into the story and save a lot of additional work.

The film was entitled 'The Sweeper of the Skies', and was full of slapstick comedy and melodrama. Mr Ramshaw, of course, played the villainous eagle, and Jean the squire's daughter, and once again the rest of us were called in to help.

The whole thing involved a great deal of faking and trick camera work. The aerial view of the village was achieved by using toy houses, the ploughed fields were of sifted earth with the imprint of corrugated card upon it. Parsley and moss made trees and bushes, and the vast cliff was a rock about three feet high. An upturned dustbin-lid, its edges carefully concealed, made a lake, and in the finished film it all looked very realistic.

A dummy child was made for Mr Ramshaw to carry. This had to be very light, for Ramshaw himself only weighed about eight pounds and could not have carried anything as heavy as a real child (quite apart from the fact that people do not usually leave their children lying about, as the legends would have one believe).

We built the eagle's eyrie in a near-by sand quarry, on a suitable-looking ledge. The dummy child was attached to Ramshaw's feet and we filmed him arriving at the nest with it. We took some still photographs at the same time, so that, by following these closely, we were able to position the real child in exactly the same way as the dummy. This worked so well that it was impossible to see the change-over when the film was done. It all took an immense amount of time and trouble, but we had a great deal of fun doing it.

To portray the consternation of the villagers when the eagle carried off the child, we filmed short sketches of their reactions. Mother, mixing some batter, sees the eagle, flings her arms up, and of course the mixture goes straight into someone's face. The lady artist, painting a peaceful pastoral scene, falls backwards off her stool into the lake. Her two admirers rush to the rescue in a boat, and in their frantic endeavours to save her, end up in the water themselves.

The naturalist, coming out of the pub in a somewhat sozzled condition, focuses his telescope on the eagle and rushes off up the street to give the warning.

I played this latter part and felt very self-conscious about it, for it was done in front of the usual crowd of onlookers who invariably gather whenever a movie camera is set up and to whom, not knowing the story, I must have appeared slightly eccentric. The telescope was made from old brass shell-cases and bent so much it appeared to look round corners. The running part was filmed at a very slow speed, so that when it was projected I fairly tore up the street.

Esmond, as the hero, had to climb the cliff and rescue the child from the Sweeper of the Skies. We built this cliff out in the park on the skyline. It was done on the horizontal, with large rocks, and in order to make it appear vertical, or slightly more so, the camera was tilted on its side.

Ramshaw had to attack Esmond when he was half-way up the cliff, and a desperate struggle was to be fought.

We got an old hood, removed the plume, painted large ferocious eyes on the outside of it, and put it on Ramshaw to make him look more evil. Esmond was well padded with cushions under his trousers to prevent Ramshaw's talons from digging into him, and Ramshaw was gently thrown onto Esmond's backside from out of picture.

I was acting as camera-man, crouching under it to work the controls. I was roaring with laughter at Esmond and Ramshaw in their mock battle, while Unk was cursing me hard at the same time in case I shook the tripod. However, all went well. Ramshaw landed on target; Esmond, trying hard to look as if he were about to fall to his death several hundred feet below instead of actually crawling along on his stomach, seized a small tree, placed there for the purpose, and, plucking it out of the cliff with the usual hero's superhuman strength, pushed Ramshaw off and rescued the child.

He was rewarded on the spot with a bag of golden sovereigns, which the squire naturally kept handy in his coat-tails. All ended happily, with the hero marrying the belle of the village.

The first time it was shown a great many of the audience, not, I suppose, so critical in those days, tended to take it too seriously and even gasped with horror when the eagle carried off his victim. All this in spite of Esmond appearing in three different sorts of trousers on his perilous climb up the cliff. So we had to add a debunking scene in order to disillusion them.

The rest of the film, entitled 'Monarchs of the Air', was serious film-work of wild peregrines, buzzards, and other birds, beautifully taken and interspersed with very amusing sketches drawn by Unk.

There was no sound-track as Unk always talked with the film from the side of the stage, an idea which not only cut the cost of making the film but also allowed him to vary his talk to suit his audience. It would certainly have made it much more difficult if there had been sound, for Unk not only gave instructions while filming but frequently made it quite clear to his cast if things went wrong.

Background music was provided by gramophone records, but they were not quite so loud and intrusive as so much of the present-day musical accompaniment tends to be. Bach's 'Toccata and Fugue' was used for the Sweeper of the Skies story, and I still have that particular record, badly scored and scratched by its much travelled life but still playable; and, as music so often does, it brings it all back to me when I hear it. The only other sound effects were a hunting horn and a 'panger'. The horn was blown off-stage when the royal hawking party set off from Knole. The 'panger' was rather like one half of a pair of cymbals crossed with a tin hat. It was beaten with a gong stick, slowly at first and then, as the Sweeper of the Skies drew closer to his victim, faster, until at the crucial moment as the eagle struck, it was smitten as hard as possible. The noise was not only awe-inspiring but deafening in the extreme to the musician.

I assisted Unk with the editing and cutting, working the splicer, making out identity tags for the dozens of short lengths of film that snaked and twined their coils all over his desk. We would discuss it at great length, running it through time and time again, on a chattering, chain-driven old projector that was turned by hand.

As he hated being interrupted when doing this sort of thing it became part of my job to answer the telephone. Because, I suppose, of my close association with him, I became able to imitate his voice. I got so good at this that even his own sister, my stepmother, was unable to tell the difference. In fact she refused at first to believe it and even when we spoke alternative sentences she failed to recognize who was who.

This led to some very amusing situations, for once I had started talking I had to work out the replies that I thought Unk would have made himself. I kept an eye on him so that he could shake his head if I went wrong and I then did my best to retrieve the situation.

At times my task of answering the phone proved to be to my own advantage, for if my stepmother rang up to ask why I was late for a meal at home, I simply pretended to be my uncle and, having made, with due apology, all the most valid excuses I could muster, would then leap onto my bicycle and pedal frantically home.

One day a friend of Unk's rang up and in the course of our conversation told me that she had a bag of cob-nuts for him. As I was very fond of cobs, I told her to send them to Phillip (myself) as I (Unk) would be away for a few days. The nuts duly arrived at home and when, some weeks later, the friend came down to see Unk, we told her how she had been fooled. At first she was very indignant at being had in this way, but she joined in our laughter finally, though not before I had given a demonstration from a near-by call-box.

Years later, after the Second World War, I rang up an old mutual friend of ours and when he heard my voice he was sure it was my uncle speaking.

So, sharing interests, and even voices, brought Unk and me very much together, and his house seemed far more of a home to me than did my own.

3 * It Looks so Easy

Try to use an adze, a tool rarely used nowadays except by wheel- and ship-wrights. Of all implements, I think this is the one that holds the most surprises for the uninitiated. It doesn't look anything out of the ordinary, and a skilled man has no trouble in taking the thinnest of wood shavings off the bow of a boat. Wield it yourself. It at once becomes the most awkward-shaped thing you ever handled, and you find yourself so cackhanded that it appears to harbour a malevolent demon, who takes charge in as fiendish a way as possible the instant a novice picks it up.

Much the same applies to falconry. It looks so easy. Any fool, you think, could feed a falcon on the fist. She just sits there eating, and when she's finished you pop the hood on. Nothing could be more simple – until you try it.

Many years ago, when we were flying falcons on Salisbury Plain, an old, retired professional falconer came over to see them. At the end of the day we asked him to feed one up. The old falconer made himself comfortable on an upturned barrel, placing himself so that the light fell on the meat and no one could pass behind him to disturb the falcon while she was feeding. Not until he was quite ready did he unhood her and let her feed. The whole time she was feeding there wasn't a flap of her wings, or a foot shifted, to show she was unbalanced or worried in any way. There is a Suffolk word, 'suent', that is used to describe anything that runs easily and sweetly, like a well-greased cart-wheel, or applied to things done without fuss or bother. Gently and suently, he gave help when she needed it. Otherwise he left her to herself.

When she had finished he wiped her beak, and let her pick up the small morsels of meat left clinging to her toes, and on the glove.

Then, when she had shaken herself, he hooded her. To the layman he was just a white-haired, weather-beaten old man feeding a falcon. To those of us who could, from past experience, appreciate his skill, it was obvious that he had fed falcons, many, many times before. He had anticipated all the possible troubles, so beautifully handling the falcon that she never had a moment of anxiety. One felt like applauding him.

I was most fortunate in having my uncle to teach me falconry. Most beginners have to learn from books, a pretty impossible task, for as yet there has been no book written that is fully detailed enough to cover all the problems likely to face the learner. To be able to see a falcon handled and flown, even if only for a day, is a great help, but to have a willing expert permanently on the spot was of inestimable value.

He was not a particularly patient instructor, and once he had shown me how to do something he expected me to be able to do it perfectly, having forgotten that there was a time when he himself did not have the know-how.

Teaching me to tie a falconer's knot, I can remember him saying, somewhat testily, 'For heaven's sake, boy, it's quite simple: over, under, round and through. Anyone can do it, I should have thought. Must be something wrong with you.'

Bit by bit I learnt, and in due course became reasonably useful to him, and eventually he considered me proficient enough to handle a completely untrained falcon.

As wild as a hawk: it is a common enough phrase, but few of those who use it can really understand what it means. Even now, after training so many, their initial wildness still surprises me, as does the swiftness with which their whole attitude suddenly changes towards humans once they learn no harm is meant.

A beginner usually starts with a kestrel or a merlin. Being so small, they are easier to manage, and their disposition is more friendly from the start. However, I had already gained a certain amount of experience from helping him with trained birds, and this particular year we didn't have anything except two large peregrines. At least they seemed very large to me.

They were both falcons, females that is, and they came in a

hamper from a keeper in Ireland. On their arrival they were turned loose in an empty shed, specially prepared for them. We had spread peat over the floor and the windows were barred with bamboo rods, placed vertically so that they could not cling to them and break any feathers. They had perches to sit on, a bath, and as much food as they could eat. They ate an enormous amount too, for they were growing fast and, although hardly four weeks old, were already nearly as big as an adult bird.

They still had a lot of the white down with which they are covered when first hatched poking out from their new feathers. The little wispy bits clinging to the top of their heads made them look very babyish. Their tails were only about two-thirds grown, and the long primaries had blue-coloured blood sheaths showing still. Until these flight feathers were full length and the quills hardened off they were to remain in the mews. Their feet were not yet the bright yellow colour of an older bird and still seemed too big for them. Their long toes – once called petty singles – stuck out in front of them and looked very odd.

At this stage of their life they were left alone to eat, sleep, preen, or do whatever they wished. Unk allowed no one except himself to go into the shed, and only when it was dark did he take in their food, remove any stale pieces left uneaten, and replenish the bath. For they might, if they once associated him with food, start screaming at the sight of him, as they do when their parents bring food to the eyrie. This can easily develop into a habit that is impossible to break, and a real screamer is something to be avoided at all costs. It will scream all day long with a monotonous, rasping, screech that you think would give it a sore throat in no time and certainly gives you a headache with its incessant, nerve-jangling clamour. Unk had arranged a peep-hole in the door so that we could see how they were getting on without their seeing us, but he discouraged its frequent use.

While they were in the mews growing, I helped him film some young herons he had brought back from the heronry in the oak wood at Allhallows. They were amusing birds. At certain angles they looked very like their reptilian ancestors, almost like some prehistoric pterodactyl.

They were free to wander all over the park and, as they grew older, found their way to the lakes, where they spent most of the day looking for eels or frogs, standing motionless in the water, their bright yellow eyes glinting, or stalking in slow-motion through the rushes at the edge. Every so often they would make a sharp jab with their ready-poised beaks. Sometimes they were successful, and their heads would reappear holding some wriggling unfortunate in their beaks before they gulped it down with evident relish.

When feeding time drew near they would come flying gracefully back, their long legs trailing behind them, their necks tucked up between their shoulders. They would land a few yards away and come rushing up, squarking for their food. This was a delicious mixture of minced-up chickens' heads, rabbits' guts, fish scraps, and poultry meal. At least they thought it delicious, to judge by the speed with which they gobbled it down their long necks, so fast they could hardly have had time to taste it. As they continued to squark while they swallowed, it sounded as though they were being strangled. Each heron thought his neighbour was getting better and bigger pieces, and they quarrelled, jabbing with their long beaks, flapping their enormous wings, and trying to snatch from one another.

When the last bit had vanished, visible only as a rapidly descending bulge in their gullets, the noise subsided as they settled to digest in a satiated stupor.

One of them was continually landing on the roof of a neighbouring house. Possibly he thought he made a good weathercock, but it ended in a broken leg. He looked very dejected when we retrieved him, but Unk put him in splints and he went off frog-hunting, splints and all, dignity soon recovered.

The eyass falcons grew fast, and soon Unk decided they were ready to start their training. He routed out some suitable leather for making jesses and laid out everything all ready. The jesses are put on to the falcon's legs by means of a cunning arrangement of slots cut in the leather, and I was made to practise putting them on a pencil, so that I should know how to do it when the time came. At least, that was the idea. We waited till dark before picking them up, as then they would not crash around in the shed. We slipped in quietly and flashed a torch momentarily to see on which perch they were sitting. Unk picked up one of them in the dark and brought her indoors. I slipped a hood on her while he held her with her feet on an old cushion to give her something to grip.

She gripped all right, but the trouble was that she didn't stay gripping the same place, and I was faced with a hissing, snatching falcon who shifted her feet just when I had got one of her jesses half on. The jess would then slip off and I would have to start all over again, getting more and more dithery in my anxiety to do the job properly before Unk's comments became too caustic and at the same time trying to avoid the clutching, grasping, great feet, whose talons I could see were making large holes in the cushion and would undoubtedly be just as happy making some in me. Finally I got the jesses on and, attaching the leash and swivel, I stood back while Unk released her.

She stood up and tried hard to scratch her hood off, but after a short while gave this up and quietened down. He took her on his glove and made her step back onto the arm of the sofa, where we left her while we jessed up her sister. Hooded falcons will always step back onto something if the backs of their legs are gently pressed against it, so one picks up a hooded falcon by pressing the glove against its legs. Because it can see what it is doing, an unhooded bird steps forward.

As I had been so slow, Unk reversed our jobs. Unk flashed the torch on and off, and I felt my way gently towards the perch. My job was to take hold of her firmly from in front and slightly above her, so that my thumbs met in the centre of her back and my fingers held her wings close to her body.

I anticipated no more trouble than Unk had had with the first falcon. I felt in the dark for the perch but, misjudging it, I touched her by mistake, to be greeted by an ominous hiss more suited to a twenty-foot python crossed in love.

From the darkness Unk exhorted me not to spend all night over such a simple job. So, taking more care, I felt again and, putting my hands over her, grasped her firmly and tried to pick her up. She had no intention whatsoever of coming, but held tightly onto the perch and refused to let go. Unk switched on the torch to see what was happening, and she promptly put her head down and bit my finger. Even at that age a falcon knows how to bite, for she has been tearing her own food up for the last few weeks, learning to rip through shin of beef, old crows and other such tough items. My finger must have been like a piece of fillet steak to her, and I, somewhat reasonably I thought, let go. She flew onto the floor and scuttled away into a dark corner in a huff. Unk informed the heavenly inhabitants above that never had he had such an incompetent, fumble-fingered, bungling assistant and asked why was I complaining about a slight nip from an innocent little bird.

In the end he picked her up and I put the jesses on. Either the falcon was satisfied with the lump out of my finger or gave up the struggle when she saw who was in command; for she was no more trouble. They were both left hooded for the night, sitting on blocks under a lean-to shelter, awaiting the start of their training next day.

To most people one peregrine is much like another, but to a falconer they vary in looks, shape, colour, size and, above all, in temperament. As with people, it is very often the most beautiful that does not turn out so well, while the less glamorous surprises everyone by her performance and pleasanter nature. Of the two falcons one was a big dark-headed bird with a smoky front, a real dusky beauty. Her sister was considerably smaller, rather pale in front and with a tawny-coloured head: good-looking but not so gorgeous.

Although both belonged to him, Unk let me choose which bird I would like to handle. I was very attracted by the big one because of her size and looks but, possibly because of my own lack of stature then, I had a sneaking regard for the smaller one and finally chose her – rather to my uncle's surprise, I think, for he mumbled something about my having possibly picked the better one, in spite of appearances.

The following morning we took them up from their blocks and carried them about, stroking them every so often with a feather. This gets them accustomed to movement, but if you use your hand to stroke them the natural grease in your skin removes the waterproofing on the feathers. Then they get far wetter than they should do if they are left sitting out in a shower of rain. A falcon can stand quite heavy rain and has only to shake herself when it is fine again to send the raindrops flying, leaving her bone-dry.

After an hour or so of carrying they were put back on their blocks, still hooded, and left while we got on with other things. It is a curious fact that, while falcons get tamer even when hooded, hawks do not, and are just as wild as before, the moment the hood is removed.

In the evening we carried them again. When it was getting dusk we brought them indoors and unhooded them, the half-light helping to prevent their getting restive, for falcons dislike flying once it begins to get dark. Both immediately tried to fly off, or bated, as it is called. Now, a two-pound falcon flying madly off the fist and not having any notion of sitting still, is quite a handful. Like any other wild thing, they try to get away, but, finding themselves tethered, they naturally tend to attack. Unk's dark glamour-puss hung upside-down by her jesses, screaming in anger and biting his hand every time he tried to lift her back onto his glove.

I was very glad then that I had chosen the smaller one, for she, after her first bate, most obligingly flew back onto my fist and remained sitting there, looking very surprised and startled.

Her feathers were all puffed out like a rolled-up hedge-pig's prickles, her beak was half open, and at any movement she hissed. Her attitude was by no means one of fear alone, indeed hostility glared out of her large dark eyes. An Army N.C.O. would have placed her on a 'fizzer' at once for dumb insolence.

By this time Unk had persuaded his hitherto bat-like bird to sit the right way up. Her attitude was the same as her sister's, but her greater size and darker plumage made her even more impressive. It seemed quite impossible to me that either of them would even deign to consider surrender on any terms, let alone ever be pleased to see us. The idea of flying them free and expecting them to return was quite ridiculous.

I watched my uncle as he slowly, so slowly, stroked his falcon's breast feathers with the hood. Very gradually he worked his way up towards her head, her hissing grew less and her beak closed, but her eyes watched every move he made. Still working quite slowly, he

c

deftly put the hood over her head and, with a neat movement of his fingers, pulled the braces tight to prevent her shaking it off.

It was like a conjuror's sleight of hand, so smooth and unhurried till the last slick movement that the falcon hadn't realized she was being hooded till it was too late to do anything about it. Like the showman's patter when he does the three-card trick, 'the quickness of the 'and deceives the h-eye'.

I tried to do the same with my falcon. I'd hooded trained falcons before, so I had a good idea of what to do. She hissed hard as I raised my hand. Her hot breath puffed out over my face with a curious scent quite unlike any I had smelt before. It was unexpectedly pleasant, like the intriguing smell of burnt horse-hoof in a smithy, or leather in a saddler's shop. It should obviously be bottled in little model falcons of Lalique glass and sold in only the most exclusive shops to very special order.

I copied Unk's movements with the hood and, to my surprise, got it on with no trouble whatsoever. For the next hour we sat quietly unhooding and hooding them every few minutes. While a falcon is still apprehensive of the falconer is the time to accustom her to the hood. Once she loses her fear of him she is far more difficult to break to the hood, for her whole attention is then riveted on avoiding it.

Hooding is an art that is either acquired fairly quickly or not at all. Some people never master the knack and so bungle things that the falcon becomes hood-shy and bates away, screaming in annoyance at the sight of a hood. If it is done properly at the very beginning, they soon learn to think no more of being hooded than we do of wearing a hat. Hoods are said to have been brought into this country from Syria by the returning crusaders. Richard Coeur de Lion took falcons with him to the Crusades, war being carried on in a far more civilized manner then.

I have had falcons that would put their heads forward into the hood; and a red-tailed buzzard from America used to go to sleep on my fist almost as soon as the hood was put on. She would tuck her head into the top of her back, and it looked most odd as I walked along with an apparently headless bird.

Next they had to be persuaded to feed on the fist. It is very easy to get them to feed with a hood on, but they get no tamer, make the hood dirty, are obviously miserable because they cannot see what they are eating, and pick up the bad habit of pulling at one's glove when they are keen, in the hopes of finding food there. So ours were to feed bareheaded on the fist and, to impress on them that we were the providers of all their food, they were to be allowed to feed nowhere else for the time being.

At first they won't even start to eat until their fear of man, and of their strange surroundings, has been overcome. Unk gave me a rough idea of how to manage and then took his bird off to another room so that we should not disturb each other.

I settled myself comfortably in an arm-chair and, holding a nice tempting piece of raw beef in my gloved left-hand, close to the falcon's feet, I unhooded her. She bated off as I had expected her to, but half flew, half scrambled back on her own. She caught sight of the meat and looked down at it for an instant, then looked up at me and just sat and stared. I remained quite still, hoping she would start to feed. She stayed motionless, still glaring. Her big eyes never blinked nor altered their penetrating gaze. Her expression was that of immutable stubbornness. More than that, for she obviously dared me to outstay her.

Just then a slight breeze from the open window lifted the curtain and made her bate. I hooded her, got up and shut the window, sat myself down and tried once more.

After about ten minutes one of my feet began to go to sleep. I shifted as gently as I could to relieve it but disturbed her, and again she bated.

I tried drawing her attention to the meat by rubbing her foot; she looked down, half inclined to eat, changed her mind and stared straight in front of her. She had obviously decided that there was a catch in it somewhere and that she was not going to be had. I rubbed her foot again, and once more she looked down but in a flash was looking back at me.

I cut off a small piece of meat very carefully, juggling the pen-knife open with my free hand, and offered it to her. She opened her beak as my hand came near, but closed it just as I was about to put the meat in. I tried again, moving more quickly, and this time I succeeded. I took my hand away, and she sat there with the meat in her beak for a brief while. Then, with a quick movement of her head, she flicked it away across the room as though it were distasteful to her, resuming her inscrutable, sphinx-like gaze.

I moved my glove under her feet; she involuntarily gripped as though to stop the meat escaping and so nearly took a bite that I drew in my breath rather sharply, and the noise stopped her.

After several more minutes of her fixed gaze, my throat began to tickle, and I felt a desperate desire to cough. Suddenly she put her head down, took a good mouthful, and swallowed it. I could stifle the cough no longer, and she naturally bated at the explosion. I was furious with myself.

Then, to my utter amazement, she shook herself, looked round the room as though to make sure it was unaltered, and began to feed steadily. The food slipped once, but she only paused when my hand caught and replaced it. In five minutes or so she had finished the lot and was sitting there contented, with a fair-sized crop. She cleaned her beak, stropping it on my glove like a razor, first to one side then the other – feaking as it is properly called. I gently hooded her without any fuss and got to my feet, appreciating my regained freedom and delighted with my success.

Just as I was stretching my cramped limbs the telephone rang with the suddenness and persistence of an alarm clock. 'Been trying to get you for the last ten minutes,' the voice said. I thought to myself that, had it rung ten minutes sooner, it might well have been at least another half-hour before I persuaded the falcon I meant no harm and that my offering was genuine.

A few minutes later Unk came in. His falcon had taken a small crop after, so he told me, a lot of encouragement on his part. So I felt very pleased. I looked at the clock. We had been over an hour just feeding them – an hour that seemed very short now it was successfully over, but that had been endless when only half-way through with nothing to show for the discomfort but frustration. A very concentrated but rewarding hour.

That evening we discussed names for the falcons. Unk was rather fussy and a little superstitious about this. He preferred not to give any falcon a name that he considered she might well fail to live up to. 'If you call her Diana you can be quite sure that all the hunting she will ever do will be for fleas.'

I must say this seemed to work out, for the previous year we had had three merlins, called Mayfly, Maynotfly and Won'tfly. Won'tfly had been by far the best.

A book on falconry that had been sent to him for reviewing made him roar when he looked at the first chapter. 'Just listen to this,' he said. 'This chap has the audacity to put a photograph of himself in the front of this book and entitle it "The author with his trained kestrel Thunderer". Ha, blooming ha! That shows you at once what an able and knowledgeable bloke he must be on the subject! Thunderer! What a name! I bet it just sits on his fist and goes "squeak, squeak, squeak" at him.'

So I was pretty wary about the names I suggested. Finally we chose Bonus for his and, because of her tawny colouring, Cheetah for mine.

For the first three days they were unhooded only when on the fist. We carried them as much as possible – two or three hours each day – and continued to get them used to their hoods and to feeding on the fist.

The second time they were fed was far easier. Though still shy and suspicious of us, they both remembered the previous feed and, after a short delay, soon settled down. They were easily put off by any sudden movement or unusual sound but would shortly be on the feed again.

In the evenings, the day's chores done, we would take them round to friends, or drop in at the local pub, and get them accustomed to noise and chatter. The regulars in the King's Head knew all about it and took quite an interest in their education, but strangers often looked a bit astonished, and would sometimes ask if the falcons talked. If Unk was feeling expansive he would give them a free lecture on falconry, but if he had already been badgered with a lot of questions he would pull their legs.

'What sort of bird is it, mister?'

'Well it's a very interesting bird that comes from the West Indies,' he would reply. 'Feeds entirely on bananas; won't eat anything else.' Quite often they would swallow it and turn to tell their friends about it with the air of superior knowledge only just learnt.

Years later, in a train, I was tempted to do the same thing myself. As we drew into the station and I got up to leave with my falcon, an old lady handed me two bananas in a paper bag. 'For your birdie's lunch, my dear.'

By the end of three days the two were showing great progress and rarely bated now except for good reasons. A violent sneeze or a strange dog rushing up were the sort of things they disliked.

Unk said that they could now be left unhooded on their blocks for an hour or so at a time. So we put them where we could watch from the sitting-room window, and, unhooding them, we walked quietly away.

After a few minutes Bonus bated off and, coming up against the restraint of her leash, stood looking bewildered. Cheetah followed in like manner. Their wings were half spread and their feathers all puffed out, and they looked as they do when about to take a bath. Cheetah walked forward but was brought up short by her jesses and promptly bent down to peck at them. She soon gave this up as a jackdaw, flying over the garden, distracted her attention. She watched it go overhead, shook herself and turned to jump back onto her block.

The block has evolved as the best possible sort of outside perch. It is very like the rock the falcon would naturally sit on, serving also as a means of securing her, while being portable too, and designed to prevent entanglement and damage to feathers. To accustom them to this perch we had put some blocks on the floor in their mews, so they already knew what they were for.

Cheetah sat there, fanning her wings hard but holding on to the block with her feet to avoid becoming airborne. Once or twice she let go, and her wings lifted her into the air a few inches, but she slowed up the beat and dropped onto her block again. It was a form of physical jerks: upwards jumping with wings flapping sideways.

After a few minutes of this exercise she stopped, bobbed her head at Bonus, shook herself thoroughly and, puffing out her feathers in front, drew up one foot underneath them, letting the feathers fall back into place, concealing her foot entirely. It was rather like a schoolgirl who, lacking pockets, discreetly tucks her handkerchief into her bloomers.

She sat there as composed as a falcon who has already spent many hours on the block.

Bonus acted in much the same way, and they copied each other, for if one bated the other followed suit a moment later – a sort of sympathetic detonation. But they quickly returned to their blocks and settled down. Everything that moved in the garden caught their attention, particularly any birds that flew past. These they watched most intently, though showing no signs of wishing to chase them. In fact they looked amiably at a hen blackbird, worm-hunting on the lawn, which hopped well within their reach at times.

Keeping falcons in no way lessens the number of other birds in the garden. Blackbirds will often eat the meat fat that a falcon has discarded while she watches them unconcernedly. In fact, birds use the feathers lying around the falcons' blocks to line their nests. One bottle-tit's nest we found was upholstered in regal style with Ramshaw's moulted feathers.

About tea-time we went out and hooded them up again. We took a piece of meat with us, but, as Unk had warned me, they both bated away and refused to jump to the fist. They appeared to have forgotten entirely and hissed at us. To me, our three days' work on them seemed wasted, but after a few minutes on the fist they relaxed, behaving in a more friendly fashion.

Now that they were both feeding without hesitation on the fist, we encouraged them first to step, then jump, and finally fly, from the arm of a chair, or from the top of a gate if we were out of doors, to the food held in our gloved hands. Bonus did this at once, but Cheetah was very reluctant to trust herself in the air even this short distance, and sidled along the perch in an endeavour to reach the food without having to fly. Finally she made it, after screwing up her courage. Once she had made the initial effort, I had a job to get my hand back into position before she was on it again.

Each day they progressed more rapidly and gained more confidence. They spent longer unhooded on the lawn, bathing with great enjoyment, splashing about and dipping their heads under the water, letting it run down their backs and rolling from side to side, before jumping back on the block, to sit wings spread in the sun to dry.

Once dry, they would preen, an operation that they were as fussy over as a girl at her dressing-table before a dance. They were very thorough about it, and would go back time after time to run their beaks down the full length of one particular primary that was being recalcitrant. As their beaks neared the end of the shaft, it would bend more and more, curving outwards, till, as the tip was reached, it flicked back into position, all breaks in the webbing invisibly mended.

Every so often they would get a fresh supply of oil from the gland hidden under the tail coverts, and so re-waterproofing was accomplished at the same time. To do their throat feathers they would draw their heads backwards and nibble at the feathers, looking rather like someone trying to hide a double-chin. They would take maybe an hour or more over their toilet, and would invariably end it by shaking themselves, or rousing. Very slowly all their small feathers would stand up, like the bristling hackles on a watchdog, then they would pause, as if a sudden, very important thought had crossed their minds, and the feathers would slowly subside, only to rebristle anew as the thought was dismissed. Their feet would grip the block instead of just standing relaxed, and they would gather themselves up, the shake beginning at the head and travelling down their bodies, gaining momentum as it went. Loose pieces of down would float away, and finally they would indulge in a spell of energetic wing-fanning before relaxing and tucking up a foot to sit contentedly, yet always on the alert for anything of interest.

By the afternoon of the sixth day they both jumped eagerly from their blocks to our outstretched gloves when we went to pick them up.

To get them used to travelling around we would take them into Sevenoaks when we went shopping. I would take one on my fist, while the other sat on the perch in the dicky of the old Austin. On the return journey we exchanged their positions, so that each got the same amount of handling. In this way they kept fairly level with each other in their training. One day Bonus might be slightly ahead, but by the next Cheetah would have caught up.

Peregrine and merlin – falcons – long wings, dark eyes

Sparrowhawk and goshawk – short wings, yellow eyes

Unk with Mr Ramshaw

Cheetah feeding on the fist

Young herons at Park Point

Filming at Knole – the cast of country cousins (*Fox Photos*)

Stooping Cheetah to the lure for exercise

Unk had postcards made . . .
            and sent them to me, altered

Two eyass falcons a
        in a hamper

The mallard drake banked away

Robert, using his enormous camera to photograph a tiny Spanish reed frog

Imping – Unk and I put a new tail on Susan the buzzard (*Fox Photos*)

Hoods – tiercel and falcon

Young sparrowhawks with spindly, pencil-thin legs and a button-eyed look

The old hobby soon got used to the noise of the camera shutter

Weighing the Cooper's hawk

The stone-curlew chick showed under
hen's wing

She looked very bedraggled after the storm

A week after being taken from the mews we introduced them to the lure. This consisted of an old pair of well-dried rook's wings, tied together and adorned with a piece of meat or a chicken's head. This tempting affair was attached to a line about four yards long. On the far end was the lure-stick, a short length of broom-handle, on which the line was wound when not in use. This also served to slow a falcon up if she tried to carry the lure away after catching it in mid-air.

Unk was very particular about the way the lure-line was wound. It had to be done in figure-of-eight fashion, the same way that a gardener's line is wound. Nothing infuriated him more than if someone just did it round and round, for then it might jam when he wanted it in a hurry, and if the culprit were in earshot, woe betide him, for he soon knew he was not in favour.

It wasn't that Unk was fussy about the way he liked things done; in fact he was most untidy as a rule and once returned from one of his American trips to discover a chicken's head still in the pocket of a coat. It was a bit fruity and his pocket was full of maggots by then. Like most untidy people, he preferred to have his things left alone, for apart from his spectacles, which, like everyone else's, were always lost, he knew where he had put things even if it was in a different place each time. But when it came to falconry he insisted on having things done his way, because he had tried others and learnt from bitter experience which was the more efficient.

I use the term bitter experience only too feelingly, for falconry is a very exacting sport that tends to make you pay rather heavily at times for a mistake. An apparently trivial error may result in a lost hawk, and may well mean hours or even days of searching before she is found, possibly even permanent loss.

The lure having been made up under Unk's supervision, and checked by him to ensure that all the knots were tight (for if the lure came loose the falcon might carry it away with her), we hooded them up and took them across the road into the park.

Here there was an area of short grass, close-cropped by sheep and suitable for our purpose. A falcon on a line, or creance as it is called, gets caught up easily if the grass is long, or there are tussocks or thistles round which she can get tangled.

We stuck an old fence-post into the ground and put Bonus, un-hooded, on this perch. Unk unwound the creance as he walked back a short way, then, whistling to Bonus to attract her attention, he threw the lure out onto the grass a few yards in front of her. She bobbed her head up and down in the curious way that all the falcon tribe have when they are particularly interested in a thing. Not sure what the lure meant, she looked away. Unk gave it a short jerk, which drew it a few inches towards him, and the movement of it attracted her again. This time she saw the meat and, after bobbing her head again and opening and closing her wings a few times, she flew down onto the lure in a clumsy, cumbersome way. She leant down looking at it closely and then struck at it with one foot and remained there looking rather foolish, not knowing quite what it was all about.

Unk stood there watching her, making no attempt to move in to pick her up in case he frightened her, as she might then try to carry the lure away to eat it uninterrupted. Once a falcon starts to carry, it soon becomes a habit, and the owner looks very silly if she takes it into an unclimbable tree and sits there eating it, ignoring both blandishments and unprintable remarks. This sort of thing generally happens when you are trying to show an important guest just how good your falcon is and how well you have trained her. So bad habits must be avoided, for once started they are almost impossible to eradicate. A falcon can only be coerced; she cannot be corrected by chastisement or admonishment, as a dog can.

So we stood and waited till Bonus got hold of the lure with both feet and began to eat. Then Unk slowly moved in towards her. Every time she stopped feeding he stood still till she started again. She was not unduly suspicious of him, and when he was within a few feet of her he knelt down on one knee and offered her a piece of meat in his gloved hand. She tried to eat from this, but, as he let her pull it towards her every time she pecked at it, she finally had to put one foot on it to hold it down. He raised his glove slightly then, so that she let go of the lure in order to put her other foot up and get herself comfortable. He now lifted her right up, at the same time deftly popping the lure into his bag with his free hand. The whole action was so neatly done that Bonus never realized she had lost the lure.

He gave her some of the meat from his glove as her reward and put her back on the post. Then he waited till she had finished picking the odd bits of meat from her toes and was in the right frame of mind to pay attention to him. Again he whistled and threw out the lure, but this time the distance she had to fly was increased by a few yards. She came almost immediately, so quickly had she learnt her lesson. The slow procedure of making in was again gone through, but this time she was offered small pieces of meat from his hand and was left on the lure to continue her meal for a time, while Unk untied the creance from her swivel and replaced the leash.

Every so often he offered her extra pieces from his hand, and soon she looked eager whenever his hand came near. When she had eaten half her daily ration he persuaded her onto his fist again, where he gave her the remainder of her meal. In this way she learnt that the lure meant food, but did not forget the fist. He hooded her, and it was now time for me to try Cheetah, who had been hooded all this time so that she would not be jealous of Bonus.

Cheetah took longer to grasp the meaning of the lure, but the second time she was called off the post she came while I was still swinging the lure in the air and I had to throw it out to her quickly.

We walked back across the park, both very pleased. Even though my falcon had only flown a short way to the lure, the knowledge that she did so solely because I had taught her, gave me a feeling of immense satisfaction and pride.

4 * Mixed Bag

Book collectors have always been a small source of annoyance to me
Unk having whetted my appetite for falconry and lent me wha
books he had on the subject, I then found that, because of the bool
collectors, the price of such works was extremely high. Yet how
many collectors ever read, let alone make use of, them?

I waded eagerly through Unk's books and learnt something of the
history of falconry. Such an odd assortment of people had been
interested. Pope Leo X kept hawks. Even Napoleon had some a
Versailles for a few years. Isaac Walton's *The Compleat Angler* ha
a falconer in it. Marco Polo saw hawks in China, and Pepy
watched the Russian Ambassador bringing falcons to the King in
London.

I read of the kite and heron hawking that was considered to be
the pinnacle of a falconer's achievement in bygone days, and c
some of the curious ways of training hawks practised in India and
Persia.

Although falconry has never died out in England, it faded to
almost nothing after the Restoration, and the Enclosures Acts spoil
the countryside as far as falconers were concerned, while gunpowde:
made it easier to take game.

Falconers were of high standing, and in Wales in the tenth century
the Master of Hawks had the honour of the Prince's rising up to
receive him in the hall if his hawks had flown well. But he was no
allowed to drink more than three times in case he neglected hi:
hawks.

Shakespeare's plays are well sprinkled with references to falconry
and he must have been very knowledgeable on the subject, for in
spite of the technicalities he made no mistakes.

Quite apart from the enjoyment of flying the hawks I became intrigued with the history and romance of it all.

Unk himself had often considered writing a book on falconry, and he talked of how one chapter would be devoted entirely to the problem of condition. So important was it that it would be printed in red.

It sounded simple. If the falcon was too fat or in too 'high' a condition, then it would tend to be lazy, to ignore the lure, to puff and blow when exercised. If, on the other hand, it was too thin or 'low', then it would be over-keen, lacking stamina to fly – like a boxer who does not do his training properly and pays no attention to his diet. Allowed to continue in this state, the bird would be more likely to pick up disease.

In those days we judged a falcon's condition in much the same way as a poulterer selects chickens. We felt the breastbone and wing muscles; and this, combined with the amount of food given her and her behaviour when flown the previous day, decided how much her day's ration should be.

The sort of food given also had a bearing on the amount to give, for white meat, such as rabbit, is by no means as nourishing as pigeon. It took a lot of experience before one became proficient.

Not long after this the idea of weighing the falcons each day solved a great many problems. Indeed this is one of the very few modern devices which has made falconry easier to practise.

The next day it poured with rain, and when feeding-time came and there was no sign of the weather letting up, we brought the birds indoors and made them fly a few feet to the fist before feeding them. This now only took them about ten minutes. After just over a week of training they looked forward to seeing us and would jump to our fists from their blocks with very little encouragement.

Next morning the local R.S.P.C.A. Inspector called in to ask Unk to help find a home for a stray swan that had been picked up in the road and was at present occupying a cell in the police station. There were several lakes in the park suitable for the swan, and as we were going into Sevenoaks we agreed to collect him on our way back. When we got to the police station there was nothing in which to put the swan; so Unk, rarely defeated, borrowed a sack and gently inserted him, carefully guiding his head and neck through a hole in the bottom of it.

On the way home he sat on my lap, waving his head about in sea-anemone fashion, bewildering passers-by with woman-driver signals as he stuck it out of the window. Next he had a look at the dash-board, peering intently at gauges and switches. Satisfied with this inspection, his head swivelled round, and, craning over my shoulder, he investigated our shopping on the back seat. I felt like Alice trying to play croquet with the flamingo. We were turning a corner when he suddenly darted his long neck between the spokes of the steering-wheel, and I only just managed to pull him out of the way before he either put us in the ditch or got himself decapitated.

We turned him loose on one of the lakes and he swam away with a grateful wiggle of his tail. A few days later he flew off on a further tour of inspection, to be brought back in a side-car this time. We clipped his wing to prevent any more gallivanting, and before he was able to fly again he was joined by a mate, who soon settled him down.

Meanwhile the two falcons were rapidly improving. The second day of flying to the lure they came some forty yards with no hesita-tion. On one flight we had trouble with Cheetah, who, coming in too fast, half stooped at the lure and went on, skimming past it, swinging round to have another go. Of course this is what falcons should do, but at this stage, being still on the creance, she got it looped round a large dandelion and was brought up short. I walked up and threw out the lure where she could reach it and then picked her up and tried again. This time it went well.

The day after, they both came the full length of the creance, which was about a hundred yards long. Unk decided they could be flown loose on the following day. To ensure that they would be extra keen, they were given a little bit less than their normal rations.

When Unk told me they were ready to be flown free I had very mixed feelings. This was what we had been working for, of course, and I was delighted that nothing had occurred to delay matters; but the idea of having them loose, after only twelve days of training, seemed to me to be asking for trouble. Surely they needed to get accustomed to the lure for a few more days before dispensing with the creance?

But Unk was very emphatic. The sooner they were allowed loose the easier it would be to teach them to stoop and to increase the distance they would come. There was a limit to the length of creance one could use. Over a hundred yards it became too great a drag and even more inclined to get snarled up. Also, he pointed out, every day the rooks, at which we intended to fly, would be getting more difficult to catch. The old birds would be through the moult and the young ones getting more experienced in flying.

I flew Cheetah first. It seemed madness to me to take off her leash and swivel and leave her loose on the post instead of tied safely to a good stout creance. I gave her a couple of mouthfuls to eat before walking away to swing the lure, to remind her that I was the source of supply. I took a last look at her, sitting there quite unconcerned, and thought I should be lucky if I ever had hold of her again.

I walked away upwind, unwinding the lure line. When still some yards from the spot where I had intended to turn, I heard a shout from Unk. Looking round hastily, I saw her already half-way towards me. I threw out the lure and stood dead still, hoping she would come to it.

She seemed to be flying much faster than usual, without the drag of the creance to slow her down. She was higher up, too, and at that moment it occurred to me that there was absolutely nothing whatsoever to stop her flying into the blue: nothing except for a mere dozen days of training. It was a very agonizing moment. Just as I thought she had gone too far to be able to stop, she hesitated and came in to the lure; I was much happier.

But her speed was too great for her to stop, and she cut the lure with her two back talons, lifting it slightly off the ground, and went on. I was back in the agony of anxiety. She swung round in a big circle and came in again, this time binding to the lure. She settled down to eat eagerly; quite composed and unconcerned with the worry she'd caused.

I made in to her and gently but swiftly put on her swivel and leash. Once I had hold of these I felt a great deal safer. She was fed, then hooded up while Bonus had her turn. She too behaved well. Because one takes extra care to see that nothing goes wrong the first time they are flown loose, it rarely happens that a falcon gets lost then. Mishaps are more likely to occur a little later on, when one gets over-confident.

We now had another problem on our hands. For some weeks Unk had had a pet rook that had fallen out of its nest. We had fed him on the same grub as the herons, and he had got very tame. He used to roost at night with one of them. The heron would sit on a low branch with one leg tucked up under him, and the rook would roost fluffed out, just where the heron's leg would come if he put it down. The pair of them looked very odd indeed.

He flew after us, calling for food and shaking his wings just as he would do to his parents. At one time he had been tame enough to feed from the hand, but because we had grabbed him then for filming he'd got pretty cunning and sly. We had a heck of a time trying to catch him. The eyasses were flying loose by then, and we were afraid they might think Rookie a tasty morsel; so we wanted to put him in the aviary for his own safety. We tried to get him one night when he was roosting in his usual spot under the heron, but we made a bosh shot. Then he roosted up on the chimney-stack, out of reach. We put down a fling-over trap one night when he was asleep. We carefully covered it with grass to camouflage it and made a pretty good job of it. In the morning we threw food down to him by the trap; but he knew exactly where the danger area was and refused to be enticed. He made short work of the bits which fell outside its range, but those that fell inside received from him a knowing look and were not touched.

We had to think again. If he's hungry enough he'll get in range eventually, we decided. So Master Rookie was put on a starvation diet. The next day he disappeared entirely. Surely one day without grub couldn't have hurt him, but nevertheless we sent out a search-party. We found him not far off, across the park, scrounging in true army style from the cook-house of a Girl Guides' camp. So we gave him best, reckoning he was crafty enough to look after himself.

He certainly seemed to be clued up, for as soon as either of the falcons was put on the wing for exercise he at once took refuge in the sycamore trees which stood close by. In fact, he was obviously amused by the whole affair and apparently thought we'd done it entirely for his benefit. He started playing 'last across' and would leave things till the last moment before he dived into cover in the trees. There he would sit, obviously chuckling to himself. But he failed to take into account all the risks.

A falconer friend sent Unk a tiercel peregrine, as the male is called from the French *tierce* – for the tiercel is a third less in size than the falcon. In all birds of prey the female is bigger than the male, sometimes a great deal bigger. Hence she is more deadly, as in the human race.

This little tiercel had been taken from the eyrie rather younger than the two falcons, and I suppose his mother had not had time to tell him that peregrines do not follow their quarry into trees like nasty common goshawks do. Unk got him flying loose, and the first time he was put on the wing Rookie played his usual game.

The tiercel chased him, but, instead of giving up once Rookie had reached the trees, he followed him in and managed to grab him by one wing in what Rookie must have considered a most unsportsmanlike and underhand manner. The two came tumbling through the branches to the ground with a lot of flapping, cawing and tinkling of bells. Unk and I rushed to the rescue, and no harm was done beyond a certain loss of dignity and black feathers. Rookie was conveyed, protesting, to the safety of the aviary, and, although a bit ruffled at first, soon regained his normal cheeky outlook.

Scottie, the tiercel, was quite a contrast to his falcon cousins. He was smaller than the male peregrine usually is, and was quicker in turning than the falcons. He was very tame indeed and had the most engaging habit of turning his head completely upside-down to look at one.

Every day for the next week the young peregrines were stooped to the lure. At first their muscles were soft and flabby, and they puffed after making one or two circuits; but in a few days they began to get fitter, and not only stayed on the wing longer but flew faster and harder.

D

It was quite a show, for Unk was a past-master at swinging the lure. This is another of the things that looks so easy to do. It is purely a matter of timing, rather like a matador with a bull or the scissors movement of the gun-limbers.

The novice is bound to make a mess of it. He invariably gets the line wound around himself, or the lure hits him on the back of the head, or the falcon, after swinging round several times, wondering what on earth the falconer is playing at and despairing of ever having the lure presented to her in a reasonable manner, decides to come in and help herself at the most awkward moment. Watch the expert at it. The falcon appears to do all the work.

She is unhooded and cast off from his fist; she circles round, gaining height as she goes. The falconer, taking the lure from his bag, unwinds the line, slowly swinging the lure round vertically with his right hand. He whistles to attract the falcon's attention, and as soon as she sees the lure she puts on speed, turns in towards it and stoops.

As she comes in to him the falconer lets the lure swing towards her, but at the critical moment pulls it away so that it is now drawn just in front of her. She redoubles her efforts to catch it, and, as it swings upwards, she too throws up after it, till the angle is too steep for her and she climbs up and away before turning to stoop once more.

The closer the falconer can work the lure to the falcon, the more she thinks she is going to get it, and so she flies harder and faster in her efforts to catch it. This is exactly what gets her fit and teaches her to stoop and throw up. Each day the time she is put on the wing and the number of stoops at the lure is increased. Care must be taken, though, not to try her patience too far, but to let her catch the lure before she gets tired or bored with the game.

The falconer varies things as much as possible by changing the direction of the lure every so often: sometimes swinging it back-handed sometimes forehanded. At times he may throw it on the ground and twitch it towards him just as she is about to strike it. When he considers she has had enough, he throws it up to the full length of the line and lets her catch it in mid-air.

It is really very beautiful and exciting to watch her circling round, stooping, throwing up again and doing her best to catch the lure: a *pas de deux* of controlled ease.

At the end of a week of daily exercise all three peregrines were putting in thirty to forty stoops, with no signs of distress after such expenditure of energy.

On the fourth day Bonus flew off out of sight over some trees. She was lost for ten minutes. We chased across fields and through hedges after her, catching up when she took stand in a tree. She took her time coming down, obviously not much interested in our enticing lure; it was clearly a case of too much food on board from the day before.

She and her sister were still carried a little each day and were getting more and more tame and friendly. They would bob a welcome as we approached and fan their wings in eagerness to be flown. Because we refused to remove our hands when they tried to bite, they soon gave this up and didn't mind being stroked.

Now that they were fit and strong on the wing, it was time they were entered to wild quarry, for they were quite capable of catching something. Indeed, the sooner they started working for their living the better. If falcons are kept too long at the lure they lose the instinct to chase and become lure-bound and unwilling to fly at wild things.

During this week of muscling them up we taught them to fly from the fist to a distant lure the moment we unhooded them; for when flying at rooks the falcon is slipped straight out of the hood, with the quarry already in the air. So in this manner we taught them to be on the alert the instant their hood was removed. At first they were a bit puzzled and seemed to expect the person with them to produce the lure. But they soon got the idea.

We only took the falcons on the first go out, as Scottie, the tiercel, was not quite ready. We hooded them up and put Bonus on the perch; I took Cheetah on my fist. We drove out along the Pilgrim's Way, the same road along which Chaucer himself, 'grey goshawk on hand', travelled. It was by no means good country for rook hawking, for it was not really open enough and there was always cover within half a mile, so that the rooks rarely tried to escape the falcon by outflying her but made for the nearest cover. We never got a good high flight there.

For young, inexperienced falcons this was by no means a bad thing; they would be unlikely to persevere if a rook started to climb but would tend to chase one that flew low. Later on, when the rooks would become more difficult to catch, we hoped that the falcons would have had enough experience to even the balance.

Unk saw how excited I was getting at the thought of flying them in real earnest, and he let me try Cheetah first. I took off her leash and swivel as we drove along and held her with the ends of her jesses tucked between my second and third fingers. The braces at the back of her hood were loosened, and she was ready to be slipped without delay. All we wanted now was to find some rooks in a suitable place.

There was still a lot of standing corn in some fields, but in others it had been cut and stooked; some had even been carted, leaving bare stubble. We passed by one lot of rooks poking about in a field; they were too close to a wood that gave them cover within easy reach.

Then we spotted a small flock feeding right out in the open on the stubble. They were close to the road, and downhill too, which would help the falcon. If she once learnt she was able to catch the rooks she would gain confidence but, if she had several disappointments, then it would become increasingly difficult to persuade her to fly them.

We drove slowly past them and, as we went by those closest to the road, I slipped her. Unk pulled the car into the side, and we jumped out to watch and assist if need be.

The rooks took flight immediately they saw her in the air, and she, not knowing quite what was expected of her, was at first undecided. It must have looked as if far too many lures were being swung all at once and were, at the same time, moving rapidly away from her. Partly, I suppose, from training, and partly from instinct, she gave chase. It seemed to me that her momentary hesitation had spoiled her chances. Luckily, an old rook who had been poking about in the long grass on the edge of the stubble was also a bit slow off the mark.

He got up to join his chums, but by then Cheetah was conveniently placed some fifty feet above him, and, seeing him suddenly appear below her simply asking for trouble, she turned over and stooped at him, just as she had been doing at my lure over the past few days.

The old rook side-slipped at the last moment and dropped to the ground. Cheetah shot past him, threw up a short distance, turned over and stooped again, this time clouting him as she went past; the feathers flew. The rook got up and made off after the rest of the flock, but he was obviously pretty shaken, and Cheetah came streaking along and grabbed him in mid-air.

Although not a very stylish performance, it was just what Cheetah needed to encourage her. Unk was, I think, as pleased as I, for after all, as his pupil, it was as much to his credit as to mine to kill a rook with the first falcon I had ever trained. We let Cheetah have a good crop and then hooded her up.

Bonus was not quite so lucky at her first slip. She seemed bewildered by the number of rooks, and by the time she had recovered they had reached shelter. Unk took her down to the lure; then on her second slip she did very well and had a young rook at her first stoop.

So we drove home to celebrate.

5 * Park Point

I used to wonder sometimes what a burglar would think if he had broken into my uncle's workroom at Park Point. It was a small room, but somehow he managed to get an enormous number of things into it. Hanging on the walls were stuffed heads of trophies caught by the hawks: a peacock's head that had been caught near Edinburgh by a goshawk; a hare's mask that, when first stuffed, looked so like a pudding that Unk sent it back indignantly and it returned looking as though it had spent a night in the Chamber of Horrors, its glass eyes bolting out from its sperimawcus-looking face. (I have never really discovered what a sperimawcus is, but the word has always been used in our family to describe any lean, thin, cadaverous creature.)

Unk's photographs, some framed, some not, jostled for place between the examples of the taxidermist's art. There were stills of eagles, herons, woodpeckers, and one of a little owl's head peering out of its nesting-hole in a tree and entitled 'No bread today, thank you, baker'. There were old posters advertising his lectures pinned up over his desk and odd mementoes from his various trips: the head of a rag doll, and a wooden chair-arm carved with a lion's head that had adorned an osprey's eyrie on Gardiners Island, ospreys having the curious habit of decorating their nests with all sorts of beach-combed bric-à-brac. Eagles will often bring fresh branches to their nests, and in Elizabethan times Shakespeare warned, 'When the kite builds, look to lesser linen', kites having the habit of taking the smalls off the clothes-line.

On the mantelpiece was a forbidding-looking baboon's skull, its vicious yellow fangs giving a good idea of the power of these animals. There were also skulls of hyrax, a small rabbit-like creature that is,

in fact, the nearest living relative to an elephant. These had come
from the remains of the kills of a large African hawk-eagle, together with the horns of a small buck and a monkey's tail.

In contrast to these gruesome exhibits was a bunch of hotel keys,
mainly American in origin, with enormous, heavy metal labels
which had failed completely to persuade Unk to return them at the
end of his stay. There was also a chart for making various cocktails.
'Clover Clubs' were his speciality, and he generally stuck to
them until the necessary ingredients ran out, when he simply made
up his own concoction from whatever drink was left, by which time
few of the guests either noticed or cared.

A brass plaque proclaimed him a member of the 'Dutch Treat'
club in New York. Primaries from Ramshaw and other eagles stuck
out from behind the pictures like pencils behind a grocer's ear.

Two large cedar-wood cabinets contained the remnants of a
once very complete collection of Kentish birds' eggs, but he had
soon given up this, preferring to film them alive. So most of the
clutches had been given away or got broken, and the drawers now
housed reels of film, press cuttings, photographic plates, leather for
hawk's gear, bells, and so on.

There was a selection of fan mail, including an envelope addressed
to:
                        Captain Nightie,
                          Eagleman,
                          England.

which the G.P.O. had successfully delivered.

Behind the door lived the heavy tripod and the cases of the movie-
cameras. The old hand-wound, 35-mm. projector stood on a rickety
bamboo table which lurched and wobbled whenever the machine
was in action. The splicer was also clamped to this table and the
surrounding area well splashed with film cement.

His desk, in the far corner of the room, was invariably covered
by a heterogeneous mass of papers: letters, forms, lists of film
sequences, photographs, lantern slides, film clippings, drawings for
titles, and requests of all sorts from people interested in falconry.
In the midst of all this stood his aged typewriter, on which he
performed with one finger at an amazing speed. Except for signing

his name with a scratchy old pen, he typed everything, even shopping-lists, which invariably started off with 'heads', meaning chickens' heads from the poulterers for the hawks and Ramshaw.

When at his desk he wore, if he had not mislaid them, a pair of steel-rimmed spectacles, which gradually slipped down till they were at the very tip of his nose. If anyone came in to see him, he would look over the top of his spectacles, and if they were not al-ready down far enough he would pull them down rather than remove them.

The telephone lived on the bookcase, as inconveniently placed as possible, being across the other side of the room from his desk, though I do not think he ever considered it inconvenient or thought of moving either desk or telephone. There was, however, a very convenient window by his desk, through which he pitched all his throw-out film clippings for disposal later on.

We disrupted traffic one evening by setting fire to a vast pile of these clippings. Negative stock was by no means non-flam. in those days, and Unk and I collected up several days' of chuck-outs and made a heap of them on the rubbish dump in the corner of the garden. We then laid a fuse of film along the path leading to the main pile. Unk lit it, and the flame went streaking along to its destination. I don't think Unk himself realized fully the explosive quality of the stuff. It went up with a wuff and a roar in one vast sheet of flame that burnt all the leaves off the trees thirty feet above it and made the cars passing on the main road squeal to a halt and their drivers come to investigate. It was over in a few seconds but it was certainly a very handsome conflagration while it lasted.

He hated writing letters or, indeed, doing anything indoors; but once he got settled down he objected strongly to being interrupted. If anybody came to the door he would stay firmly behind his desk and shout from there, 'Well, come on in then, don't stand out there.' Half turning to face the door, he would look at the intruder and greet him with, 'Can't you see I'm busy? What do you want?' This somewhat abrupt opening never had much effect on those who knew him well, but strangers would be put off and hasten to retreat. By now, however, Unk would prolong the conversation himself, especially if the job in hand was distasteful. When they finally departed he would grumble at the interruption, even though he himself had extended it.

If he was cutting film, he was even less inclined to break off. In semi-darkness the visitor would have to carry on a conversation through the chatter and rattle of the projector, being told at the same time not to move in case he trod on the lengths of film that flowed all over the room. Unk cut the majority of his films direct from negative stock and only had prints made when most of the cutting was done. The onlooker therefore had little idea what was going on; for the negative image is pretty meaningless to the uninitiated.

As he cut each length I would roll it up and attach the label with a paper-clip. When he started splicing it all together the floor would become littered with discarded paper-clips, odd frames of film, old labels; and the pear-drop scent of the film cement pervaded the whole room. Gradually the finished reel would grow, though there would be loud outbursts if a length were left out by accident and the missing piece had to be inserted. Then we would run it through again and see how it looked and what alterations and sub-titles were required.

Finally, when the whole film was assembled and finished, Unk would invite relatives, friends, and those who had helped, to run it through and celebrate.

He had a habit of taking a handful of postcards or notepaper from hotels or liners and then using them much later on. So one might well receive a postcard of the *Queen Mary* sent off from a Union Castle liner on her way to South Africa. He also had postcards made from still photographs, and I would sometimes get one of these from him with the subject altered by his retouching brush. Perhaps instead of two ospreys, he would seem to have a couple of marabou storks on his fist.

In the garden was a brick outhouse for coal and logs and there Unk kept a large block of ice wrapped up in an old army blanket. This he stabbed to pieces with an evil-looking spike and, after washing the worst bits of hairy blanket off, bunged the chips into the cocktail shaker. Next to the outhouse was an old disused lavatory in which any sick bird or animal was generally parked till more suitable accommodation could be arranged.

In a small run with an attached residence all of her own lived Lucille, a stray brown hen that had been rescued from the clutches of a goshawk. She lived there for many years and laid egg after egg with little encouragement.

Over the wooden garage where the Austin lived was a small pigeon loft which housed a few mongrel pigeons. They were presided over by a pygmy pouter which strutted up and down on the landing-board outside the loft and bowed and cooed at the hens, showing off his trimly-feathered toes and puffing himself out like an old bull-frog.

Unk hated gardening, so the small lawn, surrounded by flower-beds, was looked after by Smith the gardener. The fruit and vegetables were discreetly screened by hedges. Off a corner of the lawn was a leafy tunnel leading nowhere, called the grotto. It was here one afternoon that I became a fearsome, wild, African savage.

Unk had decided that, as an opening to his African film, he would have a dream story of Africa in its darkest, danger-lurking-everywhere, adventure-book mood.

So one sunny Sunday, we shot the story. It started with Unk lying asleep in a deck-chair on the lawn. Then the camera was thrown out of focus and panned round to the grotto, suitably lined with bamboos cut only that morning from the park and tastefully arranged to look as jungle-like as possible. Stealthily, from the bamboos, came a well-armed savage; the camera swung back to my uncle, no longer reclining, but alert and tense, and arrayed in authentic tropical kit, revolver in holster, rifle at the ready. In no time he was threatened by lions, crocodiles and snakes, and it became very exciting, though one wondered how so many fierce animals got there without bumping into each other. Finally, of course, the dream faded at the crucial moment when our hero was really in a fix. The whole thing dissolved back into the deck-chair scene, with Mrs Courtis, the housekeeper, coming across the lawn with a cablegram telling Unk that the African hawk-eagles had started nesting and he could go ahead with the film.

My part as the savage required no clothes, apart from a smelly old goatskin worn as a loin cloth. A shield was cut from a large display-card and mystic signs painted on it. A pair of buffalo's horns, that had been serving as a support for spiders' webs since their original owner had no further use for them, were tied into my hair. A broom-stick, sharpened at one end and with a rifleman's plume at the other, made an excellent spear. The only thing lacking was a good supply of grease-paint and, as it was Sunday, there was no chance of buying any. There was a slight pause while Unk pondered the problem but it was soon solved – by mixing bicycle oil and black boot-polish. When the boot-box ran dry we used stove-polish. 'You look a bit blotchy but the audience will either think it's shadows from the bamboos or that you've got some fell disease. Don't worry, just look fierce.'

Then the sun went in and we had to wait. Boot-polish being none too good at keeping out the cold, we went into the sitting-room to read the Sunday papers. The front-door bell rang. Unk went to answer it, and I heard him say, 'Come on in, go straight ahead and turn right at the end of the passage, I'll bring some drinks in.' So the unsuspecting visitors came trooping into the sitting-room to be faced by an extremely embarrassed African in full war-paint.

6 * Mr Ramshaw

Paradise. Only Unk could have given a rubbish dump that name. Whenever we were short of hawk's baths we drove over there to hunt among the scrap iron for dustbin lids. One day we found an enormous great lead cistern, which we lugged into the Austin's dicky, secured with binder twine and took back for Ramshaw. It leaked a bit, but we bunged up the holes with corks. On another occasion, when Robert, my cousin, was with us, it started to rain. Robert dashed off, to return a few moments later with a somewhat battered selection of umbrellas.

Everything possible was burnt, and the piles of rubbish, intersected by lanes so that the trucks could move in between, gradually grew higher as more and more was dumped onto the ashes. It was very dangerous to walk on these heaps, for the apparently solid ash would suddenly subside, revealing a yawning chasm of glowing red-hot cinders. The heat from these places grew the most wonderful tomatoes, which sprang from the seeds out of condemned tomato cans. Date stones, too, sprouted into date palms, though they never grew very big. Generally we would combine our visits with flying hawks on a piece of ground over the railway from Paradise. Sometimes we even flew sparrow-hawks in Paradise itself.

Hawking along the Darenth river with Anna, the gos, was always exciting because you never knew what would get up next. Rabbits and moorhens were the principal objects of the bag. Unk had a special way of cooking the latter that made most people think they were some delicious game bird. He skinned them and then inserted them into the neck-skin of a chicken, filched from the hawk's larder, tied both ends up like a sausage and then roasted them.

If we were lucky, we might find an old cock pheasant hiding in the rushes. Leaving matters just a little too late, he would get up with a clatter and fly off, all spiky-tailed and burnished copper in the sun, and be grabbed by Anna before he had got full speed up. Pheasant made a very welcome addition to the larder, and so did the mallard that we caught on rare occasions. These invariably went across the river, and one of us would have to walk a considerable distance before being able to cross dry-shod and retrieve Anna.

Going farther upstream we would cross under the road at Chipstead, wading in the stream and ducking our heads, for the bridge was very low. If the river were high it invariably went over the top of my gumboots, which were of course shorter than Unk's. The cold water would gradually warm up, only to be replenished with a further douche on the return journey. I have often wondered why gumboot-makers make those little holes about one and a half inches below the top; you think you can wade through with an inch of freeboard to spare, and the water pours in.

Sometimes we would put up a hare, but few goshawks are able or willing to tackle so big an animal, for the hare turns into a bronco when grabbed and tries to buck the hawk off. As the hare weighs three or four times as much as the gos, it is not surprising that most goshawks give up flying hares.

One day Anna flew a rabbit which beat her to the hedge. She swung up into an ash tree and sat there. As we walked towards her she dropped out of the tree onto something in the long grass on the far side of the hedge. When we got through we found her looking, rather bewildered, at a tortoise she had grabbed and wondering what sort of meal it was going to make and at which end to start. We rescued the tortoise, took him home and let him loose in the garden. Flying another gos in the same field about three years later we caught a second tortoise. The odds must be pretty long!

Flying for an hour or two every day, Anna became very quick at getting off the mark and would go at the slightest movement. So fast was her reaction that, when a lark got up under our feet one day, she snatched it in mid-air before she had realized what it was. Normally hawks pay no attention to small birds.

Most people think that a hawk kills nearly every time and is far faster than its prey. In fact the wild hawk glides quietly over the top of a hedge or slips unseen round the side of a wood, coming on top of something without being suspected; or she will sit quietly in a tree, motionless, her plumage blending in with her surroundings, and simply wait for something to come along. Then a quick drop, a grab, and it is all over. Even then, one must remember that all wild things are for ever on the alert, glancing over their shoulders, ears pricked at the slightest unusual sound, noses permanently twitching to catch the vaguest scent of danger. If gregarious, they have the added assistance of their combined senses. And reaction is so swift that, as soon as the alarm is given, legs are scampering away or wings beating hard. Escape routes appear to be automatically noted, and anything that could possibly serve to throw off the attacker is brought into play. The difference in speed between hunter and hunted is very small. Were this not so, we should be inundated with predators, whereas in fact a balance is maintained which, if not interfered with by man himself, allows both predator and prey to continue their respective races. The trained hawk is at a greater disadvantage than the wild, for the presence of the falconer warns the quarry that danger is at hand.

We flew at Knole every so often, though this was a dangerous place if Anna was not obedient, or in good yarak (a delicious word from Indian falconry), for it was very heavily wooded and the trees were extremely high; it was not a place to have a recalcitrant goshawk refuse to look at the lure. The trees were mainly beech and oak, and there was very little undergrowth; the rabbits lived mostly underground, but there were small enclosures of younger trees, fenced off to prevent the deer damaging them, and in these places the rabbits were to be found hiding in great nettle-beds.

We would let Anna fly up into a tree and then walk through the nettles. She soon learnt to follow overhead and would come swinging down, her normal speed greatly increased by the height, and hawk and rabbit would tumble over in a scatter of dead leaves.

Over the road from Unk's house lay Montreal Park. Here Unk had permission to keep the hawks in a strip of woodland that ran along the wooden-boarded boundary fence. He had a key for the gate but never used it as he had discovered that, by grasping the

top corner and pulling upwards and outwards, it could be opened
without the key. I, in my turn, being far too small to reach the top
of the gate, had my own 'open sesame' of lifting it from the bottom.
Until I learnt this trick Unk used to get very cross because he had
to open it for me.

Out here Unk built a shelter for the falcons and a place for Ramshaw. The shelter was enclosed by wire-netting; not to keep the
hawks in but to keep intruders out. Ramshaw, Unk reckoned, was
big enough to look after himself and so had no shelter beyond the
big Scots pines, whose branches came over the rock on which he
generally sat. He was chained to a ring in the ground and could
fly from his rock to a grassy hummock whenever he felt inclined.
Unk encouraged bramble bushes to grow in a semi-circle round the
eagle's area to provide a wind-break. Ramshaw was very happy and
contented here and even in bad weather refused better shelter offered
to him.

This was definitely his own stamping-ground, and he would fly
at anyone who invaded this territory unless he knew them well.
Unk could never persuade anyone to stay and see what Ramshaw
intended to do to the intruder; they always skipped hastily out of
the way. Once off his own territory Ramshaw was exceptionally
tame, and anyone, children included, could stroke him and pull his
beak or generally fuss and pet him.

As a relaxation from writing or filming, Unk would wander round
the park with Ramshaw, or possibly a goshawk, and try to catch
a rabbit. The big house in the middle of the park had lain empty for
many years and its once beautiful and cared-for gardens now ran
wild. A large magnolia still covered a portion of the front, scatter-
ing its fallen blossom over the moss-covered stone steps that curved
gracefully from the carriage drive to the front door.

A formal garden, edged with once neatly-clipped box, was so
overgrown that its intricate pathways could now only be traversed
by the rabbits which lived there, for the rose bushes, which had
nearly all reverted to their briar-root stocks, reached across to inter-
mingle with their fellows, and the whole place looked rather like
a scene from Cocteau's *La Belle et La Bête*.

Across the tennis court, now a thriving rabbit warren, was a vast

shrubbery of rhododendrons, laurels, lilacs and syringas. Here
hidden in a dark corner, was a small hexagonal summerhouse, buil
of larch with the bark left on and arranged in herring-bone pattern
We had to scuff aside the pile of fallen leaves that had collected ove
the years, to pull open the door. Inside, the walls were decorated witl
panels of sea-shells set into the plaster. The whole of the interio
was composed of these shells, thousands of them. Razor shells
clams, cowries, periwinkles, mussels, cockles, oysters, whelks – al
carefully sorted out, sized and arranged into patterns with endless
care by some long-forgotten craftsman. But now the structure wa
crumbling and rotting and the decayed wood had given way.

Below the garden, across the ha-ha, was a series of artificial lakes
Mallard, their bright heads showing first green then blue as thei
movements altered the angle of reflection, occasional teal, moorhen
and visiting herons frequented the lakes; and sometimes we caugh
a glimpse of a kingfisher, a brightly coloured streak, like a smal
torpedo flashing across the water in search of fresh fishing-grounds

Sometimes we flushed a water-rail from the reed-beds where they
skulked, and it would fly a short distance only to drop down agair
into cover. The moorhens, surprised suddenly, would swim away
hastily, their heads jerking, then half fly, half run across the wate
to the island in the centre of the lake. Here they would disappea
among the rhododendrons, flirting their white under-tail coverts
leaving only the disturbed trail of their passage, like the wake of a
toy boat on the water.

Downstream the water vanished under the park wall at Riverhead
Upstream, past a stone quarry, it dwindled to a small trickle acros
the drive, cobbled just here to lead the water over. It then dis
appeared altogether into a swamp covered with rushes and bramble
bushes, into which I would be requested to plunge, to push a rabbi
out for Ramshaw after he had been persuaded to fly up onto a dead
branch of a large oak tree, which gave him a commanding view and
added height, for him to launch himself into the air. We never
caught many, for the rabbits had such a short stretch of open ground
to cross that they were usually safe in their holes before he got going
He was very successful, though, at other quarry. Unk would be
walking along with Ram on his fist when suddenly the eagle would

go plonk onto the ground and grab with one foot a large hunk of long grass. He would pull this up and then, with his foot still clenched, poke his beak inside it, rather like a child licking the last bits of ice cream out of a cornet, and extract a mouse, which he swallowed whole with much gusto. He rarely missed at this game and when he had finished he would shake himself and jump back onto Unk's fist and allow us to carry on our search for larger prey.

Unk was in great demand for pageants, for falconry is associated so much with the past, particularly the Middle Ages. Lorenzo de Medici wrote a poem about hawking. Chaucer, in the Squire's Tale, has a description of a perch of blue velvet put at the head of the bed for a lady's hawk. One of the first printed English books – The Boke of St Albans, 1486 – is on the subject.

People took their hawks everywhere with them, even to church, and one bishop, hearing that his favourite falcon had been stolen from the cloisters while he was preaching his sermon, marched straight back into the pulpit and excommunicated the thief forthwith. Ransoms were even paid in hawks.

Performing in a pageant at Rochester Castle, Ramshaw was frightened by the band and decided that he had had enough of knights in armour, plunging horses, good Queen Bess and all the rest of it. So he took wing and, disdaining Unk's frantic lure-swinging and whistling, vanished over the castle walls.

Unk dashed after him, trying hard to keep him in sight. Eventually he was traced down to a chimney-stack, where he had taken stand. The owner of the house was unfortunately stone deaf, and by the time Unk had made him understand that there was an eagle on his roof, and had got permission to go upstairs, Ramshaw had pushed off again, and no amount of searching revealed his whereabouts. When it was dark a somewhat disconsolate party of medieval knights and ladies returned home eagleless.

The next day the police telephoned to say that Ramshaw had been found. We jumped into the car and drove to a farm several miles out of Rochester where we discovered that the farmer's wife, seeing Ramshaw sitting on a fence and causing a great deal of consternation amongst her chickens, had fetched a large laundry-basket, put it

E

beside the eagle, gathered him up in her arms, dumped him inside and swiftly closed the lid. She had been concerned for the safety of her hens and had given no thought to the damage Ramshaw's feet might have done had he caught hold of her. It was a rather different reception from that of the British chieftain, Gaufredus, who was killed in 1008 by a stone thrown by an angry henwife when his hawk killed one of her chickens.

Ramshaw was frequently in trouble of one sort or another. Unk was due to take him on a lecture tour of America and the day before he sailed had packed everything ready for an early start. At crack of dawn I was awoken by a frantic Unk on the telephone: 'Come round at once. Ramshaw's gone.' So I rapidly pulled some clothes on and leapt onto my bicycle and pedalled round to Park Point at a high rate of knots.

Unk was out in the park, clad in pyjamas, dressing-gown and gumboots, swinging a lure and obviously very worried. 'The old devil's broken his chain and pushed off on his own and, as we gave him a heck of a great meal yesterday, he won't be in the least bit keen.' I grabbed a lure quickly and, while Unk set off in one direction, I went in the other. Half a mile away I spotted Ramshaw in a tree. I yelled the good news to Unk, who rushed over, climbed up breathlessly, caught hold of his jesses and lifted him down.

When he returned from his American trip Unk brought back with him a bald-headed eagle, the emblem of the United States. She had been caught as an adult bird and been in the Washington zoo for a while. She was not actually bald but had pure white feathers on her head and neck.

Miss America was very different from Ramshaw. Her eyes and beak were pale yellow, and her tail, as well as her head, was white. Her feet were nothing like the size of Ramshaw's and her toes were short and stubby, her talons blunt from the concrete floor at the zoo. Unk proceeded to tame her as he had done the other eagles, but she was none too easy, and it took quite a time before she was allowed loose. She had a curious and rather nasty habit when she was on the fist. She would lower her head, then suddenly shoot it forward, clopping her great beak and nipping bits out of your face if you were not careful. We tried her at rabbits and she did manage to catch a few, but she was not particularly keen on working for her living and showed none of Ramshaw's zest for the chase. Nevertheless it was interesting to see her fly, and Unk filmed her in action, both on her own and with Ramshaw. The two eagles agreed quite well, but we never left them alone together in case a fight started.

Besides the bald eagle he also brought back a great horned owl called Hoogeeboo; Susan, an American red-tailed buzzard; and four young ospreys which he released a few weeks later in Scotland in the hopes of reintroducing the species, which had not bred there for some twenty years.

Hoogeeboo the owl was a most attractive creature but, apart from flying a short distance to a lure, was never of any practical use. We spent one day with a special camera team filming him in slow motion for what were known as 'Flickers', small booklets made up of a series of prints from slow-motion film. When riffled through they gave the appearance of a movie film. Well-known sportsmen were immortalized in this way, and, of course, Mr Ramshaw.

Falconry has only reached the New World very recently. However, Susan, the red-tailed buzzard, had been trained by an American falconer. When she arrived we had to repair her tail, which was merely a ragged bundle of stumps. Unk had a buzzard skin, which had been given to him by one of the American museums, and we imped the tail feathers onto her and restored her flying powers. Eventually Unk gave her to me ar d I had her for several years. She was remarkably tame and very good to the hood, but suffered at first from the nasty habit of snatching at your hand when sitting on the fist. She did this one day to Unk, and he was completely handcuffed until I managed to release him.

By careful handling she gave it up and became a most amiable old bird. She was ideal for a beginner like myself, and ever since having her I have been convinced that a buzzard is a far better bird to start with than the more generally favoured kestrel.

When Unk showed 'Sea Hawks', the osprey film, at the Polytechnic in Regent Street, I was on holiday from school. A window in Selfridge's advertised the film and was dressed to look like a Scottish moor, with a backcloth of hills and heather and a floor of greengrocer's grass. Ramshaw himself sat on a large papier-mâché rock. I was put in charge of him and used to go by train each morning from Sevenoaks to London, take Ramshaw from his perch on a flat roof at the back of the Polytechnic and cart him down to Selfridge's. I was just strong enough to carry him, and the top of his head was level with mine. This was the first paid job I ever had, and, although I forget how much Unk gave me, it seemed very generous and I felt quite rich.

Chauffeurs, waiting for their passengers, provoked Ramshaw by showing him the pet pekinese dogs left in their charge. He would stand a certain amount of cheek from these snub-snouted, over-fed pets, but there were times when a chauffeur would deliberately try to tease him by lifting up one of these pieces of eagle-bait and thrusting the unwilling creature against the window. Ramshaw would then leave his rock and, forgetting the glass was in his way, hurl himself against it, making the whole thing shiver and vibrate with the fury of his attack. Generally the chauffeur had the sense to remove the offending object, but sometimes I had to go out and remonstrate.

To while away the time I used to chat with the salesmen in charge of the tobacco department. One of them taught me that, if the handle of the cash register was pulled out a little way, the next time the machine was used the handle would come right off. I promptly put this trick into action all round the store.

In the afternoon I lugged Ramshaw back to the Polytechnic, where I parked him backstage, ready for Unk to fly him across the theatre at the end of the matinée.

Unk was a very good showman. Ramshaw had a habit that I have noticed since in other eagles. After he had flown across the stage he would be given a piece of food on the ground, bang in the centre of the proscenium. Unk would then say, 'Ramshaw, stand to attention,' and, at the same time, step just behind him. Ramshaw would naturally guard his food with outstretched mantling wings and, raising his head, gaze in a defiant attitude round the audience. This brought the house down as a rule, and Unk would take him up and go down into the stalls, where admiring children and adults thronged around to stroke him. He really was amazingly tame and put up with all sorts of indignities. Fortunately he could not understand what people said. Dear old ladies would come up and say, 'He's so like my Polly at home. Would he like a monkey-nut?' On one occasion Unk, who had been inundated with inane remarks and stupid questions and had endeavoured to be polite and tactful, replied, 'No, madam, not nuts, but he wouldn't mind the parrot.'

I was sorry when it was time for me to return to school, but the show was closing down soon so that Unk could do another American tour.

7 * The Blasted 'Eath

The Plain. Those two words must conjure up so many different feelings in different people. To archaeologists – Stonehenge, Woodhenge, Wansdyke; to ornithologists – corncrakes, quail, stone-curlews, hobbies and the great bustard, now extinct in England, whose name is perpetuated by a pub; to soldiers – Larkhill and Bulford, the ranges and manœuvres galore; to the average person – just a large tract of open country, not of much interest and damned cold in winter when the wind and rain sweep over it or blizzards block the roads across it. 'A proper blasted 'eath sort of a place,' as someone once remarked.

But to me, and to other falconers, the Plain was a sort of magical land, a happy hawking-ground where trees and hedges were few and far between; a place where shepherds still herded flocks and a horse could be ridden for miles without being brought up short against that American invention, the curse of all horsemen and falconers and the delight of invisible menders – barbed wire. But Salisbury Plain was a favourite hawking-ground long before the days of barbed wire. Sir Ralph Sadler, Queen Elizabeth's falconer, lived on the Plain. He once received a royal raspberry for taking Mary Queen of Scots out hawking too far afield, when he was in charge of the royal prisoner at Tutbury castle.

When Unk went off to the Plain that summer after I helped him train Cheetah and Bonus, I felt very much left out of things. For the past few years I had been left to my own devices while the rest of the family went off to the South of France. This year my father had rented a house on the edge of Dartmoor, and we were all going there at the time of Unk's visit to the Plain. He was to join us later, and the first weeks of our holiday couldn't go fast enough for me.

Unk joined us from Avebury with a mixed tale of success and woe. The first few days it had rained solidly every day, and they had not been able to do more than fly the falcons to the lure between showers. After that it had cleared up, and the two falcons had both done well. He had brought them with him, together with two merlins. Scottie the tiercel had been lost.

I was delighted. I took the little jack merlin while he took the female, and we flew them together in a cast, for although the moor was ideally open for flying, there was very little to fly at. On our first day out, there was bright sun, very hot, and not a breath of wind. We walked across the moor about thirty yards apart and found absolutely nothing. Even Unk was getting a bit impatient after we had covered several miles. Coming over a ridge we saw a road cutting across our line of march, and beyond that cultivated country started again.

As we walked on down the slope, up got a lark. Both the merlins went off and we stopped to watch. The lark knew trouble was on his tail and went up like a lift; the two merlins started to climb too, in order to get above him. They went ringing up, making great sweeping circles in the sky, gaining height as they went, while we lay back in the heather and Unk got his Zeiss glasses out. Eventually the lark vanished from sight straight above us, then my little jack disappeared, and finally the merlin was swallowed up in the blue. We lay there and searched the sky where they had last been seen.

Suddenly they reappeared. The lark was leading, dropping like a stone as he fled to cover, with the two merlins stooping at him, first one then the other, taking it in turns like roadmen with sledge-hammers driving a spike. Every time the lark avoided the stoop and continued his dizzy drop earthwards.

Just across the road, not more than three hundred yards from where we had started, was a field running to a sharp point. In this corner, bounded by tall hedges, was a thick bed of nettles, into which all three dived. We walked over to pick them up. Unk said, 'You know, I really hope that lark has dished them. After flying like that he deserves to. You won't see a flight like that again in a hurry.'

As we pushed our way through the hedge the nettles swayed in

one place, and we could hear the merlins' bells ringing. I slipped
down the bank, parting the nettles carefully, and bent down to the
two merlins at my feet; I could see the lark's tail feathers. I picked
them both up on my fist. 'They've got his tail but he's gone down a
rabbit hole.'

Unk was right as usual; only twice since then have I seen merlins
go up out of sight, and, although the flights were good, they did
not equal this.

I had to be content with flying the merlins, for there were no
rooks for the falcons. One day out on the moor my little jack flew
and caught a pipit some way off from us. We were several hundred
yards apart and both of us walked to where we thought the jack had
gone into the heather. We agreed on the spot and dropped a white
handkerchief to mark it.

We spent two hours searching and simply could not find him, in
spite of knowing that he could not be far from our marker. He
matched the heather perfectly and froze whenever anyone was near,
so that his bell was silent. We walked up and down, but he remained
hidden. The next morning, when we went out to the spot and swung
a lure, he jumped out of the heather within six feet of our marker.

A few days later the female vanished over a ridge flying a bird,
and we failed to find her. While we were searching the next day, a
small girl approached us over the moor and asked if we were looking
for a lost hawk. The merlin had suddenly appeared while her family
were having tea the previous day, having chased a wheatear into
their dining-room. The wheatear had gone up the chimney, and the
merlin had taken stand on the small girl's shoulder. They had put
her in the greenhouse for the night and in the morning had let her
go. We went in the direction indicated, and after a short walk the
merlin came in to the whistle.

The next day was Unk's last with us and he decided to let the jack
go wild on the moor. We flew them both in the afternoon. Then,
at the end of the day, we cut the jack's jesses off and, giving him his
day's rations, left him sitting on a rock, eating. I was to go out each
day, pick him up, fly him, and leave him out each night, either until
our holiday was over or until he failed to turn up to the lure.

I spent all the next day looking for him, my arm getting quite tired from swinging the lure. Unk waved from the carriage window, as his train went past taking him back to Sevenoaks, and I spread my arms wide to show I had seen no signs of the jack before waving in return. I returned somewhat sadly in the evening, and although I spent several more days looking for him the jack never appeared and was evidently fending for himself somewhere else.

The following year, Unk, who knew that I had been disappointed at not going to the Plain the previous year, not only took me with him but got me a merlin of my own too. Runty, the merlin, was not by any stretch of wishful thinking a first-rate performer, but it is far more satisfying to train and fly one's own bird, however mediocre, than to watch one trained by somebody else, even if it is considerably better. That's how I have always felt about it, and I think that the state of falconry now is a lot better than it was fifty years ago, when, although the standard was undoubtedly higher, nearly all the owners employed professionals to train their hawks. I am quite sure that this is why falconry books written at that time are very good at telling you how the hawks should behave but never explain how to get them to that happy state. Obviously the authors simply did not know, because they left all the hard work to their falconers.

Certainly I got a great deal of enjoyment from Runty. I was terrified to have her loose in case I lost her. At first I got her over-keen, a very easy thing for a beginner to do. Then I gave her too much, and she not only refused to fly at anything but sat in a tree and utterly disdained all my lures. Eventually I struck the happy medium and all went well.

We set off for Avebury with the Austin crammed full of luggage, hawk's blocks, baths, and the hawks themselves. Other falconer friends arrived with their birds, mostly merlins, but with a sprinkling of sparrow-hawks, one or two goshawks and one other peregrine besides Unk's two, Allan and Lundy. That season Unk had been unable to get any falcons, which he preferred because he considered that a tiercel was really not quite heavy and powerful enough to deal with rooks easily.

Not only falconers, but other friends, joined us, among them George Lodge the bird artist, whose pictures of birds of prey have never been equalled. I had met him before, at his studio in

Camberley, where I had been intrigued not only by his paintings, but also by his collection of stuffed birds, all done by himself and far superior to those of a professional taxidermist.

At Avebury that year we had fifteen merlins. To the average person merlins look as much alike as sheep do. But, in the same way that a shepherd knows each sheep, so we knew each merlin. George Lodge would wander out after breakfast armed with a little canvas-topped stool, much battered from long service in bad stations, and a small sketch-book. While the merlins were bathing and preening, enjoying the morning sun, he would quietly sketch them. In the evenings we were allowed to see his day's bag. Later on I was to know him even better and see him at work on more finished paint-ings; but it was that ability to distinguish, in a pencil sketch done in a few minutes, any one of fifteen merlins, that made me realize just how good an artist he was.

The hawks attracted a lot of people, including the Press. One poor little man, who had tagged after us all day across country, lugging an enormous great camera and a box of slides, at last packed up and decided to return to Fleet Street. His bump of location cannot have been very good, for he stood on the wrong side of the road whilst the bus he wanted pulled in opposite him. Its engine remained running and both driver and conductor, immersed in conversation, failed to hear the little cameraman's somewhat feeble cry of 'Swindon? Swindon?' uttered at intervals, rather like a young chicken with the hiccups. I suppose he was too worn out to drag himself across the road. Anyway, the bus drove off, leaving him still plaintively call-ing out, 'Swindon? Swindon?' He finally repaired to the bar and someone took pity on him and ran him to the station. Next year we had a male gos called Swindon!

In the middle of the fortnight the president of the Falconers' Club, Sir Umar Hyat Khan, came to see the fun. He arrived in a very large Rolls, accompanied by various turbaned servants.

A small fleet of cars assembled for rook-hawking the following afternoon. Leading it was Unk's very old and battered Austin, rarely washed, never polished, somewhat rusty, with a thin red waistline that Unk had added one day, 'to make it look dashing', he said. Then came Sir Umar's gorgeous Rolls, gleaming and sparkling in the sun, followed closely by an enormous yellow and black open tourer, an American Studebaker that stood nearly as high as a bus and only needed Toad of Toad Hall with goggles and cap at the wheel. There followed a collection of cars from the opulent to the near scrap-heap.

On board this fleet was an even more motley collection of people, some smart in plus-fours, some, like myself, in ancient grey flannels that had been patched after fighting losing battles with barbed-wire fences, some in riding-breeches, like Unk. Others, who had yet to find out that scrambling over fences and ditches and walking through wet stubble were not conducive to keeping a crease in one trousers, were still in smart suits. It was not surprising that our progress along the road, together with the attraction of the falcons, caused other motorists passing by to join in. We caught very little, but enjoyed ourselves a great deal, and the local farmers, who gave us permission to fly over their ground, at least got their rooks scared off free of charge, and we took care not to damage any late-season standing corn. Modern falconers are more considerate than those of the ninth century. In 821 the monks of Abingdon had to obtain a charter from King Kenulph to restrain over-enthusiastic falconers who had been trampling down their oats.

It was at Avebury that Unk, for once, much to my joy, made a mistake. Allan, one of the tiercels, had a broken tail-tip, and Unk wanted to round the ragged end with a pair of scissors. I took Allan on my fist. 'Mind you don't cut his primaries by mistake,' I ventured to say, for I could see one wing was under the tail. 'Are you trying to tell me how to do the job?' Unk replied in his snootiest voice. I kept very quiet. Two seconds later there was a bellow from him, 'Damned if I haven't done exactly that!' I had to laugh; so many times he had been able to say, 'I told you so.'

Avebury was, for me, a very happy time. The following year was even better. Unk gave me a falcon of my own, and I was allowed to buy a goshawk with my Post Office savings. Fryga cost three pounds, which was very cheap for a female gos, but she had had a malformed beak. The top mandible had crossed over the bottom one, though before she came to me her owner had succeeded in straightening this by means of a cunning contrivance of wire braces fixed to a hood, rather like a dentist dealing with rabbit-teeth in a child.

I was torn in two; to have owned either would have filled my cup of happiness; to have both, overflowed it. I had no favourite but vacillated between them. If I was carrying the gos, then I felt that the falcon might be jealous; I would put Fryga down and pick up the falcon, only to imagine that the gos's feelings would now be hurt.

Besides my two birds Unk had two falcons, a tiercel and a gos, so we had plenty on our hands. He arranged for just the two of us to stay at Shrewton, also on the Plain, before joining the usual gang at Avebury.

We started flying before we even reached Shrewton. Unk spotted a tempting bunch of rooks well away from cover, and we flew two of the falcons at them. This flying in a cast is rather a tricky business. The two falcons concerned must be exercised together fairly frequently or one may attack the other. When they are being flown at quarry they may not necessarily choose the same bird, and it is quite possible for one to fly in one direction, while the other is busy chasing another rook half a mile or more away. So the two falconers must agree as to which bird they are looking after and not waste time arguing the toss. Even more important is the fact that no lures must be shown till it is obvious that both falcons have given up or till one has killed. If all goes as it is intended, they both chase the same bird and join in the kill together.

On this particular occasion the two falcons took off after different rooks and paid no attention to each other. Unk's put her rook into a ditch, where she grabbed it on the ground; mine chased one to a bunch of stacks and had a rat hunt round and round them. I rushed up, panting hard, shouting to drive the rook out of the stack-yard. He took to the open again, but, hard-pressed, turned back to the stacks, the falcon hard on his tail. As the roundabout started again she grabbed hold of him. So we considered we had done pretty well and drove on to the Catherine Wheel.

At one time the Old Hawking Club had had its springtime headquarters here in the village. It was an august body, very exclusive, and had its own club hawks and professional falconers. There have been a number of hawking clubs at various times. In 1839 the Loo Hawking Club was founded at Apeldoorn in Holland, with the Prince of Orange as patron. In 1884 there was a Russian club in Moscow. Today there are American, British, Dutch, French, German, Italian and Spanish hawking clubs, but they no longer fly club hawks and merely try to keep the sport going.

George Lodge had been out with the Old Hawking Club many times and used to tell us all about the horse-drawn van in which the falcons were carried to the field, and how men had been employed to stand a mile or so downwind of the flying-ground to act as markers if the falcons should come their way. It was all carried out in high style and very different from our throw-the-falcon-off-and-hope-she-goes methods.

But we did have some extremely good flights, for Unk was by no means content with rat hunts, once the falcons had learnt the business. Certainly rooks are, generally speaking, easier to catch in August than in the spring. Nevertheless we found some that were prepared to try to outfly the falcons in the air, and so gave us the same sort of ringing flight that we had had with the merlins on Dartmoor. The added size and weight of the peregrines made them even more dramatic than the dainty little merlins.

My gos managed to start off in business a day or two before Unk's bird. With a party of helpers we walked in line across the stubble with a hawk at each end of the line. Hares were in short supply though, and we walked the whole of one afternoon and found only one, which, fortunately for me, got up in my half of the line and was caught fairly easily by Fryga, much to my delight. It was a three-quarter-grown leveret and even then weighed more than the hawk.

A few days later we decided to switch to rabbits, as hares were so hard to find, and in a short time Unk's score soared ahead. He did so well that I gave my hawk an evening off to find out why. I had been flying mine at the scores of rabbits out feeding in the evenings and, although she did her best, they were never far from their holes and were able to beat her to it, as a rule. The Plain was 'hotching' with rabbits then, and the whole hillside seemed to move as they dashed for safety.

Unk, however, went farther down the hill, where the grass was longer and where there were no big buries but only small isolated ones. Here we saw no rabbits out, and the hawk was not tempted to long, exhausting chases in the distance.

Walking slowly through the tussocks and kicking each likely-looking bit of cover, Unk soon flushed a rabbit at his feet, and the gos had only a short flight before she caught it. Every so often she would miss, as the rabbit dodged her in the thick grass or dived down a near-by bolt-hole. But the score steadily mounted, and I soon saw why his hawk could catch eight, twelve or even fifteen in an evening, while mine, flying far more, only took perhaps four or five.

Then the weather turned on us and for several days it rained ceaselessly. We stood in the open doorway of the outhouse where we kept the hawks in bad weather and watched the rain trickle off the pantiles and form large puddles on the path outside. We waited each day till the last moment before feeding the hawks up, in the hopes of a break in the clouds, but it remained grey and dismal, and the rain continued to fall in streaky sheets.

After four days of this Unk got desperate, so we set off, clad in macintoshes and old hats, and well gumbooted. I held an old umbrella which we had managed to borrow and kept the gos dry as she sat on Unk's fist. We put up a hare very soon after leaving the car, and the gos caught it after a short flight.

All too soon the holiday came to an end. The following year Unk was in Africa filming some more eagles, and I went to Avebury without him. Charles Tunnicliffe was there to make the illustrations for Henry Williamson's book, *The Peregrine's Saga*, and did some lovely woodcuts of a little tiercel of mine. I flew a female sparrow-hawk and lost her the first day; but I got her back ten days later, and her outing had obviously done her a lot of good as she went like a bomb and even caught a sparrow under the table in the pub dining-room.

But Unk's voice, saying to someone with a beautiful but not very successful hawk, 'The acid test, old boy, is: does it catch anything?' was sadly missed by me.

8 * A Snake in Matron's Bathroom

Up with the lark means getting up a lot earlier than one would imagine. Walking across the dew-drenched Downs before dawn, to watch some wild peregrines on the chalk cliffs of the Sussex coast, I was surprised to hear larks singing in the dark. I was also surprised to find myself at a school that encouraged such things, for previous experience had led me to believe that anything one did on one's own was likely to be banned.

But here I had not only my house-master's permission but his blessing as well. What is more, I found myself enjoying being educated. This was not one of those run-wild, do-as-you-please schools. We had set working hours and all the rest of the normal school curriculum, but we were allowed quite a lot of freedom, provided we asked permission first. We were even allowed our own dogs, as long as they behaved.

The wild peregrines didn't nest that year, and so my hopes of getting my own eyass were doomed to disappointment, but just round the corner from Rottingdean I found a kestrel's nest which I thought I could reach from below, if I could get hold of a sufficiently long ladder.

I persuaded a builder to lend me a sixty-rung ladder. Two school friends assisted me, and at eleven o'clock one evening we set out. Now a sixty-rung wooden ladder is a pretty heavy affair, and the three of us staggered along down the main street lugging this unwieldy monster between us. We were by no means a silent crew. The heavy end went first, carried by a boy who was extremely deaf and who was convinced that we were letting him take the whole load. Our efforts to converse with him must have roused the local inhabitants, but nobody stopped us on our somewhat erratic course. Reaching the sea front, we found we had miscalculated the tide; the point we had to go round was under water.

We had not lugged the cumbersome ladder all that way to be put off by any trivial stretch of salt water. It was a warm night, the ladder would float, so we stripped and half swam, half waded, pushing the ladder in front of us. Once round the point, we had a struggle to erect the ladder up against the cliff but finally managed it after a lot of puffing and blowing – only to find it was about six feet too short!

The return journey along the pitch-dark street was, in spite of our failure, hilarious. Our deaf friend refused to take the heavy end, so we put him in the middle with the heavy end behind. This time he did carry nearly the whole thing on his own, for we were laughing too much at his remarks to take our full share of the burden.

I got a kestrel in the end, a rather sad, battered little male that I bought from a pet shop. He had no tail worth wagging. I couldn't get a kestrel's tail for him, so he had to do with a black one off a dead jackdaw I found on the beach.

This process of repairing broken flight feathers is known as imping. There are various methods, but the most successful as far as tails are concerned is to cut the broken feather off at the place where the quill is hollow, about an inch from the base. The replacement feather is cut in the same place, and the two are joined by inserting a wooden peg, whittled down to fit exactly into the hollow quill and secured by glue; half of the peg is in the new feather and half in the old.

The operation is quite painless as there is no more feeling in the quill than in one's finger nail. When the bird moults, as it does once a year, the complete feather is pushed out by the new one as it grows.

My kestrel looked very smart with his new tail and was quite a puzzle for ornithologists, for the joins were hidden under the tail coverts. Having had no tail for some time, he had got used to flying without one. The first time he flew with his new tail he applied his brakes in the normal way and found them so improved that he stopped before he had reached his intended destination.

Besides the kestrel we had a lot of fancy pigeons; there were frill-backs, tumblers, rollers, tipplers, brunners, nuns, pouters and a charming little almond owl-pigeon, which had a most attractive plumage of browns, greys and greens. Lost racing pigeons often joined in with this flock, which grew rapidly.

We also had lizards, toads and a big black Aesculapian snake with a bright red lining to his mouth, which he opened wide when startled and out of which continually flickered his black, forked tongue. He was quite harmless and didn't mind being handled. He was lost for some days and reappeared in Matron's bathroom. There was also a very pretty leopard snake, who climbed trees well. When we put him on a chain, he progressed along in a flowing tandem of s's, making a most attractive pattern with his yellow and black markings.

We kept these creatures in a little brick-built shed in the garden where a predecessor had had four monkeys. These had got loose one day and taken refuge in the headmaster's room, where they sampled toothpaste, tried out his wardrobe and discovered a large bottle of cascara pills. They were there for several hours before the room was rescued.

The school had its own pack of beagles, which met twice a week. Those who followed them did so in two ways: the energetic kept up with the hounds; the more crafty and lazy, who knew that hares run in large circles as a rule, kept on cutting across and saw quite a bit of the hunt, but got left high and dry if they miscalculated.

What lovely names hounds seem to have! Nailer, Clasper, Songster, Truly, Ranter, Gracious, seem more fitting than those so often given to pampered pet pekinese. The places hounds met had nice names too: Piddinghoe, High Barn, Firle, Gore Farm, and so on.

Naturally, besides beagling, we played the normal school games. Cricket I loathed; it bored me intensely to cross over every six balls from one patch of dandelions to a similar patch on the other side of the pitch. When it was my turn to bat I was invariably missing, having wandered off birds'-nesting, or on some other interesting ploy. I am afraid I was not very team-minded. After one match I forgot myself so far that I joined in with the opposing team and cheered my own side for their gallant failure! I still consider the

F

only way to watch cricket is from a comfortable deck-chair on a warm day, suitable food and drink to hand, and armed with a good book.

Being allowed to keep hawks at school was a great joy to me. When the holidays were over I could look forward to flying them at school; my goshawk not only provided a number of people with their first sight of falconry, but, as she caught quite a number of rabbits, I was able to sell the surplus and add to my pocket-money.

We used ferrets to bolt the rabbits for her. We kept them in a hutch opposite her perch on purpose to get her accustomed to them. If you want to stop a hawk going for any particular thing, this is the way to do it. They soon get used to chickens, for instance, yet still fly pheasants unhesitatingly.

When my uncle went on his second expedition to Africa he left his trained African hawk-eagle in my care. She delighted in the name of Belli, not on account of her figure but simply because her Latin name was *Polemaëtus bellicosus*. I took her back to school by train, hooded and parked on the luggage rack. She was quite unnoticed by a lady sitting on the seat directly underneath, and would have remained so but for a slight disaster just as we arrived at Brighton Station. The train pulled up with a jerk and upset the eagle, which promptly gave the unsuspecting traveller a slice of luck all over her coat; with embarrassment I apologized and explained that it is very difficult to house-train birds. She looked up at Belli, sitting on the luggage rack, and said, 'Oh dear, it's an eagle, I thought it was a pot of cream.'

Local landowners were extremely kind to us and let us fly our hawks over their property, sometimes coming with us to watch, and invariably giving us tea afterwards.

One day, when we had been invited out to fly the hawks, we arrived at an enormous mansion to find a large house party all set to join in. It was all very grand, with stirrup-cups being handed round by a very Jeeves-like butler. Head- and under-keepers hovered in the background with large game-bags slung over their shoulders, and it was obvious to me that this was one of those occasions when everything would go wrong. The gos had one foot swollen, the crowd would probably frighten her, and I fully expected her to go bolshie. Probably she would take stand in the tallest un-climbable tree and stay there, ignoring my lure, causing me much embarrassment and loss of face.

We set out. It was a sunny, crisp winter's day, the rabbits were all sitting in tussocks of grass some way from their burrows and there were plenty of them. Fryga, the gos, despite her bad foot, was in top form. Nothing worried her, and rabbit after rabbit was caught, with enough missed to make it appear not too easy. By about four in the afternoon we had caught fifteen, and I was hoping to beat my uncle's record of twenty-three head in one day, when the keeper came up and said, 'Would you mind stopping now, please? We have a rabbit shoot on tomorrow and never realized your hawk would catch so many.' So we walked back to the house for tea. I rapidly calculated my profit if I kept two rabbits for hawk's food and sold the remainder at 2s. each. After tea we thanked our host and went out to the car. The rabbits had all vanished except for the one solitary one I had used for feeding the hawk. It was very sad, but of course my host was perfectly right.

We also had a lot of fun with the peregrines on the Downs, flying mainly at rooks, but sometimes at magpies, though they were very elusive and really needed two falcons flown together to outwit them. I thought I had one of these dodgy customers beat one day. Coming over the top of a hill I saw a single magpie poking about in the valley below. There was no cover of any sort and it would have to fly out of the valley before reaching any. I slipped the falcon and she made off after the pie, but he took refuge amongst a flock of sheep. The falcon waited overhead, and we moved the sheep on but never saw our pied friend again. He was certainly not on the ground and must have moved with the sheep, by clinging to their wool.

When the time came for me to leave school I was genuinely sorry.

9 * Business and Pleasure

I was down in the kitchens, armed with a pencil. On either side of me were great wooden tables stacked high with mountainous piles of plates. I picked up a plate, balanced it on the fingertips of my left hand and gave it a sharp blow on the rim with my pencil. It gave forth a dull, deadened sound. Cracked! I tried the next one. This responded with a more resonant ringing sound. I examined it for chips and passed it as sound.

The contents of the kitchens alone took more than a day. The day before I had been picking up gilt chairs and examining their state of health. Four of us had been doing this sort of thing for a week. We were in the Mansion House and were checking the inventory for the Lord Mayor. Two of us were seeing what the outgoing Lord Mayor had done in the way of damage, and the other two were making sure that we didn't cheat and pass on the defects to the incoming Lord Mayor.

Working in my father's office in London was certainly a change from school. Although the firm specialized in the management of country estates, there was also a certain amount of work in London itself, a lot of it dull routine: copying plans, making specifications for repairs and decorations to buildings, sending out tithe notices, and so on. Every now and then something more interesting would crop up, and, as I was trying to learn all the aspects of the business, I usually managed to go along to see what it was all about. I also went to the College of Estate Management, to help me with the various examinations ahead.

So here I was, commuting daily from Sevenoaks by train, dressed in a City suit and armed with an umbrella – when I remembered to carry the darned thing. My father also insisted that I should wear a hat, though this often got left behind, for I felt a complete idiot in it.

Our office then, was just off Bond Street, and we looked down to St James's Palace. Later we moved to even better premises in St James's Street over Lock's the hatters. This put us on the route taken by all the big royal processions, jubilees, funerals, coronations, weddings, and so on, and gave us a grandstand view. Some of these I saw, but at King George VI's coronation I was in Haslemere with my cousin, Robert, flying the African eagle Belli.

She, also, considered it to be a holiday and flew off out of sight. It was a blazing hot day and Marley Common was scorching; we got hotter and hotter looking for the eagle and were very glad to come across a cottage with a well. Glass after glass of icy-cold water we downed, to the cottagers' amazement, and then continued our search.

Eventually, we found the eagle, sitting in a tree admiring the view. Robert got her down to the lure and we went home on his motor-cycle, I on the pillion with the eagle.

Back in London the hot weather made it pleasanter to take sandwiches into St James's Park than to eat in a stuffy restaurant. The many varieties of duck here were intriguing, especially the little black and white tufted drakes, who dived down after food and bobbed up again like corks, the water running off their backs, their crests making them look very perky.

I had a Zeiss plate camera and took lots of photographs of them, with varying success. It seemed rather cheating to me, as they were very tame and required no carefully camouflaged hide; indeed, they tended to come too close. Because, after a while, it seemed too easy to photograph them swimming or standing by the edge, I tried to get some flight shots. This was far more difficult. Either the bird was too small or it was not in focus.

However, I persisted, at the same time cutting my expenses by developing my own plates by the old-fashioned dish method. I spoilt a lot of shots before I got much good at it. Unk was away, and finally I bought a book, which told me that development by inspection gave the best results, but that the plates must first be desensitized. So I dabbled in a chemical called pinacryptol green, and held dripping wet negatives up to dim safe-lights, trying hard to judge whether they were developed correctly.

Every fine day most of my lunch-hour was spent standing on the bridge in St James's Park. Every duck that took wing, I carefully watched and followed through the view-finder. On a good day I might take a dozen shots; sometimes not a duck would come my way. I learnt from the dud negatives how near the birds must be before it was any use taking a shot. One day a mallard drake came straight at me and then banked away at the last minute. A tufted drake also obliged directly overhead; and I had hopes of one other shot.

That evening it was quite exciting, wondering if they would be any good, hoping they were placed well in the negative and that I had not cut off a wingtip or a tail. When I saw the images start to appear I realized that, even if they weren't perfect, they were considerably better than my previous attempts. The tufted duck promised well, and the mallard drake banking looked just right to me. When it had cleared in the fixer I could see feather detail quite well. I washed them thoroughly and hung them up to dry.

The prints turned out even better than I expected. I was delighted and really thought I had achieved something. I got a second prize in *The Field* with the mallard, being beaten by a sunset, which, although a beautifully composed picture, could not possibly have taken the photographer so much time or used so many negatives. I showed the photograph to Unk on his return from abroad, and he was very enthusiastic about it. Years later that particular picture was very useful to me.

Office holidays were, of course, far shorter than school ones, and flying the falcons was very difficult for they needed constant exercise if they were to remain fit and continue to fly well. I had a very smart little tiercel one year, and, as he had done quite well during the holiday, I decided to try to keep him going a bit longer. So I got up early and flew him to the lure each day before going to the station. It didn't work. He was fit at the week-end but far keener on coming to the lure than flying at partridges. So I decided I had better let him go wild, turning him loose in the park till he no longer came in for food. I was loath to part with him, but had no wish to keep him tied to a block all his life, as useless as a cage bird.

I took him across the park the next morning, put him on the wing and walked towards the station while he followed overhead. When I had only a few hundred yards to go before reaching the park wall I flushed a covey of partridges, and he turned over and knocked one down, in spite of the short distance it had to go to cover. I gave him enough to keep him satisfied till next morning and left him eating. Then I cached my gumboots and hawking gear by the park wall, in a convenient hollow tree, and, putting on my town shoes, hopped over the wall and dashed off to catch my train.

On my way home, after retrieving my gear, I walked back across the park, swinging the lure idly and whistling in case the tiercel was around. To my great joy, he appeared at once and took the lure. So I carried him back and put him on his block. The next day I did the same thing, but, failing to find any partridges, I left him with his ration. In the evening he was overhead by the time I was half-way across the park.

This went on for a couple of months. Every so often he would catch a partridge as we went stationwards. At week-ends I flew him in better country. Being loose so much he became extremely fit, and, although I had no dog, he was prepared to wait on overhead for half an hour or more at a time.

Then shorter hours of daylight and early morning mists put an end to our efforts at combining commuting with game-hawking. So I took him down to the Isle of Grain one week-end, bid him a fond farewell, and, as Shakespeare so aptly puts it, 'Whistled him off and let him down the wind to prey at fortune'. It was a wrench parting with him.

I found the journeying up and down daily to London a miserable affair. In wintertime one never saw home in daylight, except at week-ends. So, in spite of family opposition, I left home and found a large semi-basement room in the Cromwell Road where I set up house. At week-ends I either went home, stayed with Unk, or visited friends in the country.

A client of my father's, who was interested in falconry, kindly allowed me to keep the hawks in his Kensington garden. He was keen to see them fly, but was confined to a wheel chair, so I some-times exercised a merlin in the garden for him to see.

Later on I had a tiercel, which I exercised very early in the

mornings in Hyde Park. I had a perch in my bed-sitting room for
him in bad weather, or at night, and he behaved so well that I never
bothered to tie him up. In the mornings, when he thought I had slept
long enough, he would fly down onto the floor, half walk, half run,
in that ridiculous gait that all *falconidae* have, jump on the bed and,
very, very gently, tweak my ear. He was a most endearing bird.

I got back most evenings about 6 p.m., and about this time a
female sparrow-hawk would come low across the rooftops from the
direction of Hyde Park and disappear towards some unknown
destination. After I had noticed her doing this two or three times, I
used to try to get back just to see her. She was a haggard, an old
bird that had moulted at least once, and she looked very smart and
clean in spite of the dirty surroundings.

Later in the evenings a tawny owl would start calling from a
chimney-stack across the way and he obviously lived close by, for
eventually his whole family joined in and competed with the cats
in keeping down the mice and sparrows, and seeing who could make
the most noise.

One day a new estate was put in our hands. It belonged to a person
who had become mentally deranged and finally had to go into a home.
We went down to see the place. Just after we had turned into the
drive we had to stop, for there was a large tree lying across the way.
We left the car and walked on, clambering over several other fallen
trees. Obviously the owner had not taken much interest in his estate.

The house was a fairly large Georgian mansion, but its garden was
now inhabited by goats of all varieties, colours and ages. Little kids,
matronly nannies, and great horned old billies, yellow-eyed and
satyr-faced; all intent on wrecking the gardens. Some stood idly
chewing michaelmas daises, some nibbled at camellia bushes, while
others stood on their hind legs to tear down the rambler roses, which
fell round their heads, giving them a more leery appearance than ever.

But the goats were by no means the least of the eccentricities.
Inside it was so dusty that we left footprints behind us. It was like
walking in snow. Upstairs, in the long corridors, spiders had taken
over and their cobwebs were draped everywhere. Brushing against
a curtain, it disintegrated and fell in small pieces like the ashes that
lift on the thermal over a bonfire and gently float to the ground,

It was very spooky, and the makers of ghost films would have been most envious.

The billiards-room had a hole in the roof large enough for a bus to be lowered through. The table had been stripped of its cloth and the slate slabs used, in a very ingenious manner, to form the sides of enormous rabbit hutches.

The large drawing-room held the biggest surprise. It was cram, jam, full of cats. All mewing plaintively. It smelt to high heaven.

I held my nose, dashed across the room and unsnibbed the window. I wrenched it open; it was like raising a sluice gate. A river of cats poured out, streaming in all directions and disappearing in the goat-ridden gardens. I rapidly joined them. The air was fresher out there.

One week-end Robert and I went up on the Downs near Chichester, flying one of the hawks. We were sitting down, having a spot of grub, the hawk sitting on a stone close by, when we saw four wild hobbies, right up in the sky. These little falcons, not much bigger than kestrels, are summer residents, coming, like the swallows, from Africa, to nest in old crows' nests or anything else suitable.

These four, consisting of Mum and her three offspring, were chasing a swift. At least the three youngsters were each taking it in turn to try to catch the swift and Mum was following on behind, presumably shouting advice and encouragement. The swift easily avoided the youngsters' efforts, eluding them with deft twists as they endeavoured to foot him.

Mum, obviously fed up with her children's fumble-footedness, decided that a demonstration was called for. She suddenly changed gear, from a slow, easy beat, to a clip of the wings that gave her a power push with each quick thrust as she climbed up.

The swift was rapidly pulling away, a great gap between them. Still the old hobby climbed, till she was some two hundred feet higher. Then she turned down in a shallow-angled stoop; her speed increased still more by her wing-beats. She turned the pace on, and the gap that had been several hundred yards began to close at a fantastic rate. It was like a racehorse, flat out, coming up on a lumbering old carthorse. Both Robert and I knew how fast swifts could fly, for they swirled and twisted round the house at home, catching insects without hesitating in their stride. Now, in just the same way, the old hobby came up on the swift. This time there was no side-slipping, no dodging out of the way. She simply put out one foot and took him with no trouble whatsoever. Both her children and ourselves had had a demonstration that was perfect. There was no doubt in my mind that a hobby was the fastest British bird.

Every so often the British Falconers' Club had a 'falconers' feast' at the Cheshire Cheese in Fleet Street, where we had their famous Steak, Kidney, Lark and Oyster Pie, followed by their equally-well-known pancakes. It was at one of these dinners that I met Carlos, a Spaniard, who was very keen to see the hawks fly.

I invited Carlos down for week-ends every so often, and we took Susan, the old red-tailed buzzard, and hunted moorhens along the river or in the park. She was rather slow, but gave us a lot of fun and caught just enough to make matters interesting. She was best flown from the vantage-point of a tree and knew exactly what to do. She would fly up onto a high branch and take stand there while we pushed about in the undergrowth below or waded into the water and prodded likely-looking hiding-places under the banks.

Every so often a moorhen would scutter away across the surface. Susan would drop out of the tree and try to grab it before it reached cover. But moorhens, though slow, are pretty sly. More often than not, just as it seemed that Susan would be successful, the moorhen would drop with a splosh into the water, sending up a shower of spray and soaking Susan as she shot overhead to take stand in another tree and shake the water off. The moorhens swam under the water and rarely reappeared, for they knew how to get under the banks and then bob their heads up for air without giving away their hiding-places.

In one particular spot along the river there was a water-rail who nearly always gave Susan a flight but whose creepy ways and expert knowledge of available cover kept him out of trouble. We should all have been very sorry if she had caught him, for he deserved his freedom after the excitement he gave us.

It is surprising how excited you get over such a chase. Quietness is the rule as you go slowly along, searching all possible places. But once the quarry is flushed voices are apt to be raised. 'He's in that reed-bed just in front of you.' 'Push him out.' 'Not that way, you ass, the hawk's behind you.' There is a great deal of splashing, an agonized voice cries out, 'Blast, both my gumboots are full!' 'Do stop fussing about trivialities, you'll lose him if you stand there doing nothing. Now you're wet, go right through the reeds and you can't miss him.' The moorhen suddenly flies off upstream in the wrong direction. 'You idiot, you've sent it the wrong way.' 'I didn't send it, it went the way it wanted to. There's another, just under the bank by you, it's your turn to get wet.'

Susan would remain quite unruffled, until, more by luck than good judgement, a reasonable chance presented itself.

We went, one afternoon, up to Boar's Hill in search of three-quarter-grown rabbits, which were about the biggest thing Susan was likely to catch. It was a hot, cloudless day and we were soon very exhausted, so we let Susan sit in a tree while we rested in the shade underneath. Suddenly she crashed down into the bracken below. We went over and found her standing in a most unusual way, feathers all bristling out, wings spread, and obviously very excited. She had caught an adder and was as pleased as a child with a new toy. She danced on it. What is more, she started to eat it with great relish. Apparently it was the one thing she enjoyed most, and she certainly showed her pleasure.

She caught two more that afternoon, for the hot weather had brought them out to bask in the sun. The last one she caught was quite close to us, so we could see how she dealt with it. She flew straight at it, grabbed it on the ground and, with her feathers so puffed out that she looked twice her normal size, kept on grabbing it and letting go. The adder didn't attack, in fact it didn't have much chance to do anything, for Susan had an extremely powerful grip. I imagine that, had it struck her, it would only have got a mouthful of feathers. Presumably that was why she puffed them out so. Considering she had been in captivity for nearly three years and had never seen a snake before, unless her parents had brought them to the nest, it was extremely interesting.

Hawking with Susan may not have been very stylish but it was not to be despised.

10 * Spain

Two very official-looking gentlemen opened my suitcase, and at once a torrent of, to me, inexplicable language poured forth. Carlos took one look inside and said, 'Of all the damn-fool things to bring with you! You couldn't have thought of anything more likely to cause trouble than a revolver.' Robert stood by hooting with laughter, and Carlos promptly turned on him. 'You'll probably land up in jail too, it's no laughing matter.' I leaned forward, picked up the offending object and, putting the barrel in my mouth, proceeded to light up the butt. As soon as it dawned on them that it was really a pipe and not a gun they all began to laugh.

We were going through the customs at La Linea, on our way to La Mocheta, Carlos's house near Seville. He had, with true Spanish hospitality, been pressing me to visit him for a long time, and now Robert and I had travelled by Orient liner from Tilbury to Gibraltar for the sum of £4 each, and Carlos had met us there to drive us the remainder of the way.

We took a tiercel, a jack merlin, and a female sparrow-hawk. These nearly brought disaster at the start, for we had very little cash to spare and the purser suddenly demanded more for transporting the birds than for my own ticket. However, as I had been informed by the company before we started that they could travel free, we managed to dodge this.

The hawks were parked down below, on their respective cadges – lidless boxes with the top edges padded for them to sit on. They were hooded except when we brought them up each day for an airing and to feed them, when they caused a certain amount of stir amongst the other passengers. Robert took charge of the sparhawk, who was still only partially trained, and the constant carrying on deck helped to tame her.

The tiercel needed no such manning, for he was in his second season and had been what we called intermewed, that is to say, he had moulted in captivity, and was now looking very smart in his adult plumage. The word intermewed comes from the French *muer*, to change or moult, and in medieval times the mews were where the hawks were kept. When falconry was practised less and less the old word stayed, but became synonymous with stabling, for the horses, which had been used with the hawks, still remained. The royal mews in Henry VIII's day stood on what is now the site of the National Gallery in Trafalgar Square and spread down Whitehall.

The office of Master of the Hawks was given to those of high rank and was well paid. In 1536 the Master received £40 per month; for his under-falconers £10 was 'one hole yeres wages'. Ten shillings a day paid James I's bill for hawk's meat, and £600 kept him supplied with fresh hawks in one year. The Duke of St Albans was created hereditary Grand Falconer of England in 1686 at a salary of £1,000 per year. He continued to receive this until the present century, when, presumably, someone rumbled the fact that he was being paid for nothing.

Hawks and falcons moult once a year and, since they must fly in order to live, take about six months to change their feathers completely. Ducks and geese, which can survive perfectly well without flying, go into what is called 'eclipse' and drop their feathers all at once, being unable to fly for a few weeks while the new feathers are growing.

Not only does the adult plumage differ in colour and markings from the immature, but the main flight feathers grow shorter for some curious reason. This is not generally known, even by ornithologists, who do not have the opportunity to keep a bird under close observation for any length of time. The difference in length of a falcon's tail can be as much as an inch. But the adult plumage seems to be stronger and less likely to break.

The little jack merlin, very trim and smart, was being flown loose to a lure before we embarked, but we kept him on a creance on board in case we lost him. Merlins were the ladies' hawk of olden days and, if the poet is to be believed, were even carried by their owners at weddings.

> The lady by the altar stood,
> . . . And on her head a crimson hood, . . .
> A merlin sat upon her wrist,
> Held by a leash of silken twist.

I wonder what the bridegroom thought.

So we drove, hawks in the back of the car, through the country. Lesser kestrels abounded, very similar to our own kestrel but with the habit of nesting in flocks, often in holes in the stonework of some old building. It was September, and the landscape was very brown and dried after the hot summer. It was still hot then, about 90 degrees in the shade. Buff-backed herons fed amongst the grazing cattle and, like our jackdaws at home, stood on the backs of the beasts, feeding on the insect pests.

We climbed up into the mountains, decidedly cooler than the plains, and a deer leapt across the road and vanished among the rocks. In the distance some vast cone-shaped heaps, dazzling white in the sun, attracted our attention: salt. The idea of all that salt made one even thirstier. We pulled up and walked into a field and cut a melon from the thousands that were growing there like common marrows. Carlos halved it and put it in the sun. 'The heat makes it evaporate. In a few minutes it will be cooler to eat.' We asked if the farmer would mind, but apparently this was the accepted thing to do. I wondered what a farmer at home would say if he found one eating his mangolds and imagined the gruff, 'That don't need no interfering with.'

After the little fields and hedgerows of England this place seemed to stretch on for ever. What a place to fly hawks in, thousands of acres of dead-flat, treeless, fenceless land! If there was anything to fly at, it would be a falconer's paradise. Salisbury Plain was a forest compared to this.

We passed a white stone by the roadside. 'Everything from that stone on the right-hand side is my land,' said Carlos, 'and, of course, yours too.' 'Thanks,' we said, and I thought, 'He's a generous bloke, though we could hardly carry a couple of thousand acres away with us.'

We drove on for quite a time and then swung through some wrought-iron gates held open by two men. They saluted as we went through. 'We've been hours coming, how did they know when we would arrive?' I was just going to ask Carlos this when we pulled up at a large white house with green pantiles and wrought-iron grilles over the windows. Two more men opened the car doors and, as we climbed stiffly out, a maid appeared from the door with an enormous tray of iced drinks. Our baggage was whisked away. It was quite a welcome.

We gulped down the iced drinks, did a quick change, and went out with Carlos to tend to the hawks and then see the stables. They were, in estate agent's parlance, 'luxuriously appointed'. Highly-polished brass horses' heads, with rings instead of bits in their mouths, were used as hitching-posts. The harness room was very impressive, with rows of polo-sticks, racks of fly-whisks and crops, saddles of all sorts – cavalry, riding, racing – and a great Mexican cowboy one that looked like an arm-chair. In an enormous cupboard were *zahones*: like cowboy chaps, but without any fur. They were made from the hide of a fighting bull, polished till they shone with the patina of antique mahogany and inlaid along the edges with white catskin, each pair different. They were obviously the pride of the head stableman, who handed us each a pair after a searching look to judge our size. He showed us how to put them on, tying the leather straps round our waists and putting the leather fittings round our legs; the fastenings were very similar to the buttons on the hawks' leashes.

Horses were led up and we mounted, Carlos looking very elegant in a wide-brimmed hat and a coat with sleeves that were attached to the body by lacing.

We rode at walking pace through the olive trees and then, as the country opened out, broke into a canter. A herd of pigs, startled by us, rushed away squealing. They were quite different from any pig I had seen before, long, lean-bodied, sharp-snouted and red-tan coloured. Carlos told us that they fed mainly on the acorns from the cork trees at this time of year. Besides the olives and the pigs, the ranch, or *dehesa* as it was called, cropped the bark from these cork oaks. Every so many years the upper branches of any size were stripped and then, a few years later, the trunks themselves.

We stopped for a breather, and my horse sauntered over to a near-by tree and, stretching out his neck, seized hold of a bright lemon-coloured fig and ate it with obvious relish. I tried one and found it absolutely delicious. We picked a few to munch on the way and went on till we came out on top of a ridge looking over a valley. Sitting on a tree, its trunk completely bare and its top looking exactly like a spread umbrella, were some vultures silhouetted against the setting sun. They took off when they saw us, flapping clumsily with great sweeps of their wings till they gained speed. Then they began to soar, wings spread and primaries whipping and bending under the air pressure, unseen movements of their wrists opening and closing the feathers very slightly as the air currents altered. In great circles they rose up, ringing like a falcon after a rook, but with considerably less effort. The up-draught from the valley evidently helped them, and in a few minutes they were mere specks above, impossible to identify. A few minutes more and they were out of sight. It was a fantastic exhibition of soaring. We turned the horses homewards.

The next morning I woke early and decided to get up at once, even though it was only 5 a.m. I looked for the old clothes I had brought with me, but they had vanished. I was still searching the cupboards and drawers for them when there was a knock on the door and in they came, carried by a servant, who put them down and vanished immediately, before I had time to think what 'Good morning' was in Spanish. She reappeared a moment later with a tray of tea and a plateful of the little yellow figs that the horses and ourselves had so enjoyed the evening before some five miles away. Someone must have got up very early to fetch them.

As I dressed, Robert came in looking for some of his old clothes, which, like me, he had brought especially for mucking around in. The whole lot, all the things we had worn on the ship, even my old grey flannels, which had been covered in mud from a wet day out in Suffolk, had been washed and pressed, and I wished I had brought a few more of my old things with me if they were to be resuscitated like this. We went out into the sun and strolled over to the stables. One of the stablemen dashed off to the house and reappeared a moment later with two chairs, which he carefully placed about three feet away from, and facing, the whitewashed stable wall. He bowed very politely to us and motioned us to sit down. It would have been very rude of us not to, after all his trouble, but we felt a couple of proper Charlies looking at the wall just in front of our noses. We were debating how long politeness decreed we should sit in this fashion when Carlos came cantering through the gateway into the yard.

After breakfast we were introduced to Don Paco, a tame eagle owl that Carlos used as a decoy for shooting crows. The owl was taken out and put on a perch in an open place by the cork oaks, and close by was a carefully-built hide in which sat the gunner. The crows, who dislike owls, came along to mob it and were too intent on annoying the owl to notice the gunner in the hide.

We had over-fed all the hawks on the voyage over, thinking that the journey might upset them, and they were none too keen, with the exception of the jack merlin, who at least flew to the lure a short distance. While we were doing this I caught a glimpse of some extraordinary animals going through the trees in the distance; they looked like immense kangaroos from their odd method of progress. The binoculars showed them to be mules with their front legs hobbled. In order to move faster than at the shuffling pace their hobbles would allow if they walked normally, they humped their backs and lurched forward with their front feet together, like looper caterpillars. They got along at quite good speed this way, but it certainly looked very odd.

Like nearly every visitor to Spain, we went to see a bullfight. In addition we went over a ranch where the bulls are bred. We took the tiercel with us, as there were plenty of partridges there. The bulls were most impressive, but seemed remarkably quiet, though we were warned on no account to dismount from our horses, for if, by accident, you get between a bull and the rest of the herd, he would attack and, unless you were mounted, you were likely to find yourself an unwilling, unpaid matador. The bulls were kept in one herd and the cows, which were considered far more dangerous, in another.

We tried the tiercel at partridges, but they were all in thick cover, and the tiercel was extremely bad, still not recovered from his voyage and also, I think, feeling the heat. Certainly on such trips one must allow time for the birds to become acclimatized.

We saw a lot of bee-eaters, sitting on telegraph wires just as the swallows do over here. They are remarkably beautiful birds, not only in their colouring but in shape too. The down-curving beak, and the two deck feathers (centre tail feathers), which are longer than the rest of the tail and narrow down to a sharp point, made them very easy to identify. We also saw several hoopoes, very jay-like in their flight, but unmistakable with their pinkish-brown crests, tipped with black, which they raised like fans. They looked very slow fliers but in fact are well able to look after themselves in the air. A lot of birds have odd-sounding scientific names; but this one, *Upupa epops epops*, wins the prize, I think.

In the evening, back at La Mocheta, we were sitting outside when we were invaded by numbers of a very large type of maybug or cockchafer. They were attracted by the light and blundered about just like their English cousins, but their added size made them quite a missile. They would go crack against the light shade and fall to the ground, then crawl about a bit before taking wing again. They had feet which seemed to stick to one, making it quite difficult to shake them off. In the morning Robert got out his enormous great reflex camera and took photographs of some of the survivors.

He also spent a hard half-hour with the camera in a swamp not far from the house, where there were a number of little green frogs which jumped from reed to reed. Their colouring matched the reeds so well that it was quite hard to find them. Robert would spot one, stalk up quite close, then start to focus. Every time he was all set to take the shot the frog would jump a few feet to another reed stalk. Then he had to begin all over again, till finally he was successful.

The jack merlin was now ready to be flown and, remembering how the tiercel had disliked the heat, we waited till later in the day when it was getting cooler. We had no idea of what he would do, for he was completely untried and it was a case of finding something he would fly. He was reluctant to go at anything to start with, but I refused to give up. Usually if you persist with a merlin it will eventually decide to go, though it may take quite a long time about it.

In the end he went very well. He flew a small bird hard into the cover of some long grass, where he tried to plonk down onto it. It dashed off to a small patch of bushes, and the two went round and round, the jack sticking well to his quarry, which proved extremely elusive though not particularly fast. Then it plunged into the middle of the bushes and, while the merlin was trying hard to do the same, but finding it more difficult because of his greater size, the little bird seized the opportunity and made off. It flew close enough for Robert to identify it as a woodchat shrike.

We preferred to see the countryside from horseback, rather than visit towns and do the usual sightseeing. We also had a morning trying to shoot turtle-doves. These were as common as wood-pigeons are over here, and I suppose they did as much damage for their size. We set off very early and, after driving some distance, turned off the road into a stubble field. Here were more people and a collection of dogs. We were taken to our allotted stand and left there with a small sack of cartridges and a large piece of cold prawn omelette.

The guns were placed along a river which had dried up, leaving scattered pools of water under the trees where they shaded it from the sun. The doves came to these from the olive groves higher up the valley sides to drink. They circled round and, if they thought the coast was clear, would drop in very quickly at a steep angle. But they were extremely wary and not easy to shoot. If they caught sight of you they just gave a flip of their wings and were away. I missed a great many of them. Robert, who was next door to me, did a bit better, but after about two hours the birds stopped coming, except for an odd one. I wandered over to see how Robert was doing. Like me, he had heard guns going off busily on either side, and we were both rather worried over the smallness of our bag. We climbed up the bank to pick up one he had shot.

A dove circled overhead high up and some way off from us. Three
shots were fired, but unless someone had an ack-ack gun it was far
out of range. We felt a lot better. Carlos came up through the
tamarisk bushes, covered with a white rime from them. He saw
our small bag and grinned. 'Not easy, are they?' However the
Mocheta party had, in fact, got more than half the total. By now it
was getting hot, and we had a breakfast of melons and wine under
some trees.

That evening we had turtle-doves cooked with mushrooms on a
long silver spit, and they were delicious.

The following day we caught the Rapido bus back to Gibraltar,
or rather to Algeciras, where we took a ferry to Gibraltar. It was
aptly called the Rapido; round hairpin bends with steep drops on
one side and a cliff on the other, it lived up to its name.

A few days later we landed at Plymouth on a cold, grey, dismal
wet day.

11 * War

Tiger O'Toole his name was, not because he was any more ferocious than most of his kind, but simply because of the large number of long-service stripes on his arm. He had been teaching us musketry for twelve weary sessions. During the first session one of us had asked him a fairly simple question; he had stopped and gone right back to the beginning, word for word, parrotwise, straight from the Instruction Manual. We kept quiet after that.

Now we were on the last session with him and he was stuck. There was nothing in his well-thumbed manual which told him how to teach others to instruct.

He had whiled away part of the time by giving us what he called 'little jumps'. These consisted of a type of P.T. armed with a rifle. The main idea was to exhaust one or to give one cramp.

'Nah, look 'ere, you lot. I've taught yer all I knows abaht musketry. Nah I'm going to tell yer 'ow ter teach others. This's what yer does. Yer teaches from the Book.' He waved his musketry manual at us. 'Yer dusn't teach nothink what ain't in the Book. See? And if there's any bloke asks yer any awkward questions, either yer says, "Sod off", or "Come and see me arterwards". And if 'e's so bleedin' stupid that 'e comes and sees yer arterwards, then either yer says, "Sod off", or yer gives 'im the basterd book and yer tells 'im to teach 'is basterd self in 'is own basterd time. Dismiss.'

The war had been going for nearly two years when I was sent on this musketry course. I had originally volunteered for the Navy. I had taken a medical on a day when apparently I was the only naval-minded recruit present, which much upset the R.A.F. warrant officer in charge. He sent me to a naval petty officer who dwelt, appropriately enough, down below and who cheered up at the sight

of me. He put me on 'three-days minimum notice', and I departed
expecting to be called up at any moment. But the phoney war was
on, the Navy were in no need of my services, and time dragged on.
I badgered the Admiralty; I returned to my petty-officer chum and
nattered at him; I annoyed several naval officers in various depart-
ments at Portsmouth; I walked up the gang-planks of both H.M.S.
President and H.M.S. *Chrysanthemum*, moored by the Embankment.
But the fact remained that I was unwanted.

I had helped move a lot of the valuable documents from the office
up to my father's house in Suffolk, and I now joined Robert at the
Haslemere Educational Museum, giving very poor lectures on
natural history to evacuated school children, and waited impatiently.

Months went past and still nothing. I was more than fed up. I
was darned annoyed. I went to the recruiting office again and badgered them. An army officer finally took pity on me and offered me
a choice of the R.A. or the R.A.C. The former I knew meant guns,
the latter I had always understood to be a motoring organization,
but I was haughtily informed that it stood for Royal Armoured
Corps and involved tanks. Never having been particularly keen on
walking, I took up the offer of tanks.

A few days later I found myself a raw recruit at Bovington Camp
in Dorset. I began training as a member of a tank crew, though for
the first month we never touched a tank but did hour after hour of
square-bashing, interrupted by P.T., route marches, and what was
known as 'interior economy'. This phrase covered a multitude of
cunningly-devised ways of passing the time. Our troop was in the
Sandhurst Block, a new building only recently opened by the War
Minister himself. It was the pride of the officers and the most uncomfortable place I have ever lived in.

It was uncomfortable in the same way that the owner of a new
car makes his machine uncomfortable. 'Wipe your feet! Do mind
the paint work! Don't spill your ash.' The hardwood floors were
polished with a 'bumper' to such a degree that one would have
skidded on them had one walked on them. But no one did walk on
them, not without first removing their boots and laying down old
newspapers. The broom and bucket, issued to each room, were never
used. The broom-handle was scraped with old razor-blades to keep

it clean, and the bucket was highly polished. Interior Economy saw to all this and a lot more.

To a normal erstwhile civilian, it was all pretty silly, but not as silly as going on guard with ·45 revolvers and ·38 ammunition which dropped straight through. 'King's Rules and Regulations say yer shall 'ave harms and hammunition. Yer've got em, ain't yer? Then don't complain.'

I then went to Lulworth, where the regiment did its gunnery. The tank-gunners-to-be stayed here for their eight-week course. The drivers, radio-operators, cooks and concrete-block-makers (the two latter were synonymous I discovered when I asked a cook his civilian job) travelled daily from Bovington by truck.

They were known as the 'Bovington Boys' by the Sergeant-major in charge at Lulworth, who disliked them because he was unable to grab them for guard duty or fatigues. One grey winter's morning, about sparrow-cheep, we all paraded as usual on the concrete square, which was surrounded by a sea of tank-churned mud. It was snowing at the time and extremely cold. The bunch of red-nosed, shivering recruits fell in, and the Sergeant-major duly walked slowly down each rank. He said nothing but marched back to his place in front of us and stamped about to face us.

'Now, you Bovington Boys,' he said in a pleasant, conversational tone, 'your boots aren't up to standard, are they?' His tone changed to one of endearment. 'Tonight, when you go home to that lovely little camp, tonight, there's going to be a change. Just for once you won't go to the canteen.' His voice now roared out. 'Oh dear me no! And you won't go to the pictures. You'll sit on your bed with a boot on your hand, and you'll polish it for an hour. Then you'll do the other boot. And while they're cooling off you'll bump the floor and clean the windows. Then you'll spend another hour boot-polishing. And while they're cooling off again, you'll blanco your webbing, and dust the top of the door, where the Commandant runs his finger when he comes round on inspection.' The tones were now steely. 'And in the morning your boots should shine, and if they don't, I shall tighten the screw and the tighter the screw the brighter the shine.'

I never actually finished my recruit training. I applied for a commission, and, finding that I should have to wait at least nine months, having nothing much to do beyond peeling onions, bashing spuds, and digging slit trenches, I asked whether I could not instruct in some way or other. All unknowingly I had touched a hidden spring. Like Beachcomber's three Turkish acrobats, 'Ho yes,' they cried, 'manure, manure, manure.' Or words to that effect. Instead of finishing my training, I did a regimental instructor's course. In no time at all I had a squad of raw recruits under me, a lance-corporal's stripe on my arm, unpaid of course, and a bunch of gunnery pamphlets in my hand. But the hidden spring also snapped the trap-door shut behind me. Instructors were needed far more than officers, and once you became one it was very difficult to change. At that time I didn't know this but, as the months went by and I remained instructing, I found out.

I was sent, after instructing for nearly a year, on an instructor's course at the A.F.V. School. This was a cinch after taking recruits for a year. Then I did a course on Sherman tanks. In between times, when recruits were not pouring in, we swept up the leaves in the wood where the camp was situated, whitewashed the stones lining each side of the paths and did all we could to ruin the camouflage effect of the trees.

At week-ends I used to wander over the ranges bird-watching, and on hot days I bathed off the cliffside. I found a peregrine's eyrie one day and spent hours watching it. With a short length of rope I could easily have taken an eyass, but food rationing made it impossible to feed one. So I left them alone, saw them start to fly and even watched one of the young falcons knock down a gull.

I spent several leaves with Unk. On one of them he was very annoyed because a fence had been put up across the park and it was in his way. I suggested he either put a bridge over it or dig a tunnel under it. He considered for a moment, said, 'Right, come on then,' and collected a couple of spades and a pickaxe. By lunch-time it was finished, a slit trench with steps going down and steps up the other side.

Coal was short at the time and he burnt wood, gathered in the park. A friend who came to stay made the unwise remark that wood fires never gave out much heat. That afternoon Unk loaded a rope into a handcart and called to me, 'Come on, we'll show that bloke whether wood gives out any heat or not.' Across the park stood a Scots pine with one great dead branch high up. After several bosh shots we got the rope over the branch and, by pulling and letting go, got it rocking. Suddenly it cracked and came crashing down. When we got back I fetched the cross-cut saw, but Unk waved it away. 'You don't want that thing, just stick the end in the fire and as it burns we'll push it in.'

After dinner the fire was burning well already, but Unk was determined to have a really good blaze. So in went our branch, several feet of it sticking out into the room and under the sofa. Staying on the tree it had dried in the wind and never got soaked like a log in contact with the ground. It caught at the end and began to flare up. The flames crept along it out into the room, we rolled the carpet up out of harm's way and pushed the sofa back a bit. The room got hotter. We retreated again. Cooling drinks were distributed. The room became stifling. We pushed the sofa back till it hit the wall. 'Good fire tonight,' said Unk. 'How about opening the window a bit?' said our friend. 'Can't do that, old boy, spoil the blackout.' 'Well, it's getting too hot in here.' 'Too hot? You were the chap who said this morning that wood never gives out any heat.'

Back at camp one of the many invasion scares flared up, and a new guard was put on duty – at Arish Mell Gap, a tiny little cleft in the cliffs that might possibly have allowed easy landing, though in fact most of the cliff along there was hardly more than a scramble. I was on duty here one night with six troopers and a sergeant. We were driven in a truck across the ranges to an old Nissen hut. As well as rifles we had a Very pistol for signalling and also a wrecked First World War tank. This rusty relic had no engine, and it was impossible to traverse the gun. One could only elevate and depress it, so that, unless the enemy came dead straight at it, it was of no use whatsoever. The only ammunition available was practice, flat-headed stuff. A range telephone was laid on to the quarter guard, some miles back at camp, and we were to ring them once every twenty minutes. If we failed to do this, they were to turn out and come to our rescue.

It was all very jolly. The orderly officer mounted the guard and
then retired by truck to his post in camp. Our Sergeant instructed
me to carry on and disappeared behind the hut. A few minutes
later, while I was opening a can of condensed milk in the approved
style, with the point of a bayonet, he came in. 'Better ring up the
quarter guard and tell 'em we're on duty.' I wound the handle of
the field telephone and listened. It was as dead as a doornail. I gave
it another grind with the same result. I was not surprised. Field
telephones are famous for not working: the wires get run over by
tanks, or a cow gets tangled up in them and breaks the connection.
The Sergeant sent a trooper back to camp to inform the quarter
guard. When we had had our grub and the usual revoltingly strong,
sweet army tea, those not on guard made themselves as comfortable
as conditions allowed. The Sergeant found an old ladder, laid this
on some brackets that jutted out from the wall and ensconced himself in comfort. Those of lower rank made themselves beds on the
concrete floor round the stove.

However, there was to be little rest. We were invaded—not by
the enemy, against whom I have no doubt we should have put up
some sort of a show – but by field mice. They did not come in vast
numbers but in ones and twos, scouting for crumbs, reconnoitring
for food, taking cover under the folds of groundsheets, making
short dashes across the open, seizing a piece of food and retiring
hastily.

They were really rather nice little brown furry creatures, and
completely harmless. But our gallant soldiers thought otherwise.
With rifle-butts, boots, shovel and poker, they went to war. But
the mice were far too quick and the only damage done was a bloody
nose on our side.

Fortunately the Sergeant was in agreement with me. 'Leave the
little flamers alone and stop all that row. You'll 'ave the 'ole flipping
camp down 'ere next. Jerry'd die laughin' if he saw the way you lot
carry on.'

The war dragged on. We ceased training recruits and became a
'holding' regiment. American tanks became our speciality. When
not instructing, we occasionally went out for a few days on what the
Sergeant-major called 'minervas'. On one of these we camped for

the night on a ridge of the Purbeck Hills, and I got permission from the farmer to shoot rabbits. I got up early and wandered off with a shotgun. Walking quietly through the gorse, I saw two cock black-birds fighting; suddenly, before they had a chance to realize it, a sparrow-hawk flashed over the top of the bushes and dropped on top of them. One managed to escape, chattering, into the gorse, but the other was carried off by the sparrow-hawk, his neck broken by one quick twist of her beak. It was a perfect example of how the wild hawk uses cover and kills by surprise more than by hard flying – a real smash and grab. I went on after the rabbits and came out on the top of the hill.

The whole valley below was shrouded with mist, except for a range of hills in the distance whose tops showed clear. This range was broken in one place by a gap, and in this gap, lit by the morning sun and standing on its own little hill, stood Corfe Castle. It was a fairy-book picture; Arthur Rackham would have delighted in it. The war seemed very far away for the moment.

I reached Sandhurst in the end, but not as a cadet. I had badgered for a change of scenery, if not of job, and was finally sent there as a gunnery instructor. It was a far pleasanter place than Lulworth, and it had its amusing moments too. Passing the square one day I saw a troop of cadets rehearsing for their passing-out parade. A Guards drill instructor urged them to make even bigger holes in the ground when they stamped their feet. The R.S.M., immaculately clad, armed with his swagger-stick, applied his binocular vision to the troop and ground suddenly to a halt. 'Mr Cadet Parker, sir,' he roared, over the intervening miles that separated them. 'You there, first man in the front rank. You've got a button missing. By the time I come to the man at the end of the front rank he'll have two buttons missing. By the time I reach the last man in the rear rank he'll be stark staring naked. And you – Mr Parker – sir – started it!'

George Lodge still lived in Camberley, and while I was at Sand-hurst I was able to visit him frequently, to talk birds and falconry and watch him painting. I spent a lot of my time in his studio. Pictures were everywhere, and stuffed birds galore. One would have tea with an ivory-billed woodpecker at one elbow, the skin of a harpy-eagle sharing the same table as one's cup, and with a

Scandinavian elk wending its way through some windblown timber as though to have a nibble at the toast.

George Lodge would talk of past hawking experiences: of seeing the Old Hawking Club falconer bring back passage hawks from Holland, where they had been trapped by the hawk-catchers at Valkenswaard; of flying at partridges in Norfolk; of deer-stalking in Scotland; of painting birds in Norway, Canada, and Japan. He would bring out a beautiful little gold tie-pin with a hood at its head, or his silver mustard-pot in the shape of a hood with the spoon made like a lure.

Out in his garden we would watch the cross-bills feeding on the pine-cones, and he would bring a discarded cone indoors to use as a model. He was a perfectionist and liked to have every detail correct in any picture he painted. He rarely went out without a sketch-book and pencil and drew anything that might be of use as a background. A piece of rock, an attractively-shaped tree-branch, all were gathered in and stowed away, perhaps for years, till he had a particular use for them. At his request I brought back such things as a branch off a walnut tree, some viper's bugloss, or a root of wood sorrel, all models for his painting.

Out on the tank runs, on Barossa, in the Devil's Punch Bowl at Hindhead and on Thursley Common, night-jars were often flushed by the tanks, for they nested on the ground in the bracken and sat very tight. In one place I saw a pair of hobbies in an old crow's nest. They didn't seem particularly upset by the tanks roaring around but went peacefully about their business.

A fox ran across the ranges one day, and, as all three tanks opened up with machine-guns, foxy put his foot on the accelerator and streaked away, his brush streaming behind him, bullets kicking up all round him. He was untouched and dived into a patch of gorse.

On one of my leaves with Unk my cousin Esmond came down to visit too. He had been blinded when on *Prince of Wales*, during the Bismark action, and one of the last things he had seen was *Hood* blowing up, 'in one vast blue flame'. He was amazingly cheerful, and we pulled his leg by handing him the pepper-mill when he asked for the fish-paste. 'Swines,' he would mutter, 'trying to poison me!' and would roar with laughter.

Ramshaw was still in good form, in spite of having been torpedoed on one of his trips across the Atlantic. He had been left on board when the passengers were taken off and subsequently rescued by Unk when the ship was towed safely into port. I took a number of shots of him flying to the fist which later went into one of Unk's books.

The war was rapidly coming to an end at last. Near Wellington College I found a sparrow-hawk's nest with five eggs in a larch tree. I knew the keeper and asked him if I could take a young one in a few weeks' time. He was anxious to get rid of the whole lot but said he would leave them alone if I took all the young.

There were two females and three muskets, male sparrow-hawks, after whom the gun is named. I turned them all loose in an aviary made of strawberry netting and gave them an old rook's nest on a dead branch.

They were old enough to pull at any food given them and soon began to climb about the branches and flutter back onto the nest. Very gawky-looking things they were. Because they have very long, spindly, pencil-thin legs, with a sharp edge in front, the Americans call them sharp-shins. Their toes are long and thin too; but do not be fooled by this brittle look about them, their talons are needle-sharp, and their grip is quite powerful enough to drive the talons into your finger, and a very painful experience it is too. Their eyes are yellow, like all hawks'. When young they are almost blue, though this changes very quickly.

They grew almost visibly every day, less and less down showed, some of it being covered by their proper feathers, and some dropping off and blowing away. When frightened or annoyed they chittered, starting fairly fast and slowing up at the end; and when they were hungry they mewed like kittens. The sound is so feline that I was once asked to help remove some kittens from a hollow tree in a friend's shrubbery and found myself looking at a nest full of sparrow-hawks when I climbed up.

Of all the birds of prey, they are the most difficult to train. Their size means that the feeding of them must be judged very exactly. But it is their temperament that can drive the falconer demented. Not only are they extremely nervous, but they will not even sit on the fist at first; they hang head down and when they are replaced seem to lose all power in their legs and flop over sideways. Just when you think their legs are paralysed, they prove to you that that is far from being the case, by clutching your bare hand and refusing to let go. When you finally persuade them to stand up they glare at you with what Unk so aptly described as a button-eyed look. Then suddenly one day, for no apparent reason, something inside their seemingly empty noddles goes click. Their whole attitude alters, they greet you eagerly, jump at once to the outstretched glove, feed with no trouble and sit fluffed out and relaxed as though they had never hung upside-down or glared like startled stoats.

All this I knew and dreaded going through all over again. So I kept this lot where they could see people, dogs, cats and traffic, and all the noise and rush of everyday life. After all, I imagine that a bushman from darkest Africa would be likely to change colour with fright if he were suddenly dumped into the middle of Piccadilly.

Now I did not, of course, want five sparrow-hawks. One is quite enough, for any austringer – the curious name for the trainer of short-winged hawks. So I picked out the female I liked best and took the others over to Unk.

My idea of taming them before handling worked out quite well, and the one bird left by herself soon became tamer still. I think this applies to most birds and animals. Fear is very easily transferred and tends to increase to panic in a crowd. Unfortunately it doesn't seem to work the other way round. You can have an old, very tame hawk sitting next to a wild youngster with no calming effect whatsoever.

When sparrow-hawks are first tied up to a perch they often take quite a few days before they learn to sit on it. I put a couple of perches into the run, and Mrs Siddons was soon using them. Then I removed the dead branch so that only the perches were left. Finally, a day or two before I thought her feathers would be hard down and ready for me to start her training, I removed all the perches but one. So, when I did pick her up, she already knew what it was for.

Training had to be confined to only a short time each day, but

Mrs Siddons was very little trouble and was soon coming on a creance to the lure. Normally short-winged hawks are trained to the fist, which leaves the lure as an added enticement if they are not quite as keen as they should be. On the other hand, if one loses a hawk which has been trained only to the fist, one has to walk round all four hedges of a field instead of standing in the middle and swinging a lure. I worked out a successful compromise with Mrs Siddons: to prevent her flight feathers getting soaked when she landed on the lure in wet grass, I swung the lure onto my wrist as soon as I saw her on the wing.

Because she had been fed by me openly when young she was a partial screamer. But this, I think, in a sparrow-hawk, is something that is not to be decried. The noise is by no means irritating. She only did it when keen, and it was better than any bell, for one heard it quite a way off even if she wasn't moving. But I still had bells on her, for if she killed in cover she most certainly wouldn't scream then.

All short-winged hawks have one very curious habit that it is as safe to bet on as anything I know. When they fly or jump onto a perch or branch, they invariably shake their tails. It is almost as rare for them not to do so as it is for a turkey not to gobble if you cough at it. Because of this tail waggling, a bell is often put on the hawk's tail, secured to one of the deck feathers fairly high up. It is not easy to do and there are various methods. I found the best way was to use waterproof adhesive tape. So Mrs Siddons had a tail bell and another on one of her legs.

She started off by catching, appropriately enough, a sparrow. But this only whetted her appetite for bigger and better quarry. Moorhens, little-owls, and other various, as the log book puts it, met their match. The score was by no means great, for I did not have much time to fly her, but it mounted steadily and her skill began to interest others. Paul, a friend of mine, came out one afternoon and we hadn't gone far when Mrs Siddons flew a small bird, probably a pipit. It plonked into some rushes as disisky little brown birds do, and Mrs Siddons flew on and pitched on top of a high hawthorn hedge.

As we walked towards her a pair of magpies appeared and began to mob her, chattering at her and flirting their long tails in annoyance at the intruder. They got bolder and bolder as other magpies joined in. We stood some way off and watched. They pitched on the top branches on either side of the sparrow-hawk but kept their distance. Every so often one would take a short flight from one side to the other, passing over Mrs Siddons, who sat disdainfully on one foot and surveyed their antics with obvious contempt.

'Let's hang on here for a bit and see what happens,' I said to Paul. 'They are getting closer and closer and one of them is going to make a mistake soon and fly below the hawk instead of over the top. When it does I don't think she will be able to resist having a crack at it.'

By this time even more maggies had collected on the hedge, and each minute they became more audacious and noisy, urging each other to cheek the hawk a bit more. Then one of them dropped off the hedge and flew along under her. All she had to do was to make one short stooping dash, and she did just that. There was a loud squawk from the maggie, and all his chums rose up and flustered over the two on the ground, making more noise and fuss than ever, but clearing off at our approach to bewail poor cousin Willie's fate from a safer distance.

After that there was no stopping Mrs Siddons. Anything that flew was worth trying. She grabbed hold of a mallard drake and held tight onto his rump and both tumbled into some thick cover across the river. I waded across, but, of course, he was far too big for her to hold. She took a young cock pheasant, just changing into his mature plumage. He tried to brush her off by sticking his head into a bed of nettles but he was too fat to get through and became a welcome addition to the larder. Little-owls she took with the greatest of ease; and she chased a tawny owl, screeching, down a rabbit hole. She even grabbed another sparrow-hawk, but left it to come to the spare lure, which Paul was swinging, not realizing that she had caught something.

But after her success with the magpie they became her favourite amusement. If we saw any around we would let her take stand in a dead tree or in some other conspicuous place and retire a short distance away to watch. Before long they would come to mob her.

A long-eared bat, whose ears, when not in use, curled like a ram's horns

'The high-speed flash stopped all movement'

'I made my way down to the eyrie'
(*James Wood*)

'Time spent in reconnaissance is
seldom wasted'

The falcons are hooded and put on the box-cadge

'So Pru, the goshawk, came to stay'

The Old Hawking Club flew rooks on the Plain

A tame butcher-bird, used by the Dutch hawk-catchers to give warning

She just waited, watching, waggling her tail now and then. If they were slow in coming within range she carried the war into their camp. She never attempted a straight dash unless they were very close but employed strategy to lull them into a false sense of security. She would fly off as though not bothering about their presence in the least bit. They would all follow her, their iridescent plumage changing colour as they flew: now black, now gold, now green; their curious cuckoo-like flight made even stranger by their long tails.

Mrs Siddons would glide a short way, then beat with her wings for a moment before gliding again. When she had gone a sufficient distance for them to be well away from cover she would swing up, twisting round, and, with a short dash, grab the nearest, now hastily retreating, maggie.

I tried hard to catch a teal with her but she never quite made it. Either they pulled away just as she was about to grab or they dived back into the river.

Then demobilization put an end to our flying. I was given my Pay Book duly marked off to show that I had completed nearly six years of 'undetected crime', and I became a civilian once more. My father had died during the war; the business had been sold, and I decided that, as I was out of date with all the wartime changes in the law of estate management, I would try my hand at photography. This meant going to live in London again, so Mrs Siddons was taken for a last fly and left, bells and jesses cut off, to return, experienced enough, to the wild.

In London I took a course in photography and then worked as a Press photographer for six months. But I found this life uncreative and distasteful and started my own studio in Salisbury.

H

12 * My Own Boss

The studio was on the first floor above a banana store. Stowaways in the banana crates became photographic models for a brief while before continuing their journey, this time by post. Insects were the commonest things, particularly large spiders with long legs and hairy bodies. And there were even larger centipedes, of a horrible khaki colour, who seemed to march like an army, on their stomachs, but who, on closer observation, rippled their many legs like a wave travelling along their sides. They were flat-bodied creatures, suitable for going under doors or through letter-boxes. When I had taken their pictures I packed them up carefully and sent them to the London zoo, marked 'Sample' on the outside, and 'Danger! Live insect. Very fierce!' inside.

We had one charming visitor, though. I had got married by then and Bill was none too keen on the insect models, having, as so many people do, an inherent dislike of them. So when our friend from the banana store brought up a small cardboard box one morning and said, 'Here's a new one for you,' she shuddered.

However, when I opened the box carefully, we found a small, cinnamon-coloured frog. But he was unlike our native frogs, for when he jumped out of the box, instead of flumping onto the floor, he went splat against the wall and stayed there. He had little suckers on the ends of his toes that enabled him to perform in this manner, and he was altogether a very pretty little chap. I took some pictures of him, put him in a box with a glass lid and thought about food.

Presumably he was short of grub after being in a crate so long. I caught one or two flies and he gobbled them up smartly; but catching flies in any number takes up a lot of time. I emptied the vacuum-cleaner bag, put on a long nozzle and sucked them off the ceiling by a steady approach from the rear. Once they felt the suck they stuck tight, and then it was only a matter of getting closer, and floop, they were in. Getting them out without losing them was more difficult, a selling point that the manufacturer seemed to have overlooked. Even so, fly catching, mechanized or not, could hardly be a lucrative business, I felt. So froggy got packed up in some damp moss and put in the post.

On arrival at the zoo he caused quite a stir among the frog experts, who, so they told us, finally had to give him a taxi ride to the Natural History Museum to identify him. He turned out to be a Cuban tree-frog with a nice long Latin name.

Of course, we had other clients, who, fortunately, paid me for taking photographs. During the war electronic flash had been improved upon. I invested in one of these machines and found it ideal for children and animals as all movement was stopped dead; apart from their parents, movement is the greatest problem when taking children.

Dogs I found a cinch to photograph. One only has to squeak like a rabbit and any decent-minded dog pricks up its ears and looks intelligent. I did have one dog problem though. A man came in one day with a Dalmatian, one of those plum-pudding dogs that used to trot between the wheels of carriages. This one had to be taken for advertising purposes, but apparently lacked the requisite number of spots, for his owner requested me to add one or two more. I had no wish to lose the job, but neither did I want someone to buy pups from this animal, in both senses of the phrase. So I said that our negatives were really too small to touch up.

One great snag was that we had no shop window, only a couple of show cases on the wall outside. The sun used to steam these up, then fade the prints and finally peel them off their mounts. We used paper sculpture and so on, but it was very difficult to make it look fresh and clean. One day, in despair, I put in a close-up of a hippopotamus's head. Later a woman came in and said, 'As you can make a hippo look attractive, you can take my portrait.'

Then, in a newspaper, I saw that Peter Scott was starting the Severn Wildfowl Trust and on impulse I looked up my mallard drake in flight, which I had taken in St James's Park before the war, and sent it to him. He replied, not only buying a copy but asking me to go down to the Trust and take some photographs. This led to an annual trip.

I would wander round quietly with the camera, gumbooted for wading, and with a bucket of food for the more wary birds. Some were easy, others surprisingly difficult. Common teal proved one of the worst to approach and the drake goosander one of the most difficult to take, because his black eye got lost in his green head plumage and his white body contrasted so much with his head.

It was hopeless to try to chase any particular bird. I got a list from Peter of the ones he would like and grabbed anything else that looked good. The very tame ones came too close and breathed all over the lens. The shy ones would swim just out of camera range, and then, when one did come close enough, either the light would be wrong or the bird would turn so that its pinioned side showed. Every so often one got something quite unexpected that made up for all the annoyances. A family of shelducklings lined themselves up so perfectly that they looked like a deputation of city dignitaries.

In the winter, out on the saltings known as the Dumbles, the wild geese come. Peter had built little watch-huts along the river wall and turned the old wartime pillboxes into watch-towers. Even so, the Dumbles is a large enough area for the geese to be well out of camera range day after day. I certainly had luck the first time I went out there. I got close-ups that included some Greenland white-fronts, a pinkfoot, and a whitefront with curious eyebrows that had been coming there for some years.

They were fascinating to watch; the little family parties stayed together in the flock, backyard-fence gossiping and arguing with their neighbours. When some three thousand wild geese took alarm, and, with a mighty clanging, rose up on waves of sweeping wings and made off for the river, it was really quite something.

One wet afternoon, when it was hopeless to attempt any photography, I sat in Peter's studio and watched him paint. I was flabbergasted. I expected dead silence: everything terribly serious, while the artist proceeded with great care. Instead the place was crammed with people, and Peter not only led the talk but used his brush and paint to demonstrate a point of the conversation and then turned the well-daubed canvas into a picture. The atmosphere was like that of a small cocktail party. The rain continued to stream down outside, the windows steamed up with a good old fug, and Peter painted steadily, nattering hard all the time, his left-handedness making it seem even more awkward and surprising.

To augment my income I took bird photographs and wrote magazine articles to go with them. I did some of a kingfisher. Then I found a little-owl in a hollow tree, put up a hide and used a flash-gun. It was very much a matter of chance, for the owl came in like a torpedo and it was too dark to see it, but when I heard a lot of scuffling, beak-clopping and squeaking going on from the young I just fired the flash, hoping that the owl was at the entrance.

A tawny owl also obliged, and then a friend who had helped over some of these projects found a stone-curlew's nest on his farm and I had an afternoon in his hide. There was one egg and one chick just hatched, the nest being a mere scrape in between the rows of barley. It was a lovely hot sunny afternoon. The old bird came stalking in, and I took a shot as she stood by the nest and some more as she brooded. The chick stuck its head out at one moment, and I photographed it before it disappeared underneath its mother's plumage. The old bird sat and fluffed herself out. She looked very smart with her gold eyes and her black polished beak.

Suddenly there was a peal of thunder and the rain came belting down. I hastily and quietly took my camera off the tripod, as the hide was by no means waterproof and the rain was pouring in. Then I looked through the vision slit at the stone-curlew. She was crouched down, her head hunched into her neck, her feathers soaking. She looked pretty miserable. I too was soaked and, until my friend came to release me, I could not get away. I knew he wouldn't come in this weather, for the disturbance would make the old bird leave the nest, and the young and the egg would undoubtedly suffer. Finally the storm passed over and the sun came out. I got the camera set up again and took a shot of the old girl still bedraggled and hunched up.

One day, out on the Plain, I happened to see a hobby fly out of a clump of spruce. I investigated and found that she had three recently-hatched young in a disused crow's nest. Now bird photography needs two people really, so my stone-curlew friend joined forces with me and we began to build a hide. The nest was about forty feet up and there was only one possible tree for the hide. This was another spruce about fifteen feet away, but it didn't have any branches that we could possibly sit on. About forty feet up they were no thicker than a broom-handle.

We overcame the problem by slinging a length of rope over a convenient fork higher up and suspending a seat like a swing. The camera had to be on a steady platform though, so I screwed two metal brackets to the trunk and fixed a shelf jutting out on one side. For the hide itself we simply ran a framework of wire from branch to branch and then, with a large supply of safety-pins, attached sacking, adding a piece more each day until at the end of the week the thing was complete. We stuck branches round the outside as camouflage and all was ready.

The female hobby always put up a show whenever we came near the nesting-tree. She was brave to the point of foolhardiness, for anyone could have shot her. She would come flying out from the clump and circle round with quick, short wing-beats, calling all the time like a peregrine but with a more plaintive note – a sort of que, que que que que. Then she would stoop at us, just shooting over the top of our heads as she threw up. We could hear the wind rushing through her sails. At the top of her throw up she would twist round and stoop again, giving a few quick wing-beats first to gain more speed. She never actually touched us, but she wasn't far off. I put my hand up once and brushed her as she went past.

But, like most birds, she couldn't count. I climbed up the tree, hauled the camera case up with a line, and closed the flap of the hide. My friend then walked away, making plenty of noise, running the gauntlet of the angry hobby.

The young were still covered in down, their feathers starting to sprout through. The old girl no longer brooded them much, but spent most of her time sitting on a dead branch which served as a look-out, some thirty yards away. Not once did she go off hunting when we were in the hide. Having laid the eggs and hatched them, she took things pretty easy.

The little male hobby, or robin, did the hunting for all the family as far as we could see. Not only did he do all the hunting, but he plucked what he caught before bringing it back and he usually ate the head, which he considered his perks. Sometimes he brought the kill to the nest, but more often he handed it over in mid-air

As he approached he would call softly, and his wife would leave her observation post and fly to meet him, circling round below him and neatly and effortlessly catching the food in her feet as he dropped it. Sometimes it fell twenty or thirty feet before reaching her, but she never missed. The timing of the two of them was as accurate as that of a troupe of trapeze artists.

When he did come to the nest he looked as smart as paint. He had beautiful russet-red trousers, cut very full in Turkish style; his black moustache gave him a very dapper look, and he kept himself well groomed. He held the food down with his bright yellow feet and knew exactly how to break it up with a sharp twist of his beak. His wings folded neatly over his back, but he held them slightly out from his body and this gave him the appearance of doing the whole thing in a nonchalant manner, with his hands in his pockets.

Both he and his wife were extremely gentle when feeding the youngsters. There was no jamming it into their mouths like a blackbird shoving a worm into its offspring's gaping maw. Each piece was offered quietly, and if the young bird had difficulty in swallowing it the old ones took it away again and ate it themselves.

Nevertheless, it took them very little time to dispose of a small bird. From the time they arrived to the time it was finished and they had feaked their beaks, roused, slipped off the side of the nest and glided away, took not more than five minutes, often only about three. So one had to be pretty smart changing the camera slides.

At first, the old birds would freeze at the slightest sound from the hide. This helped a good deal, for that was the moment to press the shutter. But after each of us had been in the hide a couple of times the old birds took no notice of our noise. Right at the end, when the young were nearly ready to fly, I had to shout at the old girl, 'Stand still!' before she would take any notice. Even then we had to be very quick.

I think most people imagine one takes bird pictures at high

speeds. It is quite possible to do this of course, but the quality of the print is not as a rule so good, because a high speed means a loss of depth of focus. We used a Luc shutter and gave exposures of about one-tenth of a second, or longer if the light was poor.

The nest was on the army ranges and at times one would hear the unpleasant whine of a bullet richocheting overhead. We were most certainly in the danger area, but they all passed harmlessly by. The old hobby took no notice whatever.

The young hobbies grew rapidly and soon were covered in feathers with only a wisp or two of down sticking out. They began climbing about the branches and exercising their wings, getting ready to venture out into the world. We hoped we might be there when they actually took their first flight, but the day we thought they might fly, there was a gale blowing. It was obviously a waste of time to try to take photographs from forty feet up in a tree which was swaying about, particularly as the nesting-tree would also be swaying, and trees rarely keep in step on such occasions. I have seen movie-film taken from a tree in a high wind, and the waste-paper basket is the only place for it. When we went the next day they had all flown, so we dismantled the hide.

A few days later a young hobby was brought to me in a cardboard box. It was at least a couple of weeks younger than the ones we had been photographing and had been picked up in the long grass, where it had fallen out of the nest, or, more likely, been blown out in the gale. I fed it, for it was obviously hungry, and then went to see if I could replace it. The tree was a Scots pine; there was no branch for the first forty feet; the trunk was too fat for me to get my arms around it; so the young hobby stayed with us, in our attic. At first she was too weak to feed herself, but in a few days she recovered and was pulling away at meat, looking considerably happier; so I had a falcon once more.

As soon as she was old enough I put jesses on her and began training. She came to the studio each day and sat on a screen perch in the workroom. At home she was loose, unless the windows were open, and she spent most of her time sitting on an old brass lanthorn clock.

Flying her to a lure was really worth seeing. A local ornithologist, who had, much to my amusement, mistaken her for a goshawk, came to see her fly one evening. Now Mimsy was a pretty independent bird and liked to have a buzz round on her own before coming in to the lure. This time was no exception. I let her go and off she went, climbing in big circles and drifting away till she was just a speck. Our guest was convinced we had seen the last of her. I was quite happy, because I knew her little foibles pretty well by now.

After she had been on the wing for about ten minutes and had caught herself a few crane-flies as an appetizer, I got out the lure and whistled to her. 'She'll never see it from that distance,' our friend remarked. Well, of course, birds of prey have fantastic eyesight, provided the thing is moving. Often, when we have had several trained falcons sitting on blocks, we have noticed them all looking up, with heads turned at the same angle. By using powerful binoculars and following the direction of their gaze, it is possible to distinguish a tiny speck wheeling round in the blue. From the way it flies and the interest shown by the falcons, it is obviously another bird of prey. But it can be anything from a falcon to an eagle as far as we can tell. I am quite certain that they know exactly what it is, and probably its age and sex into the bargain. So my lure, swinging round, was quite plain to Mimsy.

Provided I gave her long enough to expend her energies eating up the sky, the moment I swung the lure she would come. But if she thought I had cut her time short she simply ignored me. On this occasion she was ready and came at once, not in any particular hurry till she was almost overhead, when she changed gear, stopped coasting along, and began to show off.

Now Unk had shown me, years ago, how to swing a lure properly, and I was pretty good at leading it just in front of a peregrine or a merlin; by now it was second nature. But when Mimsy was in top form I had to concentrate very hard on what I was doing, for she was extremely fast – and not only fast but clever too. Her judgement of distance was fantastic. You could put a piece of meat about the size of an oak-apple on your fingers, and she would pick it up in her feet at full speed without touching your bare hand. It looked very spectacular. She would eat it on the wing, as she did the insects she caught. I had exercised her more and more each day, and by now

she was so fit that she could put in forty or fifty stoops without
showing any signs of being out of puff. I always ended up by throwing the lure as high as I could and letting her catch it in the air.
Our ornithologist was most impressed.

One day I was pushed for time to exercise her and decided to
fly her across the street, outside our house, to my fist. But a passing
car frightened her, and she was up and away over the rooftops. I
grabbed my bicycle and rode off to the nearest large open space,
which was a playing-field for children down by the river. There were
a number of people about and they all looked somewhat astonished
when I shot onto the field, dropped the cycle and began to whistle
and swing the lure.

I must admit it crossed my mind that I should look rather silly
if nothing happened, and it would have been rather embarrassing
to have had to pick up the bicycle and go off empty-handed. But
Mimsy saw me, and we gave a free demonstration to the surprised
onlookers before I let her catch the lure, took her on fist and rode
home.

Being extremely tame, she came for walks with us and was quite
a family pet. Naturally she commanded some attention from passers-
by and, according to how they felt, they would murmur, 'Oh how
sweet!' or, 'Quite disgusting, the bird should be let go.' A lady who
was admiring Mimsy asked if she could stroke her. 'Of course you
can, she doesn't mind in the least.' The elegantly dressed lady put
one finger towards the hobby, who leaned down and bit it hard, a
thing she had never done before. Only then did I realize why. The
red-painted nails looked very like a tasty piece of meat.

But as a falconer's bird she was a dead loss. Except for insects,
she never caught a thing. She would fly alongside a small bird, turn
her head to look at it, raise her hat, and politely say 'Good afternoon'. She had only to put out a foot to catch it, but she was just
not interested.

At one time hobbies were used for daring larks. By putting a
trained hobby on the wing the larks were frightened into crouching
down on the ground, where they were taken by nets – in much the
same way as a kite in the shape of a hawk used to be flown to enable
shooters to get within range of partridges. But larks had no fear of

Mimsy and didn't even bother to hide themselves when she was flying.

Naturally I took photographs of her, and I wrote a short article which I managed to get published. This led to an old friend of mine, Geoffrey, getting in touch with me again. We had flown hawks together before the war. I went over to Surrey to spend a week-end with him and took Mimsy with me. It was October and, whether it was because at that time of year hobbies migrate to Africa, or whether it was the strange place, or merely that I had overfed her, I don't know, but I lost her in a rather high wind and never saw her again.

I decided to get a goshawk. Like John Paston in 1472, who wrote from Norfolk to his brother in London, saying, 'I desire nothing but that you shoulde sende me a mewyd goshawke', I wrote to friends in Holland asking for one, but it so happened that the people who were trying hard to catch me one just didn't have any luck. They are generally caught in a cage-type trap which has a decoy pigeon in a separate compartment at the base. The pigeon serves two purposes, for the trap is so made that, once the hawk is caught, the pigeon is released and flies home to tell the good news.

I was working in the dark-room one afternoon, the hawking season was over and I was hoping for better luck next year, when I heard footsteps on the stairs. I went down to see who it was and was greeted by a gentleman who, without any preliminaries, simply said, 'Do you want a gos?' Feeling somewhat nonplussed – a word I feel really refers to my bank balance – for, after all, none of my clients had ever offered me such a thing before, I stammered out a hasty 'Yes'. My visitor went on to explain. 'I've had her a couple of years; she's moulting now, and I'm going to live in London. I must find a home for her.'

It ended up in my buying her for a small sum. I went by bus to collect her and walked the last mile or so. In an open cartshed, sitting on a falcon's block, looking very uncomfortable, for gos-hawks dislike the shape of a block, was a very handsome female gos. Her primaries were somewhat battered, which was not surprising, for she was on a pile of wood-chippings and every time she bated she wore a bit more off her wingtips. One jess was broken, so I approached her very quietly, to avoid making her bate, for the remaining jess looked very weak. She stepped up onto my fist, and I took her into a shed and put on some new jesses that I had luckily brought.

'How are you going to get her home?'

'Oh, on the bus with me.'

'She'll crash all over the place, I expect,' he said. 'She's never been on a bus before.'

But she didn't. She sat very tight-feathered for the greater part of the journey but by the time the bus reached Salisbury she was relaxed.

So 'Pru' came to stay, and once more I had a hawk of my own.

13 * Pru and Joanna

During the day Pru lived in the garden of some friends, since there was no room at home. The approach was up a short drive from the main road, and a high wall hid her from passers-by. She could hear people walking along the pavement, but took no notice until I went up to collect her or to see how she was getting on. Then, long before I was in sight, she would start to scream in a high-pitched whistle which was so piercing that it carried an immense distance. Her hearing must have been very acute to distinguish my steps from the hundreds that passed each day. It was certainly not a matter of time, for I went there at any old hour and she would always greet me.

She was deep in the moult, and because she was badly in need of a new set of feathers I left her to get on with it. So when Unk offered me a merlin, I jumped at it. He brought Joanna down with him for a week-end visit, during which he first silenced the crammed bar of the local and then had them all in fits with one of his many stories. He had no intention of enthralling anyone apart from Bill and myself, but once he had started on his story it was inevitable that the whole room should stop to listen.

Like Mimsy, Joanna became very tame with the constant carrying between our cottage and the studio. There was a tiny yard at the back of the cottage which I had wired over to keep out stray cats. Joanna found herself a perch on a piece of wood that stuck out of the wall and would sit there sunning herself. I came in one day to find that she had flown into the kitchen and was eating some cold ham on the kitchen table. It didn't have any ill effects on her, however.

Joanna was soon going loose, and I started flying her. She was doing very well and had a few head to her credit, when, one afternoon, a pair of wild hobbies came out of some trees and started to mob her. Obviously she had gone too near their nest.

I swung the lure to get her back, but the hobbies were between us and she was chased out of sight. I ran through the clump of trees that blocked my view, expecting to find her on the other side. There was nothing moving. She had vanished. I followed the usual procedure for lost hawks: waiting a short while in case she circled round back to the starting-point and then, as she didn't turn up, walking on downwind, for hawks tend to take the line of least resistance. Still no sign of her. Remembering Unk's advice, 'When you've gone as far as you think she can possibly be, then go on twice as far', I continued, swinging the lure and whistling for her. Finally I had to give up.

I was up early next morning and took the bus out to the spot. A male hobby came sizzling overhead with something in his feet. I thought for a moment he was Joanna, but his longer wings and different style of flying soon undeceived me. I spared as long as I could, but had to return without her.

In the late afternoon, just as I was finishing at the studio, I had a telephone call to say that she had appeared at a cricket match in Bulford Camp, had sat on the umpire's head for one over, thought little of her perch, shifted to a better view-point in a tree and, finally, come down to an improvised lure, which my informant, who had seen her flown a few days earlier, had made up. He had picked her up and left her on a piece of meat obtained from a passing butcher's van. I caught the next bus, but she had had as much as she could eat and had vanished again.

I spent several more days looking, but neither saw nor heard anything of her. It had been the fourth of August when I had lost her. On the fifth she had watched the cricket. On January the sixteenth the next year the R.A.F. rang me up to say that they had had a trained hawk in their Guard Room for the last three days, and would I please remove it. I dashed over there, wondering what hawk it could possibly be; and there, sitting on the edge of a coal-bin, covered in coal dust and with her tail all broken, sat Joanna, my jesses and bell still on her. Someone had seen her sitting on the roof of a Nissen hut. They had thrown a piece of meat to her and she

had remembered her training to the lure and had come down. She
had been out 162 days, a remarkably long time for a lost hawk, but
by no means a record. In 1610 James I, endeavouring to show the
French royal falconer how much better the English hawks were at
kites, lost his hawk, which disappeared into the blue after the
quarry.

In 1792 it was reported that a hawk had been picked up at the
Cape of Good Hope. Round its neck was a gold collar, inscribed:
'This goodlie hawk doth belong to His Most Excellent Majestie,
James, Kinge of England. A.D. 1610.' As the hawk would then be
at least 182 years old, it seems a dubious story. Peregrines have been
known to live for some twenty years and eagles for fifty or more.
But 182 years needs a very large sack of salt.

The gold collar was more likely to have been the varvels: flat
metal washers which were sewn onto the jesses before swivels were
used. These varvels often had the name or the coat of arms of the
owner engraved on them.

I took Joanna home and, as it was quite clear that no ordinary
bathing would remove the grime and coal dust, I mixed some Lux
in a large basin of tepid water and dunked her in. It was not the sort
of weather for a soaking wet bird to dry out of doors. So I dried her
with an electric hair-dryer. A few days later I gave her a complete
new tail and she was as good as new.

I flew her the following season, but she did exactly what the old
falconers warn one about. She 'flew cunning'. She knew very well
that she would be fed whether she caught anything or not, and she
refused to expend her energies needlessly. Only if she considered
she could catch a bird easily would she go, flying low over the ground
and then swinging up into a flock of small birds and, presumably
because it is harder for them to manœuvre in a flock, just grab one.

So flying Joanna became rather a dull affair. Then she started to
carry whatever she caught into a tree. When she happened to pick
an unclimbable one, I had to wait till she had finished eating. She
would then fly down and I would take her home; for I had learnt
that it was hopeless to go on. She had done her stuff, and enough
was as good as a beast as far as she was concerned. So I let her go
back to the wild.

Meanwhile Pru had finished her moult and was looking very spruce in her new plumage: blue-grey back, long, white-tipped tail and barred front. She had been flown by her previous owner, so it was merely a matter of refreshing her memory, getting the superfluous fat off her and muscling her up.

She was very tame and had a most amiable nature. Almost too amiable for Bill, on whose head she liked to sit at times. Fortunately she didn't grip when on this somewhat curious choice of perch. After a bit Bill got used to her and even thought of going to a fancy-dress ball as 'Perch: Mark 2: Goshawks for the use of'.

I bought two ferrets, Chloë and Snowy, and Pru was introduced to them so that, when the time came, she would not catch them in mistake for a rabbit. The Wilts and Dorset Omnibus Company served as transport out to the ranges, where I had permission to fly. Pru travelled on my fist, Chloë and Snowy curled up in a warm nest of hay at the bottom of a sack. The conductors sometimes looked a bit troubled, but luckily the Company's Rules and Regulations said nothing about goshawks or ferrets.

We would walk across the ranges, looking in all likely places for rabbits. Sometimes we were lucky and caught two or three; but Pru had her off days when, for some reason or other, she muffed rabbit after rabbit. It wasn't a question of flying, she was simply fumble-footed, or thinking of other things.

Sometimes we failed to find rabbits anywhere. Then I would look for a small bury in the open; either Chloë or Snowy would be tipped out of the sack and, shaking her bottle-brush tail, would disappear underground. Pru and I stood back a little and waited. Sometimes nothing happened, and the ferret reappeared, blinking at the daylight and sniffing the air with a look of disgust. Sometimes a rumbling in the chalk below would perk Pru up, and a rabbit would shoot out of a pop-hole and make off to the next bury with Pru in hot pursuit. If it was a biggish bury then both the ferrets had a go.

Quietness was essential. If you stamped around on top the rabbits were not at all keen on coming out and would bolt out of one hole and scoot down the next, leaving Pru on the ground at the entrance, peering down. By giving the ferrets half their day's rations before we set out, I avoided their lying-up on a kill and saved having to carry a spade to dig them out.

One week-end two of us went to one of my old hawking-grounds near Devizes. We caught a number of rabbits and walked back along the Wansdyke, Pru eating her fill on my fist. A wild merlin came flying past us in close pursuit of a pipit. The merlin was too intent on the chase to notice us, and the pipit was too busy avoiding capture to bother; so we had a grandstand view. It was a very different style of flying from that of a trained merlin. The little falcon never let the quarry get any distance away. There was no high flying, but little short stoops, a matter of twenty feet only; but put in with a vigour that was very pretty to watch.

The pipit, too, was exceedingly clever and used his head. A wire fence gave him good protection from the merlin's stoops, and he flew along this, dodging between the wires so that the merlin was always placed on the wrong side. He zig-zagged his way along, looking hard for a thick patch of grass to hide in, but it was late winter and there was nothing thick enough. He tried one or two places, but the merlin was so hot on his tail that he had to move on hastily or she would have had him. It looked as though he must eventually get caught.

Evidently he thought the same, for he changed his tactics. He zig-zagged through the fence once more as the merlin put in another stoop at him, then he half went to ground, so that she plonked on the deck and tried to grab him through the fence; but he got up at the critical moment, left her temporarily thrown out and struggling to get on the wing again, and doubled back down the fence. The merlin came after him hot-foot; but he had enough lead on her to leave the fence, swing low over the Wansdyke, and dive down a rabbit hole. The merlin knew when she was beaten and just threw up over the hole and then pitched on the strainer post at the fence corner. She roused, looked around her, saw us and sped away across the Plain.

The speed at which birds fly is something about which very little is known and it is certainly grossly over-estimated by writers of popular fiction. I have seen it said that a peregrine in a stoop goes at over 250 m.p.h. I would hesitate to make any statement on speed,

I

except that on the level a peregrine is only just faster than a grouse, while in a stoop the experienced grouse stands a very good chance of avoiding disaster by dodging. I don't think a peregrine would ever miss at 250 m.p.h., and I doubt if it could pull out of a stoop if it did miss; certainly at that speed it would hurt itself severely when it struck. It clearly comes down at a pretty good lick, but I shall be most surprised, when speedometers for birds are invented, if it clocks over 100 m.p.h., and it may well be considerably less.

At the studio not all our clients were human ones. After a night of strong gales, we had a little auk brought into the studio to be photographed. The gale had blown a number of them in from the sea, and they had landed, exhausted, all over the country.

Next came a tame badger, a whacking great old brock, whose owner had quite a struggle to lift him, he had grown so big. He was very tame and no trouble to photograph, which was just as well, for a rampant badger has a hefty great set of snappers and could undoubtedly do a lot of damage. After all, he is a member of the stoat and weasel brigade, and they are exceedingly sharp about the teeth.

Someone brought in a long-eared bat that curled up its ears when they were out of use, so that they looked like ram's horns.

A knock on the door one evening heralded a gentleman with a brown paper bag, in which, he stated, was a live falcon. Somewhat naturally, I was doubtful, for only a few weeks previously I had been given a crate, large enough to hold an eagle, in which I was told there was a kestrel; but when I opened it, a swift had blinked at me instead. The paper-bag held a beautiful haggard peregrine, a tiercel, but alas so thin that it died a few hours later. It had one shotgun pellet in its head. If only it had been found a few days earlier I might have saved it. Another creature that arrived, this time dead, was a salmon that I had won in a photographic competition. But alas it had spent too long on its journey and was no longer edible.

I was asked to rejoin the British Falconers' Club, to which I had belonged before the war. At an annual dinner I met James Robertson Justice, who wanted to see Pru fly and was keen enough to provide transport, in the shape of an elderly Rolls-Royce, to his home in

Hampshire. He also had a black pointer, who joined in and wallowed in the reed-beds by the river, pointing moorhens for Pru.

Friday was quite a character; he was deaf, or pretended to be. He chased hares as though he were a greyhound and no amount of bellowing on his owner's part would make him desist, but he pointed extremely well. Pru caught a rabbit that Friday had pointed; and when he arrived hot on the scent, he blundered into Pru, who, resenting this, promptly fetched him a smartish swipe across his nose, which surprised him more than somewhat and he never came near her again. He was a large dog, with a great flail of a tail; but he curled himself up in a basket more suited to a toy poodle.

I took Pru and a little tiercel called Adolph, which Unk had given me, over to James's one week-end. Adolph was only just learning and had achieved nothing of note. When we arrived I was introduced to the Duke of Edinburgh, who had joined the party. It is on occasions like this that things go wrong, and that day was no exception. We tried Pru first and hadn't gone more than a few yards when an enormous great hare, 'big as a donkey', as they say in Suffolk, ran off, ears flat, its great hind legs pushing along. Pru, who normally avoided such large creatures, evidently had been overcome by our chief guest and shot off after it to grab it. But it was too strong for her, she had a poor hold on it, I got in the way, and the hare made good its escape. Pru flew up into a tree and sat there in a huff, refusing to come down. It was all very embarrassing, and I began to get hotter and hotter under the collar. I sent an emissary to fetch Adolph, thinking I would leave Pru to come to her senses and fly Adolph meanwhile. But by the time he arrived Pru had come down.

After lunch I put Adolph up to wait on while we walked a field where a covey of partridges had been seen. Suddenly he started to chase a green woodpecker which had appeared, rather unwisely, on the scene. As he was gaining on it, James remarked, 'God help that woodpecker!' The woodpecker, uttering its chippering note, dived into the safety of an oak tree. 'James, God has helped that woodpecker,' said Prince Philip. We didn't actually lose any hawks and we even caught one rabbit. But it was by no means a good demonstration.

The next week-end was even more disastrous. I lost Adolph, and the day after he was picked up with a broken wing. He had been shot and died a few hours later.

I flew Pru every week-end that weather permitted. Geoffrey, James and I had a day in the River Test with Pru and Geoffrey's gos, Medusa. I say in, because that was what it was. The Test is very wide and shallow at that particular place, and we all wore waders and spent most of our time in the river. Friday of course joined in, snuffling his way along and galumphing through the reeds.

A friend from Holland brought his gos over for a week-end. Out on the ranges, we had a job to find any rabbits, but Pru managed to catch two and our guest-hawk one. Pru also had a crack at a short-eared owl that suddenly got up. She flew right up to it, put out her feet to grab, and the owl suddenly noticed her and, with great sweeps of its wings, rowed itself up in tight circles and left an annoyed goshawk as though she were standing still.

Then, one evening, Pru got ill. One moment she was sitting quite happily on her ring perch; the next she was on the ground, twisting round and round, obviously in pain, getting thoroughly tangled up in her leash. I picked her up and took her indoors. I had seen this sort of thing happen before, and there was no cure for it as far as I knew. After all, very few vets ever see a trained hawk; and except for poultry, their knowledge of bird disease is not very great.

A doctor friend prescribed 'M. & B., keep the patient quiet and feed it often'. Bill, always good with sick birds, helped me; and although Pru got very thin, she managed to recover. The hawking season was over by now and I fed her up well and left her to moult.

Then Unk asked me if I would help him. He was making a new film for the National Geographic Society. There was an eagle's eyrie in a rather unusual site, on a sea-cliff on the Mull of Kintyre; and he proposed to go up and film it. Would I go with him? It was a foregone conclusion.

14 * Wild Eagles

The aged van in which we were to drive to Scotland needed a bit of an overhaul before attempting so long a drive. Unk was even less mechanically minded than I, and while we waited for the garage people to sort out the van's tappets, gussets and gudgeons, or whatever was wrong with its innards, we found a cuckoo in a hedge-sparrow's nest.

We built a hide and gave the bird a day to get used to it. Little birds like this are fairly tame anyway. Then Unk and I rigged up the movie camera and he left me in the hide to get what I could.

The old birds were busy hunting for insects to feed their enormous foster-child, which could not sit in the nest properly but bulged out over the sides. Every time the old birds came near, it opened a vast cavity of a mouth lined in bright orange. It never stopped being hungry.

All day long the little hedge-sparrows searched for caterpillars, moths, flies, and so on and brought home beakfuls of wiggling food in their endeavour to satisfy the creature; and as soon as it saw them anywhere near it it wheezed away with its great gaping, insatiable maw.

The second day it flew, or rather fluttered, out of the nest and sat on a post near by. The hedge-sparrow returned to find the nest empty, but the inevitable wheeze soon told her where to go. She flew over and had to sit on the cuckoo's head and lean over to feed it, for there was no other perch within beak-reach.

By now the van was pronounced to be as fit to take the road as it was ever likely to be. We packed all our gear on board; cameras, tripod, film, clothing, binoculars, maps, and so on. Esmond had given us instructions how to get there: 'Go straight through

London, get onto the Great North Road, turn left at Scotch Corner, and there you are.'

We left Sevenoaks slightly before dawn. Ramshaw stayed behind with friends. We got through London before the daily rush had begun and slogged our way steadily northwards. The film was to be a very different affair from those that my uncle had made previously. This one was to show the beauty and romance of Scotland, and so we stopped at Gretna Green, Burns's house and other places of historical interest.

We put up for the night and, setting off again the next day, soon found ourselves along the western shores of Loch Lomond. The road here follows the lochside, twisting and turning continually. After several miles there was a large road sign, which stated, to the already giddy driver, 'Bends for the next 3 miles'.

Although it was the middle of June, the bluebells were in full flower, which seemed rather curious to us, for back in Kent they had been over for some time. In Scotland, one must not, of course, call these bluebells but wild hyacinths; the bluebells of Scotland are our harebells.

Foxgloves, too, grew in profusion amongst the scrub birch, and little sand-pipers flitted along the shore and even in front of the car. We stopped at one place and talked to a keeper, who showed us a fly-catcher's nest in a dry-stone wall. The old bird was sitting very tight, so we took a short length of film of her then and there, without bothering to build a hide.

By tea-time we had made our way over the Rest and Be Thankful, down through Inveraray and arrived at our destination, a small pub on the west side of Kintyre looking over to the isle of Gigha with the hills of Jura standing behind.

We dumped our kit and then drove out to a shepherd on the Mull who knew where the eagle was nesting. She had two young ones on a sea-cliff ledge, an unusual site, and, being a good hour's walk out from the nearest road, she had not been disturbed in any way. So, after hearing this good news and having a cup of tea in the shepherd's house, we drove back to base.

That night I was kept awake for some time by the corncrakes, which made a curious noise rather like a motor-cycle far away in the distance. This was the first time I had ever heard them – though at one time they were so common that the rent of certain land was paid in the form of corncrakes, caught by trained sparrow-hawks in the flax fields around Ely.

Hawks themselves were sometimes paid as rent, and the Duke of Atholl held the Isle of Man from the Crown on that basis, the rent a cast of hawks to be presented at the sovereign's coronation.

While I was in Scotland I was very anxious to get a peregrine for myself, and so the next day Unk stayed behind while a farmer friend, one of his shepherds and myself drove over to an eyrie some ninety miles away. It was a bit late in the year to get eyasses, but we hoped for the best.

It was a long, weary, wet day. The car broke down, not entirely, but so that it could only be driven at little more than walking pace.

At the first eyrie we visited the eyasses had flown, and the next two eyries were both unoccupied, but at the last one we found two beautiful young falcons, nearly ready to fly, and brought them back in triumph, finally getting back about 2 a.m. very, very tired.

Unk, after his day of rest, banged on my door the next morning, all set to get cracking. We had another possible eagle's site to look at, to which our farmer friend had promised to take us. So we set off with him and his two small daughters and drove to a small hill lochan. It was calm and sunny, very different from the day before. Unk stayed by the car, as he was unwell and not up to walking far.

The rest of us set out over the heather. We walked for about an hour, seeing little lochans everywhere, climbing up and down, ridge after ridge of small hills, till we reached a wide glen, on the other side of which we hoped to find the eagle nesting.

As we walked down to the burn we saw two eagles soaring over the opposite hill. We watched them through the glasses for a bit, but they went over the top out of sight. We crossed the glen and climbed up the other side, and there was the eagle's eyrie: a vast collection of sticks, piled up on top of each other, perched on a wide cliff-ledge. By going up to one side and peering over we could look into it. It was empty.

We turned to go home. The sun had gone in and it had suddenly turned cold. We crossed the burn again and had started up the hill when the mist came down. One moment it was clear, the next moment we could only see a few yards in front of us. The mist made us all damp and cold in a very short time. We trudged on, climbing up a steep hill, steeper than I could remember having come down. At the top we suddenly had to stop. We were on the edge of a small cliff and, as the mist swirled and cleared for an instant, we could see the black water of a lochan below. Then, through the mist, came a most eerie cry and two strange-looking birds swept past us like little torpedoes, calling as they went. They were red-throated divers, close relatives to the North American loon.

We made our way along the cliff edge down to the lochan and, skirting this, we plodded on, getting wetter and colder and more and more tired. The two children, who, at first, had thought this something of an adventure and had been chattering gaily, were pretty silent by now.

Personally I had no idea of where we were, and it seemed to me that we had been walking considerably longer than the time it had taken us to do the journey out. However, we were still crossing the ridges of hills and must eventually hit the road. Sure enough, the welcome sight of a telegraph pole loomed up and we were there. I had no idea which way to turn to reach the car, but we turned right without any hesitation, so I gathered our friend knew what he was doing.

'I'll walk on and fetch the car and Unk, if you follow slowly.' And, with amazing energy, he strode off into the mist. An hour later we were having tea with lashings of hot toast and sausages in front of a blazing fire and Unk was telling us how, when the mist came down, he had blown the car horn at frequent intervals and that the only reply he got was the gulls laughing on the lochan.

Before we could build the hide for the sea-cliff eyrie all the wooden uprights, the sacking and other materials had to be taken out, an hour and a half's walk, on our backs.

Three days later, after six trips to the hide, it was ready for occupation. On the last evening we loaded up the camera and checked over everything carefully, and early the next morning the shepherd and I set off with the gear. I got the camera set up, made

One of the leverets successfully reared on the bottle

'I am the cat that walks by itself, and all places are alike to me'

In the back-end of the year the frosts come and turn the birches gold

'Another ground nester is the hen-harrier'

Caterpillar of the northern eggar. 'You could
make several busbys for toy soldiers out of one'

'I found a merganser's nest by the shore'

The old eagles add to the eyrie each year

The young eagles crouched down
on the nest

Hill hares usually choose a less open site for their form

This young knobber was lying behind a rock. He stood up when I squeaked, and stared at me

The Lord Chancellor's seat – a woolsack being filled

No park stag this – and you must stalk a lot nearer with a camera than with a gun

Winter is a bastion against civilization

The cold creeps in and the deer come down early from the tops

Things already lovely become even more so when the snow comes

Mrs Murdoch weighed nearly fourteen pounds and needed a strong chain to hold her

She took an interest in the T.V. team – not too much, they hoped

Her powers of flight improved gradually

Her great feet coming forward to grab the lure

A golden eagle coming to the fist is liable to knock you back

After nine months' training I had taught her all I could and I let her go back to the wild

a slit in the sacking for the lens, another for the view-finder and one for me to see through at each side. The shepherd left and I settled down to wait.

The hide was right on the edge of the cliff, the posts on that side being kept upright by wire stays, with heavy rocks on the ends hanging over the cliffside. I could see the two eaglets, nearly full-grown now, lying down sleeping on the nest. The sea-cliffs ran away in front of me, becoming higher in the distance. I had a good view of the moor on my right, and on my left I could see over to Rathlin Island, off Ireland.

I looked along the shoreline, and there was a whacking great eagle poking about among the rocks. One of the parent birds, I thought, but what a curious place for a golden eagle. I reached for the binoculars to get a closer view. It wasn't a golden eagle. It was a sea-eagle. It had a great heavy beak, a pure white tail, and its legs were bare, not feathered to the toes like a golden eagle's.

This really was something. I hastily cut a hole for the camera in that side of the hide. It was too far away for filming but it might perhaps come nearer, and then I should regret not being ready. After all, I could film the golden eagles any time, but a sea-eagle was a really rare bird. They have been extinct as a nesting species in Britain since the early 1900s. This one had probably come over from either Norway or Iceland.

As I watched it ran across a flat stretch of the shore and, with great sweeps of its wings, took off. At first it lumbered along, but as it gained speed its flight became more graceful and it rose up and circled round, getting higher and higher. It was too far for photography, even with the telephoto lens.

Then, as it came in towards the cliff and I had my fingers on the camera-trigger, positively itching to press it, the two golden eagles came belting over and proceeded to mob it, buzzing it like a couple of Spitfires at a bomber. The sea-eagle turned away and made off.

In the air it looked entirely different from the other two. Its wings were far broader, and its white tail showed up an immense way away. It got smaller and smaller; the golden eagles gave up mobbing once it was away from the eyrie locality, and it vanished towards Ireland.

I swung the camera back onto the eaglets, who had woken up now and were doing a bit of exercising, flapping their wings and jumping about. I took about twenty feet of them and then stopped in case the old bird should come in and catch me short of film.

It was stiflingly hot in the hide. The flies buzzed in the bracken outside; the eaglets went to sleep. Two hours later, and still nothing much had happened. The eaglets had woken up a few times, but they soon dozed off again. There was no sign of the old birds. The day wore on. It seemed to me that the old eagles were rather neglecting their offspring.

Then, suddenly, the eaglets began to get very excited. They crowded to the edge of the nest, flapping their wings and calling 'Kewp, kewp, kewp' in quick succession. In the distance, about a mile away, I saw one of the old birds. She was flying along the edge of the cliff, taking full advantage of the updraught. She came rapidly closer, the young getting more and more excited. I got the camera ready. As she came nearer I could see her wingtips turning up under the pressure, her tail fanning out now and then and her wings being slightly folded or extended, according to the needs of flight. She rocked very gently from side to side.

Then, about three hundred yards away, she dropped down below the cliff-top. Still not a wing-beat. Lower and lower she dropped, till she was at least a hundred feet below the level of the eyrie. I tilted the camera down and started shooting, following her in the view-finder. Just when she was almost immediately below the eyrie, she swung up, the speed at which she had been flying bringing her easily up to the ledge, where the eaglets were now beside themselves, dancing about and jumping up and down like children at a Christmas tree.

She braked with spread tail and turned wings and, with effortless grace, landed gently on the nest, a blue hare firmly held in one great, gnarled, yellow foot.

The camera was still whirring, and then, as one of the young took the hare from her, it stopped. I hastily rewound it and went on shooting. The old bird stood on the edge of the nest looking at the young, who were having a tug-of-war. She paid little attention to this childish bickering, but turned her head and looked all round. She really was a magnificent bird; the sun caught her hackles, and at that angle she did look gold around the head, the rest of her quite a dark brown. She looked like a big edition of Ramshaw – a good deal bigger.

I looked at the footage counter; not much left. I had better go on shooting, though. It was very lucky that I did so, for she didn't bother to feed the young, they were old enough now to pull for themselves. She turned into the sea breeze, spread her wings, dropped off the ledge and sailed out of sight behind me. The camera gave a small hiccough and changed its note. The film had run out.

I changed film, shot some more of the young, feeding, and packed up the exposed reel. About an hour later the shepherd came along and let me out. I took a few feet of the hide from higher up the hill and then we walked back to tell Unk of our success. That night we celebrated and sent the film off to be processed.

A few more days filming the eagles, and then we dismantled the hide and said good bye to the eaglets.

We spent a day or two more, taking other things of interest, eider duck, fulmars and so on; then it was time for me to go back to Wiltshire.

The two falcons came with me, in their hamper.

15 * Do It Yourself

The two falcons had been very near flying when they were taken, and they had grown even more while I was filming the eagles. So they were only about a week in the mews at Salisbury before they were ready for training.

New peregrines meant that I should need hoods, and by now all my old hoods were getting very shabby and in need of renovation. There are several types of hoods. Indian hoods are fairly easy to make, but are very easy for the bird to remove. The Dutch hoods are much better-looking and, if well fitted, quite impossible for a falcon to get off on her own. There is a third alternative, an Indian hood with Dutch fittings, but these are ugly and lose shape quickly.

Dutch hoods were no longer being made in Holland for there was not sufficient demand for them. At one time in the village of Valkenswaard there were as many as eighteen professional falconers, chief amongst them being the Mollen family, who not only made hoods, hawking-bags, bells, swivels and other gear, but also caught passage and haggard falcons and supplied them to falconers from all over Europe.

Each year, when the autumn migration of birds came over the heath, a few miles from the village, the hawk-catchers would go out in the early morning to the huts they had previously built for the purpose. These huts were made of turf with a large cart-wheel on a pole to support the roof. From outside they looked like a small hummock. The catchers took work with them: hoods to be made, shoes to be repaired, and so on, for only a small portion of their time was taken up by the actual catching.

They had with them, tethered outside, a pair of tame great grey shrikes, or butcher-birds, whose chattering warned the catcher when a hawk appeared. Then, by use of various decoys, the migrating falcon or hawk – for they caught peregrines, goshawks and sometimes, gyrfalcons, the big falcons from Norway and Iceland – was enticed and finally caught in a bow-net. It was an extremely complicated set-up but very efficient. When the migration ended, the birds which had not already been sold to order were auctioned.

In due course, the demand for passage falcons ceased, the heath became built over, the migration route altered, and the practice died. The Mollen family still made gear up to 1939, but the war put an end to this and they never started again.

So I decided to try to make my own hoods. I knew roughly how they were made: sewn inside out, turned, soaked in water and then blocked like a felt hat to get them into a good shape. I managed to get hold of a couple of hood-blocks from Holland, but little did I realize the problems I was up against. First I had to have a pattern to fit the block. Taking an old hood to pieces was useless, for the leather stretched when wetted and a pattern from it was too big. I solved this problem by covering the block with plasticine, cutting it to shape, bisecting it, and then laying it out flat on paper and tracing round it.

The next thing was the leather. The hoods are sewn so that the edges butt against each other and no stitches appear on the outside of the finished hood. I tried all sorts of leather. If it was too thin it ripped and tore, if too thick it didn't remain light-tight when turned and was also too heavy. The right kind of thread, the best sort of needle, the material for the eye-piece covering, leather for the braces which opened and closed the hood, how long to soak them, how best to turn them; all these problems, and others besides, had to be solved by trial and error.

Then they had to fit when done. Even with a hood-block to help, this was far from easy, for the size could be altered simply by the way one cut and trimmed. I pegged away at it and looked through the old falconry books to see if I could glean any information.

In one of them there was a coloured plate of various types of hoods, including an odd-looking Syrian affair. I examined this closely and then realized that, by crossing it with the Dutch style, I could devise a type that might well be easier to make.

I fooled around with pencil and paper, worked out a pattern of my own, cut one out and sewed it up. It looked rather attractive when I had turned it and put it on the block to dry. I couldn't wait for it to dry normally, so I put it in front of an electric fan fire, which dried it in half an hour. Because the process had been speeded up the hood had been stiffened too. I had discovered something useful, quite by accident.

I trimmed it, put some braces on the back and, without bothering to put a plume on it, tried it on Greensleeves, the falcon. It fitted. I took it off, put on a plume and marked the number inside: Number 42. The other forty-one had all been duds.

I was lying in bed that evening, reading, and the hood was on a near-by table, sitting on a nicely bound book that was tooled in gold-leaf. Suddenly I thought how nice it would be if I could put gold-leaf onto the hood.

The next day I went to the local bookbinders, taking the hood with me. I told them what I wanted to do and they were most helpful.

'It won't be as easy as tooling a book because the whole thing is on the curve,' said the expert, 'but I think you could get a tool specially made to overcome that difficulty.'

That sounds a bit expensive, I thought, but apparently it was only a matter of a few shillings. The amount of gold-leaf I should use would not break the bank either. I became even more enthusiastic. I left the shop armed with various bits and pieces and a headful of instructions. At least I had plenty of dud hoods to try it out on.

About ten hoods later I was able to turn out something that not only fitted a falcon but had the looks of a craftsman-made job. My fingertips were torn by endless recalcitrant needles, and I had a sore ridge on one finger where the thread had bitten in as I pulled the stitches tight. My thumb had been burnt guiding the hot iron that put the gold-leaf on, and, had I known what was in front of me, I should probably never have started. Still, I had a very satisfying feeling of achievement.

The two falcons each had a smart new hood, but, as I really could only manage one bird, I gave the other to James. We flew them at rooks, on the Plain and around Winchester, and they were also used

in a film he was making for Walt Disney in which I, also, had a
very minor part. There was no flying in the film, as there had been
in Charles Laughton's Henry VIII film, for which Unk had done
the falconry piece, but there was one scene in which the falcon
made her mark. James, as Henry, was sitting on his throne, feeding
the falcon a pigeon's wing. The French ambassador, with retinue,
strode up between the ranks of the assembled courtiers, bowed, and
made a long and boring speech. During this time the falcon went
on plucking feathers out of the wing, taking no notice.

The cameras whirred, the lights blazed, sound experts held
microphones in strategic places from queer, mechanical crane-like
contraptions. The French ambassador ended his speech. There was
a pause as Henry drew himself up to reply. Before he could do so
the falcon stopped feeding for a moment, looked up, slowly went
'Yak, yak, yak', then continued madly throwing feathers about. It
was the perfect reply. Yet for some extraordinary reason it was never
used.

Back at the studio I went on taking whatever came my way:
portraits, poodles, pewter pots, all sorts of odd things. The local
museum wanted ancient Saxon iron work photographed. It looked
more like the gleanings from a scrap-merchant's to me, but they
knew what each bit had been, in spite of their incongruous shapes.

At week-ends I flew Pru or Greensleeves. James went off to
America to do some more filming and came back with an assortment
of birds of prey in a zip-bag. There was a very beautiful prairie
falcon, a little Cooper's hawk, and six tiny western kestrels. He
gave me the Cooper's hawk and also one of the western kestrels.

We had a few days at Whitchurch with Pru and then took the
falcons out after rooks. It was a day of disaster. James's flew a rook
over the skyline and disappeared and, although we searched for
hours, we found no trace of her. I flew mine, who put a rook down
by a wire fence and then broke her leg on the wire. I carried her
home and put her in plaster, but it was an awkward break, the
feathers made it extremely difficult to set, and she never recovered.

We got James's falcon back the next day. She had chased the rook
into a shepherd's hut, where she had been accidentally shut in a

few moments after. I had searched under the hut but had never thought of looking inside.

The following Friday I took Pru over to James's house at Whitchurch, where Geoffrey joined us with his gos, Medusa. We all three piled into the old Rolls shooting-brake and drove up to Norfolk. Here, James had arranged a rather special day's hawking at Sandringham.

We tried his falcon first, at rooks, but she was obviously put out by the importance of the occasion and refused to fly them. Instead they mobbed her. Geoffrey and I then tried our two gosses. Pru was a bit uppish to start with, missed an easy chance at a rabbit and went off to sulk for ten minutes in a tree. I got her down and, rejoining the party, found myself faced with the problem of greeting the Queen in a dignified manner with an irate goshawk bating off my fist.

Geoffrey's gos had a good flight at a pheasant, and we then parked the hawks on the lawn and had lunch at Sandringham House.

Afterwards, we had a rat-hunt with the two gosses at the moorhens who lived on the ponds in the gardens. It was quite a show. Moorhens were flying in all directions, the goshawks after them, and the onlookers, royal and otherwise, joined in, shouting instructions and information from their various points of vantage. Pru caught two, one of them eighty feet up an enormous Wellingtonia. Medusa caught four, so, although it was not by any means a stylish exhibition, at least we were not disgraced.

The week-end after high tides and a heavy gale flooded vast areas of the countryside. The wind stopped my flying Pru, and I brought her indoors to feed her up. But her old fits started, and in three days she was dead, in spite of nursing from Bill and advice from doctor friends.

16 * Falcons and Film Stars

'M.G.M. here. We want two dozen trained falcons for a film,' said the voice on the telephone. It was October; all the trained falcons in Britain wouldn't add up to that number. Even the Old Hawking Club in its hey-day had had less than that. I thought quickly over the various possibilities.

'You won't get that number over here, but you might be in time to buy untrained ones in Pakistan. There is a hawk fair there each year. Do you really need two dozen?'

'At least that number. We have to allow for losing a lot of them during the film,' the voice went on. 'You see we want shots of them in flight.'

'But there's no reason why you should lose any, certainly not more than one or two at the most. You'd need a lot of people to look after all that number, and if you bought them abroad you'd probably need a plane to yourself to bring them back. It'd be extremely expensive.'

'Filming is always expensive. Can you suggest any other way of doing it?'

'If you didn't want them till late July or August I could get half a dozen from this country, I expect.'

'Well, we'll think it over and let you know. Thanks for your help.'

I heard nothing more for some months. I went on with the normal studio work and took a lot of high-speed flash-shots of Geoffrey's gos in flight, when a wet week-end spoilt our plans for flying her. I was rather pleased with the results. I typed out an article to go with the best shots and sent it to one of the better-known sporting magazines, which published it a few weeks later and then asked for more. By that time I had had their cheque, and as it hardly covered the

K

cost of taking the photographs, it certainly wasn't worth while doing any more.

Then Bill and I found a cottage a few miles out of Salisbury and decided to move. Having no garden where we were made it difficult to find room for the livestock.

James had given me one of two young Bonelli's eagles which he had brought from the Pyrenees. He lived in the attic over our sitting-room and, because of the strange noise his feet made over-head, we named him Trog, after a radio character who had similar foot trouble.

Besides Trog and the Cooper's hawk, we had acquired a Siamese cat, Bung-ho, and a most endearing dachshund, Emily, whose owner had decided that Tanganyika was not a good place to take her.

Then Bill, knowing how I had found Friday, the black pointer, so useful, had found a family of German pointer pups who were eating their owners out of house and home and therefore going cheap. Pointers and setters have been used for falconry for several hundred years. In 1624 setting dogs, together with hawks, were given to James I by the French king. There were three gangling great pups to choose from, and I picked the smallest of the two bitches and took her home, snuffling down the backs of our necks as we drove along.

With that lot, not to mention the children, the house was really bulging, and we looked rather like a circus when we went out. So the new cottage, with its decent-sized garden, was a great joy. Besides, the livestock we already had seemed to act as magnets for others. Any lost, sick or unusual creature automatically arrived at our door in some container or other.

The local detective-inspector parked a tame grey squirrel on us. As we already had one of our own, I built a cylindrical cage of wire-netting round an old apple tree for them. For technical reasons I had to work from the inside during the course of its construction, and my family considered this a huge joke. They were convinced that I could not get out and proceeded to offer me nuts through the bars. However, I extracted myself without much bother and, having closed the top, we introduced the two squidgers, who found it a wonderful place and raced in spirals round and round the trunk and dashed in and out of the sleeping-box hung on the tree.

Our next guest was Mr Ramshaw, who came to stay for a few months while Unk was on another trip. The wild buzzards that drifted over, high up, from the big wood behind the cottage, intrigued Ram no end. By now, he was nearly thirty years old, but when he spotted these buzzards he acted exactly like a young eagle in the eyrie when Mum comes along with some grub. He jumped about excitedly and called in his strange piping voice.

No sooner had Ramshaw returned to Unk than his vacant place had another claimant. An eminent naturalist had just died, and his heirs and assigns were left with a bear, a monkey, a lesser spotted eagle and an eagle-owl. The bear was soon removed by a zoo. The monkey missed its late owner and pined away. Only the eagle and the owl were still homeless. I drove over with a friend to collect these two. When we arrived a number of onlookers gathered round, convinced we would be torn to pieces by one or other of the birds.

We tackled the eagle-owl first. She was in a big shed with an outdoor flight, and we spoilt the onlookers' fun by shutting the shed door. The owl was frightened, and all we had to do was to position ourselves one at each end of the shed and grab her as she flew past. I missed her; she went up the other end; Ian grabbed one leg; I rushed up and grabbed the other, and she was in the hamper and we were out in a matter of minutes. The audience seemed disappointed that there was no blood around, but they gathered round the eagle's cage hoping for better things.

This time there was no shed to spoil their view. The eagle, quite a small one, sat calmly on its perch and watched as I slipped through the door. It didn't seem in the least alarmed.

'Mind 'e don't peck yer, Guvner,' came from the crowd.

The eagle still remained motionless on the perch. I attracted its attention with my left hand, waving it just out of range, and then grabbed both its feet from behind with my right hand, rendering it quite helpless. I carried it across to the door and popped it in the hamper. Our onlookers' attitude changed immediately. A few moments before it had been a case of, 'Cor, look at 'is beak, I wouldn't go in with 'im for a week's wages.' Now it was 'Oh, the poor thing, what's 'e going to do with it?'

What, indeed, was I going to do with either of them? I thought as we drove back home. The eagle-owl could go loose in Ramshaw's apartment. I had really not got much room for the eagle and, like most birds of prey in small cages, it had broken primaries and tail feathers and it would be at least a year before it moulted out and was able to fly properly. Also I had noted it had very small, stumpy feet; obviously it was a vulturine thing and would never be much use as a falconer's bird, being more inclined to feed on carrion than to catch its own meals. However, I knew a bird artist who might give it a home and use it as a model. He was delighted and I packed the eagle off the next day.

Meanwhile Aunt Jobisca, the eagle-owl, settled down in her new quarters. I put a pair of jesses on so that I could pick her up easily if I wanted to, but I left her loose, for she was wise to wire and never crashed against it. I gave her a shelter, but she disdained it entirely and never made use of it even in the wettest or coldest weather. After a heavy frost at night she looked more like a snowy-owl, but her thick layer of down, under her feathers, kept her insulated against the cold.

She really was a most handsome bird, with long ear tufts, which were actually nothing to do with her ears and which she raised or lowered at will. Her eyes were the most striking point about her. These were the size of half-crowns, and of a deep glowing, orange colour with black pupils. They were bright and shining, like wet glass, and the pupils dilated and contracted to an enormous degree. Her feet were feathered, as in all owls, right down to her talons. She had an immensely powerful grip too, and the ordinary falconry glove was by no means proof against her. When angry she would puff herself out to twice her size, clop her beak and, if the dogs came too close, spread her great wings and lean forward and make herself look very dangerous indeed. This was most effective.

We had thought that so large a bird would be accompanied by a taxi-sized hoot, but Aunt Jobisca disappointed us by remaining quite silent. Then, one summer evening, some three months after her arrival, I heard a peculiar noise coming from her area of the garden.

Quite soft and gentle, a rather delicate, flute-like, little 'Twuit, twuit, twuit' came floating across the lawn. We listened for a while and commented on the call being rather like Ramshaw's, unsuited to the size of the bird. The night air was making us chilly, and I leant out to get hold of the window catch to shut it. The owl stopped calling and there was dead silence. As I was about to pull the window to, suddenly, out of the night, came a thunderous Hoo . . . hooooooooooooooooo, rolling and echoing across the village, setting the dogs barking furiously and making the cat's hackles stand on end, bristling like an old shaving-brush. The noise died away; the village turned to sleep. I shut the window. Aunt Jobisca had done us proud.

Soon afterwards M.G.M. got in touch with me once more, and this time I managed to persuade them that six falcons would be ample. In fact I only managed to get five, and we only used two of them properly, the rest being understudies and having small walking-on parts.

Because of the shortage of time, I concentrated on the two tiercels, who, being smaller, were ready before their sisters. Alistair and Brounie soon learnt what was required of them and after nine days of training they were both coming loose to the lure. Brounie being the more amiable, I picked him as our star performer, with Alistair as understudy. We took them daily to the studio and, every morning, when we brewed coffee, they took a bath in a spare developing-dish on the workroom floor. They enjoyed this and splashed about so much that I had to spread newspapers around the bathing-area.

Brounie became so tame that you could walk up to him, put your hands round him and pick him up, bodily, from his block. I was reasonably confident that he would be ready in another week when the film company rang up to ask if we could start right away.

The Boreham Wood Studios had built a shelter where I could keep the peregrines when they were not being used. This was on the back of the lot, and so, on arrival, I drove up to the main gates. Now these, apart from stars, directors, producers and other high-ranking film people, are sacrosanct. So the gatekeeper, who was accustomed to sleek, slinky sports cars or luxuriously appointed limousines, was reluctant to let the old and battered two-seater go through.

I drove between the various enormous buildings that housed the stages, to the workshops behind, where all sorts of fascinating things were being built or dismantled. The craftsmen here, from a few bits of wood, metal, sacking, plaster and paint, turned out anything from a Roman chariot to the latest type of submarine, good enough to fool anyone until they actually touch it. They had made a wonderful job of the falcons' enclosure, and I still use the blocks they made from my designs.

I parked the falcons and then went off to find out what was happening. It is very easy to get lost in such places and, as several films are being done at the same time, one is apt to get mixed up in the wrong one. However, the producer sent one of his many minions to tell me that we were on location at Trent Park, several miles away.

Out at the Park I got Props to bang some posts into the ground and link them up with rope, enclosing a little area of my own where the falcons could sit without being trampled over by horses, eaten by dogs, or run down by any of the assorted vehicles that milled around. I left them hooded till things had quietened down a bit, except for Brounie, whom I carried around unhooded to get him used to the scene.

In due course the more important members of the company arrived. Chairs, with their owners' names written large on the back, were placed out in a point of vantage: Ava Gardner, Robert Taylor, Stanley Baker, Ann Crawford, Felix Aylmer and so on.

The man in charge of the horses came up and asked me if I would try one or two out, to see what they thought of having someone on board carrying a falcon. Some object very strongly, and this can make things rather awkward. The leading man never has more than one horse. This animal, chosen more for its looks than anything else, is all-purpose, goes hunting, hawking and even into battle, and is never allowed to be mud-splashed, even after galloping hard for some hours.

Brounie was introduced to the stars, some of whom were somewhat diffident in shaking hands with him. I was hoping that our first day's filming would be fairly simple and would serve to accustom the falcons to this somewhat strange life, so very different from the cliff ledges on which they were hatched. Instead I discovered that

Brounie was to be unhooded by Robert Taylor mounted on horse-back, and flown off into the blue – hardly a walking-on part for a beginner.

I explained to Robert Taylor how to handle Brounie and asked the director where he wanted Brounie to fly and how close I could come without appearing in the picture. He waved his hand and said he must fly up. As we were already on top of a hill and anywhere I stood would be lower, I explained that upwards was the one direction he would not go, unless I were placed higher. In the usual way of film companies, this problem was solved not by moving the scene slightly, but by erecting a small platform, some fifteen feet high, made of tubular scaffolding. On top of this I stood and, when the cameras were turning and Brounie was unhooded, I showed him some meat on my fist and he flew up to me immediately. 'Cut,' shouted the director. 'Next shot.'

I scrambled down with Brounie from the platform, somewhat surprised. In my previous experience of filming, two takes at least were normal, very often far more than that. Perhaps Brounie had not performed well enough and they had decided to cut the falconry shots entirely. But the director beckoned me over and said he was delighted. The falcons took part in several more shots, and when we stopped shooting for the day everything had gone well. We had no retakes. I left the falcons in their enclosure on the lot overnight.

We were on a different location the next day. The chippies had built a wooden track for the cameras to run along, parallel to the scene they were to shoot. This was of the whole hawking-party: thirty or forty horses and various foot-followers, moving along, first slowly, then breaking into a canter. Several people were to carry the falcons, and this was the only time I used all of them.

It happened to be a Saturday, and by the afternoon there was a crowd of onlookers watching us. The whole shot took quite a lot of rehearsing, and by the time everything was set clouds started to drift across the sun and time and again we were delayed.

I wanted to keep Brounie and Alistair exercised each day because the script called for some flight shots. So I took advantage of the delay and flew them to the lure. I put Brounie on the wing, and the sound of his bells overhead attracted the attention of the waiting crowd. He flew round in circles, paying no attention to the people below, and I got the lure out and started to stoop him properly. He went like a bomb, flying hard at it, stooping and throwing up in fine style. By now everyone was watching. When I thought he had done enough I shouted to him as usual the next time he came round and, as he came towards me, threw the lure up as high as I could; he caught it deftly and landed some way off.

Now film people are fairly used to seeing stunts, performing animals, and so on, and are pretty inured to such things, but Brounie's performance to the lure brought the house down. As he landed there was a spontaneous burst of applause and even shouts of encore. It was all very gratifying.

Then the sun obliged, and the tracking shot was filmed. It had taken four days to lay the track; several hundred people were taking part, from the stars in the foreground to a poor little man, dressed as a monk, who had spent all day pretending to fish by the lake in the background. I fully expected at least one retake, but no, the cameras stopped, there was a moment's pause just to check that they had run properly, and then the track was dismantled. Our director certainly had plenty of confidence in his actors and technicians.

The next three weeks or so were spent filming either in the studio or round the castle on the lot. This castle was a magnificent affair. Behind, it was simply a framework of tubular scaffolding and lath and plaster, with here and there a platform for the actors to stand on. But from the front it was a medieval fortress of stone, complete with drawbridge, portcullis, battlements, little turrets for fair damsels in distress to wave from, and everything that a proper castle should have.

We spent one day out on location, purely to take flight shots of the falcons. We did this near Winchester, on the farm of a friend of mine, right up on top of the Downs. We were all gathered on the top: two camera crews, producer, director, technicians, props, chippies, even a continuity girl. Besides all these people, plus the usual lookers-on, there were lorries and cars in profusion – all this to film two little tiercels flying about.

In the valley below, just out of sight, one of the farm workers

was starting to burn the stubble. Our director, seeing a small plume
of smoke rising and thinking it might spoil the sky background,
leapt to his feet with a cry of 'Gee, the canyon's on fire!' Ever since
then that little valley has been known as the canyon.

When the assembled company was finally all ready, with cameras
in position, and so on, the director asked me to get the tiercels to
fly. 'We want them coming right at the cameras, and circling round
high up, and diving, and so on.'

It was a gorgeous, sunny day, with big, white cumulus clouds
scudding across the sky. The director sat between the two cameras.
Both tiercels were really fit, and a breeze gave them plenty of lift
as they circled round. The camera crews were screwing their heads
off trying to follow them, nearly falling off the platforms. After a
brief halt for some clouds that came across the sun, we started again.

'Let's have them coming right at us this time,' said our director.
I cast Brounie off, and the cameras started to turn; I moved in
closer and began to stoop him to the lure. He stopped his lazy
circling at once and turned, coming in hard and just lifting to clear
the camera crews, who all ducked instinctively. 'Gee, that's fine,'
came from the central chair. Brounie circled round and came in
again. He wasn't just stooping, he was giving an extra clip of his
half-closed wings every so often and really piling on the pace,
obviously enjoying the game. He came in even lower, threw up, and
stooped again. The camera crews were swinging round to face him
as he shot over their heads, and round they all pranced once more,
but by the time they were facing the right way he had stooped
again and was behind them.

He came in lower still, this time between the two cameras and
right at the director. After all, this was the guy who had asked for
it. At the critical moment he threw up, about six inches above the
director's head. 'That's the stuff. Keep him going.' Brounie came
in again, he was determined to show off that day. He knew exactly
how close he could get. After all he would be judging distance in
the wild state just as well. The director was now his target. He had
had his fun with the camera crews, now he meant to show the
instigator of all this that he could work to the fraction of an inch.
He flipped over his head; he came in from behind, from in front;

the wind pressure pushed the bells against his legs and the wind screamed through the slots in the bells as he stooped. Our friend was now getting worried. 'Take it easy!'

But Brounie wasn't satisfied yet. He climbed up higher, turned and came streaking down, tearing up the sky. The target, who up to now had stood his ground, ducked. His chair slipped and over he went, his hat flying off.

I threw the lure to Brounie, who caught it as usual and then left it to jump a few feet to my fist. I walked over with him. 'That what you wanted?' He nodded. 'It sure is. Right, boys, break off for lunch, I reckon we've earned it.'

There was little more to be done after lunch. They had exposed over 2,800 feet to each of the two cameras. Unless something had gone very wrong indeed, they couldn't have failed to get some first-class results.

We did one more little bit on location close by the studios. This particular shot, I thought, was bound to need several takes to get it right. Brounie was to fly into the picture carrying a dead bird and to land in a tiny patch of sunlight not more than six feet square. I got them to build another small platform, like the one we had used on the first day, climbed to the top with Brounie and gave him the dead bird on the floor. As the cameras started to run I picked him up round his body and gently tossed him, bird and all, in the right direction. It was purely a matter of luck where he would land. The cameras followed him and he landed bang in the middle of the sunlit patch.

With the little car laden I set off home.

But M.G.M. needed one more shot of Brounie. So Bill and I spent a final day at the studios. We got there in good time, to find Robert Taylor being rescued by Berwick, his faithful horse, from a rather watery-looking and very messy bog. This shot went off well, and then Berwick was required to nod his head. But it wasn't Berwick's day for nodding. The girl in charge of him impatiently tapped her boots with her riding-crop and called 'Berwick'. Nothing happened.

Two hours later, and several hundred feet of film wasted, we were still nodless. We broke for lunch.

'Give him some oats,' said the camera-men. But the oats did no

good. Another hour and a half went by. Everyone was murmuring
'Berwick'; his handler was really worried. He had done pretty nearly
every trick they could think of in the film and performed beautifully.
This should have been easy to so talented a creature.

Time was getting on. I tentatively suggested we might do the
shot of Brounie before it was too late. The camera position was
altered. I slipped into Robert Taylor's costume, for my arm would
show in the picture. The cameras turned; I picked Brounie up from
his kill, hooded him, and it was all finished. I went to change and
then back to the studio to say good-bye. Berwick was still there,
without a nod. As I went out I heard the exasperated voice of the
usually patient director: 'Oh, take him away and give him a mare.'

That winter, at home in Wiltshire, we had heavy falls of snow.
Aunt Jobisca still persisted in refusing to take shelter and sat on
her tree-trunk with a hat of snow on her head, her two ear tufts
sticking up through it.

The squirrels stayed snug in their nest box on the apple tree.
The children's tame hedge-pig also retired to bed, a spiky ball that
moved only very slightly as he breathed slowly. The dogs stayed
fire-bound and did their best to melt their brains, so close did they
lie to the blaze.

At the studio we were busy with the Christmas rush and were
knee-deep in film, mounts, photographs and packing.

One evening James came over and offered me a job. He was
considering buying a house near Inverness and wanted me to look
after the place generally and to train and fly falcons for him. And
so I became a professional falconer.

17 * Migration North

The old van was packed tight. Besides my own luggage and a suitcase of Paul's, who was coming as co-driver, we had a small circus on board. There were two peregrines, Kate and Brounie, Trog the Bonelli's eagle, Trudy the German pointer, Emily the dachshund, Bung-ho the Siamese cat, Clementine the white pigeon, and a couple of rabbits. Trog was in a hamper, the rabbits and the pigeon in boxes; Kate and Brounie sat hooded on a cadge; and the dogs and cat roamed around loose. We tried putting Bung in a hamper, but he objected strongly and so was allowed to join the dogs. Bill and the children were to join me later, when all the furniture had arrived and things been sorted out.

It was early March, and very cold as we left Barford about three in the afternoon. Crossing the Plain it started to snow and, about half an hour after, a lorry, trying to overtake where there simply wasn't room, put us into the grass verge and gently smacked us on the nose.

After repairing the damage and spending the night in a pub, we drove on. The old van forged ahead and hour by hour we pushed on, through the industrial Midlands, then over Shap, covered in a thin coating of snow, and across the border at Gretna. Every so often we stopped to give the dogs and cat a run and to stretch our legs. By eight that night we had reached Stirling. 'Let's have a real blow-out here and drive right through the night,' Paul suggested. So we trooped into the Golden Lion and discovered that the road north was blocked by snow.

We decided to risk it and, after a whacking great meal, we pushed on. Apart from a few mountain hares in their white winter coats and some deer, we saw no living thing till we got to Croft Downie at five the next morning. James greeted us and helped to unload the livestock; and we slept on a couple of mattresses in front of a blazing log fire for a few hours.

We woke up to find that Bung-ho had vanished from an apparently sealed room where we had put him with the dogs. However, yowls from the chimney gave away his retreat; and I had to climb on the roof and push him down with a mop-head tied to a long pole. We spent the morning getting the livestock sorted into more permanent quarters. Then the removal-men arrived and the normal chaos ensued before things began to look slightly more orderly.

A few days later the snow melted and the sun came out and blazed away all summer.

The rest of the family arrived, and we began to explore the countryside.

We were on the Black Isle, in Ross. It was not in fact an island, though to get to our main town, Inverness, meant crossing the Moray Firth by ferry or else a twenty-five-mile drive round. The Firth was at our door and full of, to us, new and interesting things. Seals came in quite close, though the local inhabitants shot them if they could.

I found a merganser's nest in some bushes by the shore and filmed her on the eggs. She sat so tight that I had no need of a hide. Her long, thin red beak, with its saw-toothed edge for holding fish and eels, was the only thing that showed much, the rest of her greyish plumage merging into the background. She hatched a few days later and, like all ducks, as soon as the ducklings were dry, she led them away to the water.

There were a lot of mute swans on the Firth and one or two whoopers, whose straighter necks, angular heads with the yellow patch on the bill, and way of holding their feathers tight in, made them easily distinguishable. It seemed strange to see swans on salt water after being used to them on rivers.

The common gull really was common here, instead of being the rarity it is in the south. Kittiwakes, as well, frequented the shore. One dived in and caught my minnow one day, and I had the rather odd sight of my line being taken up in the air. It was hooked just inside its beak, and I released the gull, with no more than a fright and a scratch.

On a steep grassy cliff a mile or two away I found a large heronry. The nests were in the tops of some pines on the slope. It was a marvellous site for photography because the slope was so steep that, by building a hide near the top, on the ground, I could film them without having to do any tree-climbing.

Sitting in this hide one morning, I watched some cormorants on the branches of a dead tree below me. One was a curious coffee-coloured bird; a freak of pigmentation. They had quite a job landing on the branches with their webbed feet, which weren't very suitable for such an undertaking. They frequently missed their footing and flapped away clumsily, to wing round and come in again for another try. One of them landed successfully only to have the branch break under its weight. As the bird had half folded its wings by then, it dropped downwards once its support was gone and, by mischance, its head got caught in a fork. It flapped madly, but its own weight stopped it from getting free. It hung, like a victim on a keeper's scrag-pole. It made one last desperate effort; its frenziedly flapping wings made it swing and, for a moment, its paddling feet came in contact with the main trunk and lifted it free. With a somewhat laboured flight it made off to the water below to recover itself.

The herons were very graceful as they flew around, their necks tucked into their shoulders and their long legs protruding beyond their tails. But the young were most ungainly and kept up an incessant chakkering, their throats pulsing like a croaking frog. I spent two days filming them and then left them for a week, so that they would be farther advanced before I took any more. During that week a fire swept round the hill and my hide was completely burnt. The herons were safe, high up in the trees.

I wanted to complete this little bit of filming with some shots of a heron actually fishing. So many nature films seem to me incomplete because of the difficulties involved in getting shots away from the nest. I wasn't sure where the best place would be to get such pictures; herons fly great distances and, even if I found where they went, I might still spend a great deal of time in a hide and never have them come near me. But luck was on my side, for once. We drove over to the West Coast one day, cameras in the back, purely to see the countryside. One bit of the road ran along the shore of a sea loch, and I noticed two herons standing on a sandbank not far out.

I pulled the car into the side and got the movie-camera out and all set. Birds and animals soon get used to cars and take little or no notice of them, though if you get out they all depart hastily. I took some distant shots of the two herons wading about, and then a third one came in. Apparently his presence was unwelcome, for one of the others promptly flew off in my direction and came gliding along, very low, and pitched bang opposite the car. He folded his wings, looked around him, and then, rather like a guardsman doing a slow march, waded along looking for food. I didn't have the luck to get him catching anything, but the film gave one a good idea how herons do fish.

We found a ringed plover, only just hatched, crouching in the sand pretending it was a stone, which it certainly resembled. I took a shot of it sitting in the sand and then we picked it up to examine more closely. I filmed it as it was put down, and it ran off at a fantastic rate for so young and so small a thing, its little legs twinkling so fast that it looked like one of those wooden toy birds which have four legs on a wheel, two only showing at a time.

There were terns nesting here too; they flew round overhead screeling, stooping if you got too close. We watched them fishing just off the shore, diving in head first with a splash and appearing with a small fish or sand-eel. Quite how they manage it I don't know, but they bring several back at once, held in their beaks.

On the way home we came across a bunch of stags, their horns well grown but still in velvet, and I had time to take some movie-shots of them as they made off, in no great hurry, up the hill.

Then it was time to take the new eyasses, train them and try my hand at grouse-hawking, something I had never attempted before. Our first season was pretty poor, for several reasons. We were new to the game. It was a very hot summer, really blazing; one of those summers that one reads about and so rarely sees. There were very few grouse on the moor where we flew, and they were extremely difficult to find because there was little or no scent for the dogs.

We had Trudy and also a Gordon setter called Stroma, a handsome black and tan dog with a feathery tail. Both dogs did their best, but the heat tired them very quickly, and their tongues lolled out, getting longer and longer; they would wallow in every damp patch of ground they came across in an effort to keep cool.

Trudy was by no means steady on a point, but would run in unless restrained. The lack of grouse made it extremely difficult to get the falcons going at all, and we made the mistake of having tiercels too, whose lack of weight makes them unsuitable for grousehawking unless they have done a season at partridges first. But we learnt a lot, and Trudy improved and stopped running in or chasing hares.

The pollen from the heather, kicked up by our feet plodding across the moor, was like the wake of a car on a dusty track. It made us sneeze, and the dogs too. It was in one of these thick bits of heather that Trudy came onto the point one afternoon. I unhooded one of the falcons and put her on the wing, and, when she was well placed, I called to Trudy to flush the grouse. To my surprise, up got what I thought was a blue-hare, and Trudy, much to my horror, gave chase. I called her off and she obeyed at once. But Polson, the keeper, shouted out, 'It's a wildcat!'

We had been talking about wildcats only a few minutes earlier and Polson had been saying that there were far more of them than most people imagined and that they did a lot of damage to the grouse and also to chickens during the winter. So I urged Trudy to take up the chase again, and off she went. The cat was looping over the tall heather. Trudy, with her long legs, soon caught it up and was wise enough not to get too close, but bounced around it and kept on turning it off its course. I ran as hard as I could and had just caught up when the cat vanished down a draining-ditch cut in the peat.

Polson arrived panting and, as he went one way up the drain, I took Trudy the other way. The heather had grown over the top and we had no idea which way the cat had taken, or how far it had gone. Polson was armed with a stick; I had nothing. We had drawn apart a hundred yards or so when Trudy put the cat out of the drain and bounced away after it again. It was spitting and snarling at her and, what with my shouting at Trudy, the noise of the cat, and advice from the onlookers, there was a considerable commotion going on. I ran in, grabbed the cat by its tail and, with my gloved hand, held it down.

Wildcats may look like common domesticated pussies in a lot of ways, but I can assure you that the resemblance ends there. The wildcat is a writhing bundle of muscle and tendon; its twenty long, black talons are as sharp as its white, curved fangs. To try to hold one is like trying to hold a conger eel. I had partially immobilized it, but only at the expense of completely immobilizing myself. Had Polson not come to deal with his enemy, the stalemate position would have been resolved fairly soon by my being forced to let go.

Polson, whose ancestor was responsible for the demise of one of the last wolves in Scotland, was delighted. He measured it: three foot six from nose to tail. He weighed it: eleven pounds. And he lugged it home in his game-bag. Poor pussy, his skin adorns my wall, for, after all, not many people can say they have caught a wildcat with their hands; but even so, in this extraordinary country of ours, the Government had the last word. I had to pay three-and-sixpence purchase tax on the skin.

Looking back on it, I should certainly never attempt to do the same thing again, for two reasons: first, one would be very lucky to get the same hold without being seriously mauled or bitten; and second, because, although they do a lot of harm from man's point of view, they are, let's face it, the only wild feline left in Great Britain. And I have a great admiration for the way in which they have adapted themselves to what must be a remarkably tough existence. The wolf, the wild boar, the beaver, the reindeer, the bear, have all given up the struggle. The mammals of this country should have some kind of protection before it is too late. Even those which eat the same food as man should be allowed a share. At least they catch without fire-arms, fish-hooks or other aids, which makes me feel that *Homo sapiens* is not really so *sapiens* after all.

The wildcat is a very handsome creature. I once met a tame wildcatten, taken before its eyes had opened and brought up on the

L

bottle. Most people will tell you they are untamable; but this one was perfectly domesticated when I saw it. It was friendly with strangers, and only when it was given its food did one realize how different it was. For then it rumbled like a small and very active volcano, in a deep bass voice, its ears flattened, its green-yellow eyes smouldering. It should have been called Susie, for it was a real wild child.

Now and then, when flying on the hill, a wild peregrine, probably curious about its trained relative, would come and investigate. What happened then depended on the temperament of the two birds concerned. Some trained peregrines are extremely jealous and will try and catch a wild intruder; there is a chase which is very exciting indeed and invariably goes on very high up, so high sometimes that little wisps of cloud hide the two.

Most books on falconry state that no trained falcon is ever as good as a wild one. I venture to doubt that statement. On more than one occasion I have seen the wild bird hard pushed to avoid being caught; once a wild tiercel vanished over the top of the hill, screaming with terror, with our falcon hard on his tail. What happened, I never found out, but she reappeared half an hour later, her legs and thighs soaking wet. At least that wild peregrine, like myself, didn't agree with the books. After all, a trained falcon, flying every day at grouse, probably flies more than a wild one, who only has to kill once every two or three days and can spend the rest of her time in idle contemplation of the world from a rock on a cliff-face. From that same rock, when some unwitting quarry flies past, all the wild falcon has to do is to slip off, keel over, and help herself.

Sometimes the trained falcon just flies over to pass the time of day, and then comes back to the lure. Now and again the wild one may join in and stoop at the same grouse; but, as this brings them closer to the hawking party than they care to be, they don't stay long but sheer off.

Grouse being so scarce and hard to find, we turned our attentions to hoodie crows. If you look up the hoodie crow in the bird books, you will find that it is smaller and more gregarious than the carrion crow. You will also find that it crosses with the carrion, and that the young are likely to be queerly marked. After flying peregrines at hoodies, I am inclined to doubt whether the ornithologists are correct about this cross-breeding. None of the other *corvidae* interbreed, though some rooks and crows often feed together and so do jackdaws. There might be some very interesting results if they did : we could have jaypies, and magdaws, and even crooks. But, whether the ornithologists are right or not, I am quite certain that there is a black hoodie. In the spring, it is very common indeed to see a greybacked hoodie paired off with a totally black one. In winter, one sees both sorts, in large flocks, all mixed up together : and the carrions do not flock. If you fly a falcon at either a grey hoodie or a black one, they always act in hoodie fashion, and not in carrion fashion.

In October, I received a passage peregrine from India. A passage hawk is one caught after it has left the eyrie and is killing for itself, but before it has moulted into adult plumage. Once it has done this, it becomes a haggard, in falconry parlance. Passage hawks were used a great deal in olden times and are preferable to eyasses; but, because of the difficulty of catching passagers in this country, eyasses are more often used.

The advantage of a passage hawk is that it has already learnt that height is essential, how to stick out a foot sideways when the quarry tries to dodge, and various other useful accomplishments that only come with experience. This particular falcon was no exception. In spite of having broken tail and wingtips from her journey over, she was a very good flier.

I started her off at rooks, and she showed me at once that she knew a trick or two. She would circle round, paying no attention until she had gained height. They took little notice of her if she did this some way off, and some were foolhardy enough to remain feeding on the ground till they had left it too late; for, once she had got up two or three hundred feet, she made straight for them. They would at last realize the danger and make for cover; and she would turn over and stoop at them. I never saw her knock one down, for apparently that was not her way. They would dive down, twisting and twiddling to avoid the stoop, and then throw up as she went past. She, too, threw up and, because she had greater speed from her great height, just when they were at the top of the throw-up and half stalled before flapping on their way, she would come up behind and grab them. This never failed. Hoodies she treated the same way, and, by this trick of hers, they too were grabbed unceremoniously from underneath.

Unfortunately I lost her before the next season, so I never knew how she would treat grouse. She flew some rooks, which dived into cover, and a farmhand threw stones at her and drove her off a herring-gull she had caught. I spent several days looking for her but never caught up with her. I had various reports of her in the neighbourhood; but they always came in just a few hours too late, and, by the time I got to the place she had last been seen, she had moved on.

We also had another type of Indian falcon, called a Lugger. This was a very odd bird, like a great big kestrel, but with the soft brown plumage of the desert falcons such as the sakers.

It had blue feet and a blue cere and a very long tail. In India they are used to catch crows, but the Indian crow must be a very different thing from our crows, for the lugger had neither the strength, speed nor weight, and certainly not the inclination, to catch hoodies. It was amazingly manœuvrable, though, and would swing in and out of trees like a kite. I gave it away finally. Had we got suitable quarry for it, it would have been worth persevering with, but, like so many foreign species of falcons, it failed to make the grade.

At home we acquired the usual pets. Two young leverets were brought to us and successfully reared on the bottle. Ross and Cromarty, as they were called, were given their freedom once they got big enough to look after themselves. They were followed by two young rabbits, survivors of myxomatosis. One had been brought in by a cat and the other had gone through the reaper and binder and had been found struggling his way out of a barley shock.

They, too, were reared on the bottle, graduated to dandelions and lettuces and turned loose to make up the rabbit stock. Nuts and May were their respective names, not anything to do with the nursery rhyme but as a shortened form of 'Nuts to myxomatosis and May rabbits increase and multiply'. This may have annoyed local farmers and foresters, but, in spite of all their outcry against the rabbit, I never observed that they lowered the prices of their crops when the disease increased their yield.

We also had some rather odd chickens. The story went that a Norwegian ship had been wrecked on the Island of Coll on the west coast. A number of these hens had survived, and their subsequent offspring had found their way around the coast because the hens laid remarkably pretty blue eggs. This was not like the blue-green of a duck's egg, but more like the colour of a heron's egg. The hens themselves were a bit odd too. They wore feather beards and feather umbrellas on their heads and were mottled all over, but not with any particular colour; greys, whites, browns, they didn't keep to any scheme. In spite of their umbrellas, they went off the lay if it rained or was cold – not very profitable birds to keep in Scotland.

As the back-end of the year drew on, the wild geese began to come in from the north. Their wide-spread, clangoring skeins advertised their coming, and they flew over, high up, and then rapidly began to lose height and settled on the Firth to rest, sleep and preen. Sometimes they came down in a steep slant, sometimes they wheeled round, losing height more gradually; but if the wind was strong, they would pretend they were falling leaves and would suddenly twist and turn and spin, whiffling down, apparently out of control until the last moment, when they flattened out and pitched quite gently on the water. They fed on the stubble and potato fields, and you could see them gleaning away as you drove past. If you stopped their heads would shoot up, looking like a sea of umbrella handles in a lost-property office. Pinkfeet and grey-legs comprised the greater proportion, with a few Canada geese, and now and again, a whitefront.

As the nights started to get frosty, I brought the falcons into the mews. In the wild they can choose their own roosting-places and have an early-morning fly round to warm themselves up. As they had not this freedom, I thought it better to provide shelter for our trained falcons.

18 * Peregrinations

The black shape of a wild falcon swung out from the shadow of the cliff against the blue sky, and the harsh angry 'heck, heck heck' of a nesting peregrine came clearly across the glen to us. A smaller but identical shape, higher up and with faster wing-beat, added an echo to the falcon's call. The tiercel had joined in from farther along the cliff.

'Am thinkin' th' nest's at yon end of th' face. I seen her comin' aff there eairrly in May, whin goin' eafter th' foxes. But I hadna time ta git oiwer here since.'

'Well, in that case, we'd better get under the cover of that big rock and see if we can pin-point the exact place. "Time spent in reconnaissance is seldom wasted".'

So the three of us, John the stalker, Paul and myself, went on through the heather, over the burn, and then up the slope to a big rock I had spotted as being a good place to watch from. We dumped the ropes and the crow-bar, made ourselves comfortable and lay in the heather, binoculars ready.

I thought of one of the first eyries I had ever been to, several years before. Paul had also been with me then, on what I call a 'peregrination', and we had been over-enthusiastic. The old birds had been hecking like mad and we were sure they had young, so we had climbed up to the top with hardly a preliminary look at the place. I had gone over on the ropes time and time again, till my hands were smarting and blistered, and still we hadn't found the right place. Paul was frozen sitting on the top handling the safety line, and I was alternately too hot from climbing, my shirt soaked with sweat, and too cold in the intervals of resting. Finally we had had to give up because the light was failing.

We had come down off the hill, stumbling in the semi-darkness and glad to see the car after the long walk back. It was then that I learnt that you can rarely see anything much from the top and that it is far better, and considerably less exhausting, to spend an hour or so below, not only to pin-point the eyrie, but to study the rock-face and work out the best way in to the nest. We had gone back the next day, found the eyrie and returned triumphant.

Since then I had been to many eyries, inland and on sea-cliffs: some so easy that one could walk in, and some needing 300 feet or more of rope. One or two had been quite impossible to get at, and not even the skill of the Everest team and all of the London Fire Brigade's appliances could have managed it. At each eyrie I had learnt a little more and by now I realized that, no matter how many you went to, each presented a different problem. Under the Bird Protection Act, you must apply to the Scottish Home Department or, in England and Wales, the Home Office, for a licence to take the young before you can go off on your peregrinations.

The old tiercel soon made off over the hill once we were under cover. He does most of the hunting, so he has his work cut out to keep the family fed and leaves the falcon to guard over the eyasses.

What he catches depends on what suitable prey is in the area and also on his own particular likes and dislikes. Some eyries are fed on a remarkably monotonous diet. One, although on the edge of a well-stocked grouse moor, had puffins to eat the whole time, for I picked up the heads of seventeen puffins that had been brought to the nest over a period of some weeks. I think this comes about because a young peregrine kills, let us say, for his first kill, a puffin. The next time he is hungry he will tend to fly faster at a puffin than he will at anything else, simply because he has gained confidence in his ability to catch them. This builds up until he becomes a specialist. He learns what sort of place to find them, what kind of evasive action they take and how best to deal with it. I have seen a trained tiercel that wouldn't look at a wood-pigeon right underneath him, but who went like stink at a covey of partridges a few moments later. Obviously a peregrine hunting in an area where food is scarce soon learns to fly at anything, and, the older he is, the more versatile he becomes.

As the eyasses grow up they need brooding no longer and start to pull at the food for themselves, instead of having to be fed piece by piece. Then the falcon may occasionally join in the hunting, though it is rare not to find her at home. Some tiercels bring the food in and help feed the eyasses, but more often they pluck the kill and, as they near home, call to the falcon to meet them and catch the food as they drop it. This aerial pass is a neat piece of timing; though, for a bird that can stoop at the speed a peregrine does and knock down a grouse going flat out, the skill of catching a dead bird dropped in front of her is nothing more than that of a Londoner hopping on to a passing bus.

The old falcon flew round a while longer and then pitched on a pinnacle of rock, which, it was obvious to us from the white marks of her mutes all round it, was a favourite look-out post. She still hecked at us but gradually quietened down and became silent.

I looked at her through the glasses and then borrowed John's telescope for a close-up view. There is something about a wild falcon on her own crag that never fails to give me a thrill. This one was no exception. Her feet and cere were a bright yellow. Her black head and salmon-pink breast, with its darker markings, made her look very handsome. The wind ruffled her flank feathers, making them stand out from the leading edges of her neatly crossed wings.

As I watched, she roused, and a moulting secondary was shaken free and spun slowly down to land on the scree, far below her. She put her head on one side, quizzically, and watched it drift down. She was really beautiful.

I handed the telescope over to Paul, picked up my binoculars and began systematically to search the ledges where John thought she might have the eyrie. If the ledge it was on happened to be narrow, then I might be able to spot the down shed by the eyasses as they grew up. This down is very clinging and looks rather like cotton grass.

I slowly looked over each ledge in turn, some were sloping outwards, others were damp from the water that trickled over the cliff in places, and she would not choose a spot like that. But there were a great many suitable ledges, and I finished the search without any success. I had seen an old raven's nest under a great overhang; if

Edwina the tame fox

The bobbery pack

Arthur treated people as though they
were tree trunks

Concentration

A falcon is one of the Queen's Beasts . .

. . . and makes a good heraldic device

Falcon argent on a field of sable

Grouse being scarce, we turned our attention to hoodie crows

The day starts with each falcon having an opportunity to bathe

Spinningdale lies on the Dornoch Firth

Upstream the salmon go

Upright and otterwise

The guests come out with the falcons

the eyrie was there we could pack up and go away, for it was in an impossible place, even with ropes to help. We lay there for nearly an hour, talking in undertones so as not to disturb her. She sat on her rock, preened herself for a while and then rested on one foot.

'There's the tiercel again, coming in on the right,' said Paul.

I put the glasses up and found him, gliding along, high up, silhouetted against the sky. 'He's got something in his feet, a kill of some sort.'

He called, not the angry hecking we had heard previously, but a sharper, shorter call, almost a fox's bark. The old falcon went out to meet him and, as he dropped his kill, she caught it deftly about twenty feet below him and, turning, came in towards us. 'Keep your glasses on her, don't lose sight of her,' I cautioned.

She swung up and pitched on a ledge away to our left and stood there looking round, the food held in one foot. We sat motionless and waited. She called quietly, a plaintive, almost peevish, cry and then flew off again, carrying the food to another ledge. She stood there, looking around, and still we waited.

After ten minutes had slowly gone by, she suddenly turned and, dragging the kill with her, went in to the back of the ledge, very quickly. She was out again in a few moments and without the kill. 'Keep an eye on her, I'll watch the place she's just left,' and I resisted the temptation to follow her and kept the glasses on the ledge. There I caught the flick of an upraised wing. 'That's the place all right, I saw one of the eyasses move.'

The waiting was over.

We stayed there for a few minutes longer, watching the ledge. 'If the eyasses move again, we might see what sort of age they are, though they obviously are big enough to pull for themselves, because she just took the food in and left them to get on with it.'

While we watched I had a good look at the situation. The ledge was about half-way up the cliff, two hundred feet or so from the base. About ninety feet above it there was another, much wider, ledge, which, it seemed, we could all reach, with only a slight scramble. There was a dead rowan tree that would serve as a signpost when we got up there. If I put the crow-bar in about fifteen feet to the right of it I should be bang in line, but the cliff was a bit overhung there and it might pay me to go farther still to the right, have an easier climb down by a little gully, and then crawl along the ledge. A yellow bunch of globe flowers gave me an indication of where I should work from, in that case.

We talked it over, memorized the sign-posts and got to our feet. The eyasses hadn't shown themselves any more, and there was little point in waiting. The old falcon flew off her pinnacle and started hecking again.

We made our way slowly up a gully towards the top. We came upon the remains of a kill, a cuckoo, a bird that peregrines seem to be very fond of eating. I have never seen one caught, but I imagine that they are a pretty easy prey. The dead rowan gave us our bearings and, after a bit of a scramble, we were all standing on the broad ledge. While John and Paul took off the straps which kept the ropes coiled neatly, I looked for a loose rock to use as a mallet to knock the crow-bar in. In some places it is very difficult to find a crack in the rocks under the heather, and you may have to try several times before getting the bar firmly fixed.

I secured the hand-line to it with a few half-hitches. The binoculars, camera and telescope were put in a safe place, and I threw the hand-line over the cliff. It snaked out into space and came up with a jerk as the crow-bar took its weight. I tested it to make sure it was secure and then, holding it with both hands, I backed to the edge and leant out to see what it was like below. The overhang was considerably more than it had appeared to be from below, and I decided to move along to the little gully I had marked down as being an easier route.

This meant shifting the crow-bar, for it is always best to have the rope as vertical as possible, otherwise you swing like a pendulum, if you slip, a most unpleasant feeling and likely to be painful.

It wasn't a very difficult place but, as we had the safety line there, I tied it on, put the sack round my waist and was all set. I had the whistle on a cord round my neck, and we ran through the signals to make sure everyone knew them. One blast meant 'lower away', two 'haul up' and three, 'keep me where I am'.

The old falcon had stopped hecking and had disappeared altogether. With my face to the cliff and my head turned down looking for footholds, I made my way down, the strong-arm men on top paying out the safety line as I went. This is not as simple as it looks. If they held too tight, I would have to pull at the line all the way, and if they didn't keep a good grip and I happened to slip, my weight would snatch the rope through their hands and I would probably end up fit only for a raven's dinner.

This is rather different from rock climbing. You have very little choice of route. Very rarely do you start at the bottom. In a lot of places the rock is bad and crumbling, and pieces as big as a football come away if any weight is put on them. But today we were in a good place, and down I went as fast as I could to a ledge some fifty feet from the start. The faster you go the less tired your arms get.

As I reached the ledge there was a woosh of wings, and the falcon stooped overhead and pulled out about fifteen feet above me, hecking angrily. I have never had a peregrine attack me, and some never come near but stay just out of gunshot range, having learnt how dangerous man can be.

There was a sheer face dropping straight down to the eyrie ledge, but the eyrie itself was out of sight round the corner. I rested a minute or two, spotting the remains of a gull. With a warning blow on the whistle down I went again, hand over hand, my feet pushing against the cliff face.

The ledge was a good wide one. There was one awkward place on the corner, where a big rock jutted out, but there was a passageway under it that I could squeeze through by lying down and wriggling my way along. Popping out the other side, like a cork from a bottle, I could see, only a few feet away, a young falcon, nearly ready to fly. She looked a bit surprised at this strange apparition coming towards her and puffed out her plumage and hissed defiance. A few feet beyond her was another eyass, lying down sunning. This was a tiercel, smaller than his sister and with a flatter head. He jumped to his feet and scuttled along the ledge a bit.

I got the sack untied and made my way cautiously towards them. The falcon backed away and then hecked at me. I got closer and judged the distance between us. I thought I could just about reach her now. I spread the fingers of my right hand out, palm down, and grabbed for her feet, catching them between my fingers. She tried hard to bite but I drew her quickly towards me and, folding her wings with my left hand, I put her, head-first, into the sack.

The tiercel too had backed up against the cliff in a corner, but he was too far for me to reach. I crept forward on hands and knees, taking the sack with me. Once I got within range I put it on one side, with my knee on the mouth so that I shouldn't lose the falcon. I caught him the same way, but, being hampered by the sack, he managed to grab me in return. I removed his talons gently and he joined his sister, where she greeted him with angry hecking, somewhat muffled now.

Now I was free to examine the eyrie. There was no nest, only a scraped depression in the peaty earth. There was a very cold, bleached egg lying in it, surrounded by the down off the eyasses and by the litter of the kills. I picked over the remains: three more cuckoos, a hoodie crow's wings, two grouse, a curlew's beak, some feathers from a mallard and, a bit farther on, a freshly killed common-gull, half plucked. This was what the tiercel had handed to his mate when we were watching from the cover of the big rock.

I put the gull into my pocket and began to make my way back. I had to hang the sack over the side of the cliff and hold onto it with one hand as I wriggled back under the corner rock. I crawled back to where the ropes hung, tied the sack securely round my waist, blew a couple of times on the whistle and, as I felt the safety rope tighten, I began to climb.

In a few minutes I was back on top. They opened the sack and admired the eyasses. 'Afraid she's had some of your grouse, John, but she's done you a bit of good by killing a hoodie.'

We pulled up the hand line and, sitting down, coiled up the ropes: under the foot and over the knee; and put the straps back on. Doing them like this makes a coil that slips over your head onto your shoulder and is comfortable to carry, though 125 feet of rope is still quite a weight on a long walk. Paul worked the crow-bar free, and we collected the rest of the gear and made our way back.

I apologized to the old falcon as she flew overhead. I don't like taking all the young, but on a grouse moor they would only be shot if I didn't.

If you are going to train falcons, it is far more satisfying to take your own eyasses. After all, both the eyasses would be flying loose in about six or seven weeks' time and enjoying themselves nearly as much as if they were wild. Better than being dead.

We trudged back across the hill, over the burn, past the old summer shielings, now marked only by bright green patches of grass and crumbling walls. I picked up a horn dropped by a stag. It had already been nibbled by other deer, short of calcium. The trout were rising as we passed the lochan, making little expanding ringlets in the water. The two eyasses protested now and again in a half-hearted way when I stumbled and jostled the sack.

Back at the car we transferred them to the hamper and put the gull in with them. Food was the next thing on the programme and we sat in the heather and got out the grub basket and the reviving flask.

You meet all sorts of new and interesting things on peregrinations: rare flowers, deer, birds. You see the countryside from a very different view-point from that obtained from a car window. Up on the high tops it is an utterly different world and you discover things of beauty that make the sweat of climbing well worth the effort.

You may see a hill fox trying to catch a mouse, stalking up very quietly and then jumping high in the air to land, all four feet on a tussock of grass, and snapping up what is evidently a delicate morsel. You may come across his earth and find a litter of lamb's legs that the cubs play with, after they have eaten their fill. The deep gullies are cold on the hottest day. Ravens croak their annoyance at being disturbed. You come across tragedies of the winter, a dead deer, or, where there are feral goats, you may pick up a horned skull of some old billy who has slipped and fallen to his death.

Once, finding a previous year's eyrie empty, I decided to go below and watch. There was an old ewe and her lamb grazing close to where I had been climbing. The ledges were covered in wood-rush and very slippery after a night's rain. I knew that already, and it had been one reason why I had not gone on searching on the cliff face. While I waited, the lamb suddenly butted her mother in hopes of a drink. The old ewe slipped, scrabbled hard to find a footing, and a shower of wood-rush and peat came over the edge. The old ewe nearly made it, but the slippery surface gave way again and over she went.

She was dead long before her body finally came to rest. She hit a rock ledge, bounced off and came crashing, thumping down. She thudded onto the scree at the base of the cliff and rolled at least a hundred feet before a large rock stopped her. The lamb looked over and bleated. There was nothing I could possibly do. I was alone, and the lamb was not get-at-able, even with ropes. On the way back I met the shepherd and told him. 'Ay, we lose a puckle there every year. No' much we can do aboot it. I doot the lamb could find its way up.'

It didn't. It had joined its mother when I went there three days later, and the hoodies and ravens had an easy meal.

You don't want to take risks on the high tops.

19 * The Hill

Mountain is a word used only by tourists in Scotland. To the inhabitants, regardless of height, it is simply 'the hill'. At first you think that some particular hill is meant but it is an all-embracing term that covers any large tract of uncultivated ground from Ben Nevis, the highest of them all, downwards.

Here on the hill it is possible to get away from all signs of civilization and to walk for miles with not a house in sight. This, I think, is its greatest charm, though man is doing his best to wreck it with vast hydro-electric schemes that spoil the fishing, and thousands of acres of forestry with its huge ploughs scarring the land only to be followed by rank upon rank of militarily planted conifers, which are boring to look at, impossible to walk through, and devoid of nearly all animal and bird life; for these plantations are wired in and the deer denied access. The squirrels are trapped and shot and so too is the capercaillie, that turkey-sized game bird whose liking for pine needles to eat makes it unpopular.

Just as the trees are getting to a size when the animals could do no harm and people could enjoy walking among them, the whole lot are clear felled, leaving an army of stumps standing in disconsolate conquered rows while the bodies are dragged away to be dismembered and the whole process is begun again. Two excuses are made for this despoliation; firstly that trees were there long before the forestry commission, which is true as you can see from the old stumps still to be found in the peat. But then they were sparsely spread and in decent disorder. Lastly that there is nothing much apart from growing trees or sheep that can be done with such land. 'It simply isn't economic, my dear fellow.' That is the moment when I wish

I were a very rich man and could buy great lumps of hill and just leave it as it is, with a large notice:

BEWARE, ECONOMICALLY UNSOUND.
FOR ENJOYMENT ONLY.
TYCOONS KEEP OUT.

Spring comes late on the hill. Even in June there is often still snow in quite large patches on the tops. In some of the gullies, it may remain there till covered again by the first falls of winter. The heather is still brown and only showing a few signs of new life. But heather is by no means the only plant. I am not a botanist by any stretch of the imagination, but there are plenty of plants which seem interesting to me.

Bog myrtle, once used for brewing, and sometimes called sweet gale, gives off a delicious scent when its leaves are crushed in your hand. The white tufts of cotton grass, like tiny rabbits' scuts, grow in wet places, as does the sundew, with its red-whiskered leaves, each with a sticky blob like dew on it, a trap for the insects on which it partially feeds. The butterwort also does this, and it has a pretty blue flower on a tall, straight stem growing from the centre of its starfish leaves. You may find some antler moss creeping through the heather; a single stem may be several feet long, rooting at intervals like a strawberry runner, and its green, almost prickly, covering looks very antler-like. These moss-like plants suffer from the technical term *Lycopodia*, but they are none the less fascinating. Another kind has flat scaly leaves like fallow-deer antlers.

Up among the rocks are other plants that are only to be seen in such places: saxifrages, rock roses, wild azaleas, globe flowers and so on. You are forced to buy a book on wild flowers just to find out what they all are. On the rocks themselves are lichens of all colours and varieties: bright greens, bright yellows, and little red-cupped ones. To say there is nothing but monotonous brown heather to be seen is to admit that you go about with your eyes shut. It is no use thinking you will see much just by driving around in a car. You must get out and walk.

Among all these plants live a great number of different creatures. Emperor moths, whose caterpillars, bright green with black bands around them out of which sprout little shaving-brush clumps of pink bristles, are very beautiful. The caterpillars of the northern eggars are the biggest 'woolly bears' I've ever come across. You could make several busbies for toy soldiers out of one skin.

Now and again you will catch sight of a lizard sunning on a rock and watching you with a beady eye; or you come across a pair of adders enjoying the warmth. They are very local these snakes, and some places are well renowned for them. You even see notices reading 'Beware of adders'; to one someone has added in pencil, 'and subtractors'.

Right up on the high tops, you may be lucky enough to see a dotterel, a pretty type of plover that breeds on the highest parts, on the bare ground; it is so tame that you may photograph it without bothering about a hide. Ptarmigan, too, nest up in such places and, like the blue-hare, change to white in the winter.

Although you will see the eagle hunting up here, she prefers to nest lower down on some cliff-face or even in a tree. Year after year, the same nest may be used, more sticks added to it, until, in time, it becomes an enormous structure; eventually its own weight may well destroy it. Like the raven and the buzzard, the eagle feeds on carrion a great deal; and dead deer, dead sheep and dead lambs are all welcomed. This often leads to both buzzard and eagle being accused of wholesale killing of lambs: a ridiculous thing to apply to a buzzard, which only weighs about one and three quarter pounds; and it is only rarely that you get rogue eagles.

The raven nests very early, and by the end of May her young have flown. The peregrine sometimes takes over the raven's nest, instead of laying in a scrape on a cliff-ledge. After wintering on the estuaries and in the marshes, the curlews come to the hill to nest and, of all the non-singing birds, their call is, I think, the most attractive. Snipe nest in the boggy parts of the hill; the vibration of their outspread tails as they dive down makes a noise that sounds like the faint bleat of a goat.

As the days grow warmer, the red deer retreat to the tops during the daytime, out of the way of flies and humans. The pretty little roe-deer stay more in the birch and alder scrub; but now and then you may see one suddenly jumping up and bouncing away like a

M

big boxer dog from where it has been lying up in a patch of bracken.

The sun brings out the insects and the summer bird visitors that feed on them; wheatears, whinchats, swallows and martins arrive. There are not many banks suitable for the sand martins to tunnel in and so, instead of finding their colonies high up and inaccessible, as you do in the south, here they may be only a few feet from the ground.

The cuckoo invasion starts, and, within a few days of hearing the first one call, the hill seems to be full of them, the male cuckoo-ing away, and the female, heard less often, making her strange noise like a bottle of water being emptied. Here they lay mostly in meadow pipits' nests and go far out in the hill in search of them, flying from rock to rock, or perching on the power cables that march through the hill on their meccano-like pylons. The small birds mob them as they sit, tail up, wings drooping; but they pay no more attention to their irritated audience than does the short-eared owl that comes to nest in the heather and hunt voles and mice.

Along the burns the dipper flits, always appearing very business-like with its white dicky, only lacking a briefcase and a rolled umbrella to be a complete city gent. It walks about quite happily under the water, looking for insects, bobbing up again nonchalantly just when you think it must have got washed away. It is an expert water jay-walker, dodging the places where the current is too strong as though nipping across the road between traffic. You rarely hear its song because the noise of the running water drowns it, but some-times you come across one singing on a rock at the side of a hill lochan. It has the same perky stance as a wren, and its song is very similar and amazingly powerful for so small a bird. Higher up the hill, in among the rocks, you may come across the dipper's cousin, the ring-ouzel. It is more like a blackbird with a white shirtfront and not a relative really, though their colouring is very similar, and the dipper is sometimes called water-ouzel.

The black-headed and common gulls come to the hill to nest. Really swampy ground with clumps of rushes is the sort of place they like: too shallow and muddy for a boat and not firm enough to walk on. In spite of their choice of such spots, their first clutch is often taken, for the eggs are considered quite a delicacy and on a par with green plovers' eggs. Taking them is a muddy and somewhat acrobatic proceeding. You arm yourself with a couple of planks and something to put the eggs in and, by a process of picking up the plank you have just walked on and putting it in front of the one you are standing on, you can progress, at times knee-deep in slush, across the quagmire, collecting eggs as you go. Black-headed gull is a misnomer, its head is a chocolate-brown colour, and that only in the summer, for in winter it moults out white.

On more grassy hills, the green plover lay and are for ever on the look-out for hoodies or gulls, which would take eggs or young if they could. As soon as one of these predators comes anywhere near, the plover stoop at it and drive it off.

Coming along a track one day, I saw an old plover brooding some young in the middle of the track. She flew up as we approached and the three little downy young, only a few days old, scuttled off into the rushes. Two went one side of the road, but in different directions, and the third crossed the road before disappearing in the grass. The old bird flew round calling plaintively, and we sat and watched. After a few minutes she quietened down and settled on the ground about ten yards from the nearest chick, and a good thirty from the one farthest off. I had the binoculars on her all the time, and she never opened her beak, nor did we hear her call. Only the fact that one of them had to cross the bare track allowed us to see any signs of the young. In a few minutes we saw it walk across and wade through a shallow ditch towards its mother, looking like a tiny short-necked ostrich. How they found the way, I have no idea, but within five minutes all three had gathered under her. She got up again as we passed her, and we stopped once more and got out to see if they were all present and correct. The grass was cropped short by the sheep, and yet, even from a few feet away, it was exceedingly difficult to spot the crouching young, so well did they match their surroundings.

Close by here was a small pine wood, in which a pair of herons had built a nest, though unsuccessfully, for the river had just received several tankfuls of salmon parr, and the keeper was not keen on giving the herons a free feed. A tawny owl lived in the wood, too, nesting in an old rabbit-hole under a pine stump. Her two

young, covered with a grey down, clopped their beaks and hissed
at us when we looked at them. They looked like two beery, bleary
old men with fur coats on, their eyes pink-rimmed from a severe
hangover.

Up in a gully, on a small rock cliff, was a kestrel's eyrie with six
rusty-brown eggs in a scrape on one of the ledges. The two old birds
took it in turn to brood, and to work hard to provide the family
with food when they hatched out. At such times kestrels, in addition
to mice, lizards and beetles, turn to catching small birds, but not
so successfully as the merlins, whose greater flying skill and audacity
enable them to feed almost entirely on pipits, larks and wheatears
and who spurn insects and furred creatures. I watched a little jack
merlin, who did most of the hunting and brought his kills to a
big rock, close to the nest in the heather, where he plucked them
before handing them over to his mate. Merlins are becoming rapidly
scarcer in Scotland, though for what reason I don't know. Most
keepers leave them alone, and the rarity of the merlin cannot be
blamed on them.

Another ground-nester is the hen-harrier. The male is pale grey
with black primaries, his mate brown. Both have a white rump like
the wheatears. If you go too close to the nest they will stoop at you,
putting on a performance that makes you wonder why, when they
can fly so well, they hunt in so lackadaisical a fashion. They seem to
have a good turn of speed and are certainly very manœuvrable. They
quarter the hill like well-trained pointers, ranging up and down and
searching the ground as they go, only a few feet up. Sometimes they
will hang in the wind like kestrels; and they have the same way of
catching their prey, not stooping like a peregrine with wings nearly
closed, but hanging over it and dropping down suddenly by simply
raising their wings straight above them and letting gravity pull them
down. They look as big as buzzards, but their legs are nearly as
spindly as a sparrow-hawk's.

The hill varies a great deal, sometimes gently rolling, sometimes
rounded slopes, sometimes very steep with rocky outcrops and inland cliffs. Up on the tops the wind keeps the plants low and short,
and in places there are just bare rock and scree. Up here in a gale you
have to turn your back to the wind in order to breathe. Yet the

grouse sits it out, sometimes right in the open, keeping her eggs covered till they hatch and she can lead the young away to a more sheltered place.

Where the hill joins the coast, on the sea cliffs, there is a different group of birds to be found: puffins nest down rabbit-holes, kittiwakes, razor-bills, guillemots, herring-gulls, fulmars lay on the ledges and crowd every available space. In the caves the rock-pigeons, bright red legs and black bars on a grey wing, lay their white eggs and rear their ugly, soft-beaked squabs. The air is full of the incessant screaming of the gulls. If anyone lands on someone else's bit of ledge, there is a snapping of beaks and the intruder is left in no doubt as to his mistake.

The air coming up the cliff-face makes it very easy for the cliff-dwellers to spend hour after hour on the wing. They glide along, only a few yards out from the cliff, their heads turning to watch for any possible food below. Anything edible that floats, or gets washed ashore, is soon cleared up by those scavengers, the black-backs and herring-gulls. Anything that is sick is attacked; and the young ducklings must stay close to their mothers or the gulls will snatch them up and swallow them whole, still wriggling as they disappear down their throats. There is no sentimentality in nature.

A number of sea birds nest on the hill. You would think that they would be better off closer to the water and their food supplies, but a lot of the duck family, eider ducks, shelducks, and the like, whose life is otherwise spent either on the mudflats or in the sea itself, fly off, sometimes quite a long distance away from water, to nest. This means quite a trek for their young when they are hatched; and a number get lost in one way or another.

I saw a hoodie crow acting in an unusual way as I was driving through a hill road. I stopped and saw a mallard duck wending her way towards a small pond, her brood trailing behind her. The hoodie was stooping at them, trying to frighten and scatter them so it could snatch one. It managed to get one and was returning to the attack when our shouts sent it off. The old duck, though quacking to her young to keep by her and to hurry up, didn't seem all that put out by the loss, but rather to accept it as just one of those things. Of course, birds and animals that are subject to a heavy mortality rate make up for their losses by producing more young than those who do not suffer in that respect.

The hill is full of variety and of strange happenings. You never know what you will come across. Along the shore of a sea loch our two pointers put up a hare. It wasn't chased, but went off at its own pace along the edge of a small creek. Suddenly it turned off, waded into the salt water and swam across to the other side, where it splashed its way out through the shallows. Reaching dry land, it shook itself and lolloped away in the grass. The distance was at least three hundred yards, of which two-thirds was out of its depth.

In broad sunlight I once watched a pipistrelle bat fly out over the Firth, settle on the water and commit suicide for no apparent reason. I picked up its body as it was washed ashore, and there seemed to be nothing wrong with it. Can bats go bats?

Some of the inhabitants of the hill are very rarely seen, though they leave signs of their presence: an otter's pad-marks in the bare peat on the edge of a burn, bark torn by a wildcat ripping at a tree. I have always supposed that the idea of cats sharpening their claws is wrong; surely they are really wearing them down a bit to stop them getting too long.

By midsummer most birds have at least hatched their young, if they are not already nearly on the wing. The hill lambs are well grown and getting too big for the foxes to pay much attention to, and the shepherds arrange to help each other over gathering. The hill is swept by dogs and men and, down from the highest tops, the sheep are driven, a moving carpet of walking hearth-rugs, bleating and baa-ing, till the whole air seems to shimmer with the sound. Every so often one tries to break out, but the ever watchful dogs streak out and turn it back. In the morning they will be sorted, marked, clipped and then allowed to make their way back to their grazing-grounds, looking, and no doubt feeling, very odd without their shaggy coats. The woolsacks, so long that they have to be hung up on a tall frame, rather like a child's swing, in order to be filled, are sewn up with the inevitable binder twine and an enormous packing needle and stowed away in the shed to await collection.

Now the heather is coming into bloom, first the bell and then the ling. The red-deer calves are losing their spots and no longer lie dead still in the heather or bracken, waiting for the hinds to come and feed them, but are following on foot.

Keepers are repairing the grouse butts for the coming shooting-season and looking anxious when the clouds gather in case heavy rain or hail should kill the chicks, though, if rain does come, it will mean more water in the river and the fish will start to move. A hot summer and no rain spells disaster to the salmon; they cannot get upstream to spawn, and they may well die if the water gets too low or too warm.

A highland river in spate is well worth seeing. No longer is it a gentle, tinkling burn, trickling, crystal-clear, between the stones, but a rushing, roaring, foaming, surging, all-powerful mass, peaty brown in colour beneath the foam, pushing rocks and trees before it. In places where the rock is softer, little whirlpools drive stones round and round till a hole is worn and the whirlpool becomes greater, and at each spate the hole grows bigger. The little islands and shoals disappear under the water and the oyster-catchers and gulls have their nests swept away.

But it brings life to the fish, and upstream they go, where you would have thought it impossible. The water itself supports their weight and allows their muscles to be used almost entirely for driving them forward. They reach the falls and gather in the pools below, every so often making an attempt to get up, jumping a foot or more clear of the water and landing again only to leap once more. A poor jump, a misjudged landing, and they are swept back to rest and try again. But some make it and, reaching the top, disappear in the deeper water with a joyful shudder of their tails.

By July the stags are growing their new antlers, covered in velvet. They are fattening up again after the winter and look very different. The young eagles are nearly full-fledged now, and the old birds only come to the eyrie once or twice a day, bringing in food and leaving almost immediately.

I watched a pair of eagles hunting one day. One of them crossed my vision as I was driving along, and I stopped the car and lay in the heather. They seemed to be in no hurry as they searched the moor below them. A few wing-beats and then they would glide, their primary tips bending upwards. I could see their heads turn from side to side as they flew. Cars passed on the road, but no one stopped, though both eagles were never far from the road. The male stooped at something in the heather and a blue-hare raced away, its ears flat. The female joined in the chase, and, as the hare turned to avoid the male, she came in with a swoosh and, picking it up, carried it away out of sight over the hill. Her mate followed. I drove on and stopped for lunch at a hotel. 'What were you looking at so intently?' a man asked me. 'I saw you a few miles back by the road-side.' I explained. 'Eagles!' he exclaimed. 'I wish I'd known, I've been up here for twelve years and never seen one.'

A few days later, I saw another eagle, and, as there was a party of people picnicking by the road, I thought of the man who had wanted to see one. I pulled up by the picnic party and leant out of the car, pointing out the eagle to them. They looked at me as though I had escaped from a lunatic asylum, and, without looking, or saying anything, continued with their meal. I drove on.

It depends on the weather, of course, but generally by August the heather is in bloom. In a hot, dry year, it lasts only a very short time, but given a shower of rain every so often, it goes on blooming for several weeks. In some parts of the hill, white heather is quite common, but in others, you can walk all day and find none. Strangely enough, it doesn't stand out like a sore thumb, and visitors will walk right past it without seeing it; though a trained eye can spot it from quite a distance.

By the middle of September, the stags are breaking up from their bachelor parties, and each big stag is rounding up his harem of hinds, coming miles to find them. The velvet has been rubbed off their horns in the peat hags, and they roar their warning to the other stags to keep away.

The hinds pay little attention to their lord and master, but gently browse along, or lie down in a sheltered place, their legs tucked under them, ears atwitch and black damp noses on the wobble, always seeming alert. Once they were beasts of the forest; but the trees have gone and left them, and they have adapted themselves to the situation. Their sight is poor compared with their hearing and sense of smell.

On a day when the clouds are rolling in over the tops and the wind is blowing up snow showers, it is like a scene from *Macbeth*. The clouds hide the deer, but through the mistiness you can hear the stags roaring. Then, suddenly, the wind opens the clouds for a moment or two and you can see the stag, looking enormous in the mist, his neck stretched forward and his horns lying back as he bellows out with a curious grunting roar, almost like a lion. The cloud closes in again, and the visibility is down to nothing. You expect the three witches to appear at any moment from a peat hag. It is worth the cold and discomfort, the sting of sleet against your face, the weariness of climbing, just for one glimpse like this.

It is in the last week of September or the first half of October that the hill is at its best. The frosts have come and turned the birches gold and the bracken brown; the first snows are on the high tops; the salmon are red-gold; and, on a crisp, frosty, sunny day, the blue sky makes the river blue too.

Stay on the tops and watch the herring-boats come out from harbour in the evening and go racing each other up the Firth to the fishing-grounds. As the sun sets, the Firth changes from moulten pewter to dazzling gold, each wavelet reflecting the light so fiercely that the eyes are almost hurt by the myriad dancing specks that shimmer as the water moves.

The distant hills beyond change from hazy blue, to purple, to a translucent grey, as the sky goes from gold to flame to red. The gulls skirl and wheel as the nets come in and the fish come aboard. It grows darker, and no longer is there any visible detail in the hills, only a charcoal-black outline of them against a dull glow of red, like the back of some spiky prehistoric monster.

The trawlers' mast-lights, faintly visible at first, grow stronger as darkness falls and replace the great blazing path of the sun across the water with a number of separate little lanes.

On one such evening I felt like a spectator in a theatre, held by the play. I was almost reluctant to move off, even though the show was over. Eventually I made my way back home, and it was only after dinner, when I went outside to see the falcons, that I realized that a second act was about to begin. There was a curious flashing in the sky, like summer lightning, and then I realized what it was: the Northern Lights. We stood and watched from the window. The flashes stopped; filling the sky was a fantastic veil of light, gathered at the top, widespread at the base, it shimmered with pale greys, pastel pinks, faint apple-greens. It was translucent and, because of this, no artist could have imitated it, for his very canvas would have taken away this quality. As we watched, some unseen hand released the gathered folds at the apex and it spread wide, across the southern sky like a gigantic curtain, fading away at each end into the black night. From each end the light rippled across it, playing along it as though the folds were being shaken. The Firth and the hills beyond were a perfect setting. The moving water reflected the sky and made it seem even more wonderful. The light faded and dimmed and let the darkness close back in. No one said a word till it was done.

Snow can transfigure even the ugliest object into a thing of beauty. But things that are already lovely sometimes become even more so. The hill under snow is really something. The great open spaces seem even bigger than before; and yet there is a softness about it, and it is only when you see the bare face of rock cliffs, too steep for snow to settle on, that you realize its hard cruelty. It is a bastion against civilization.

At first light the sun tips the peaks with a rosy hue; the rest of the land is still in shadow, not the black shadow of summer or the grey of the back-end but a blue translucency that hides none of the details.

The sheep, their fleeces looking very yellow against the purity of the snow, keep closer together and scrape with their feet in a search for food hidden beneath. You can spot grouse a long way off, but more often they are hidden, sheltering in the hummocks or feeding underneath, where the long heather supports the snow. The hill hares are now white but for the black tips of their ears. They are hard to see unless they move; but their tracks are everywhere, and it seems that the hill must be covered in hares until you realize that one hare can make an awful lot of footprints.

The ravens, paired off already, call to each other in their harsh, cronking voices, strangely attractive and, in spite of the cold, they play in the sky at their aerial courtship. Blacker than ever they appear against the sky, which itself seems even bluer than in the height of summer. Flocks of snow buntings, crested waxwings with gay red pearlets of wax on the tips of their secondaries, hunt for food.

On the tidal stretches of the rivers and in the estuaries, the duck gather in huge flocks. Widgeon, teal, mallard, golden-eye, tufted, and eider. Long-tail duck from Iceland dive into the water, looking for food, and their tail streamers give a delighted wiggle as they go under, like a lamb's tail.

The lochans are frozen, the tops of the reeds showing through the ice as though it had forgotten to shave for some days. The burns still tinkle their way, half hidden under the snow, great clusters of icicles hanging from the banks where the water has dripped so slowly that the frost has caught it before it could reach the burn. Only a few yards away, the noise of the running water is muffled and deadened by the snow. Scrub birches on the lower slopes have broken in places under the weight and show raw stumps of newly splintered wood.

In the birch woods the deer find both food and shelter, nibbling at the bark and searching with their hooves for grass and moss. The intense cold and the lack of food have made them less scared of man, and they are loth to leave such places.

The days gradually lengthen, and when you see the skeins of geese going north, it is not long till spring.

20 * Mrs Murdoch

'Could you train a young golden eagle to earn its own living in the wild?'

'I don't see any reason why not,' I replied.

'Right, there's an eagle in Benbecula that was rescued by a crofter when the old birds were shot. If it's turned loose now it will die because it has never been taught to kill. You'd better deal with it!'

So, in a few days' time, I collected a tea-chest from the airport at Inverness and took it home. I opened the chest up in the gun-room and out stepped not a male eagle, as I had expected from the name Murdoch, but a whacking great female. This wasn't going to be as simple as I had thought. Unk's two females had both turned a bit awkward; and, deciding they were too dangerous to have flying loose, he had let the first one go and exchanged the second for her brother, Mr Ramshaw. However, she seemed quiet enough at the moment, apart from knocking a landing-net off the wall and sending a box of cartridges flying as she jumped onto the chest above her. I cautiously put a pair of leather jesses on her, added a swivel and chain, and carried her out to a big log.

She jumped onto the log and roused herself. Her tail and wings were a bit bent from being confined in the tea-chest, and I got a large jug of hot water and a cake of soap and cleaned her up and straightened her feathers. She didn't show any resentment at this treatment. I offered her some meat; she refused, having been obviously very well fed by her previous owner. I left her to settle down in her new surroundings.

It was late October. If I got this eagle going now it would be late December or early January before she was fit to be let free. I could teach her to chase rabbits and hares from the fist, like a goshawk, but I couldn't teach her how to hunt from a height; for trained eagles will not wait on like a falcon. By January the hill would be snow-covered. Suitable eagle quarry would be hard to find for so inexperienced a bird and the odds would be against her survival.

I decided to do nothing much beyond handling her a bit to keep her tame and to start her training proper in May. By the time she was ready to be set free there would be plenty of young inexperienced things for her to learn on, and the weather would also be in her favour. Young eagles leave the eyrie about the end of July, and if I let her go a bit earlier than that she would have a good start on them and that might well make up for the training that her parents should have given her the previous year.

So I measured her up for a hood and got a saddler to make up an extra thick glove to go over my normal hawking-glove. She had enormous great yellow feet with long black talons, which, I knew, could drive through quite a thickness of leather when they gripped tight.

It was just as well I had made that decision, for the winter was really bitter and long. By Easter there was still a great deal of snow on the hills, and the deer were coming right down in the early afternoon, to scrounge what food they could find on the low ground. Not that there was much food for them, both deer and hill sheep were dying, and the crows and ravens were about the only well-fed creatures on the hill.

In May I started in earnest on Mrs Murdoch, as she had been renamed. I had received all sorts of letters suggesting Gaelic names for her that I could neither spell nor pronounce, but a man in Norway, who was interested in eagles, had called her Mrs Murdoch, and so Mrs Murdoch she became.

I did a short film with her for television with Fyfe Robertson, and she behaved very well in front of the cameras, though she refused to fly to me for food, being still too fat from her winter's feeding against the cold. I cut down her food supply, for she must learn to return to the lure before I could fly her loose and teach her any more.

This is one of the main difficulties in training eagles. Their powers of fasting are so great that ten days without food is nothing. In the

wild state, in winter, they may well be weather-bound for days on
end and just live off fat built up previously. They probably don't
kill any more than once a week then; for, in spite of their size,
once they are fully grown, they eat very little, about the same as
two falcons.

So it was a slow process getting her going, but once she got the
idea she came along very well. I didn't teach her to jump to the
fist very often, because a female eagle coming hard to your outstretched arm is liable to knock you back when she lands; besides,
once she is on the fist you have no control over her till you can get
hold of her jesses. This is the moment when, if she felt that way
inclined, she might snatch at your hand, thinking you were going
to take her food away.

If an eagle does get hold of you, there is not much you or anyone
else can do about it. You certainly can't prize her talons out of you.
In fact, even someone else, using both hands, can't so much as
wobble one of her toes. I know, because she got hold of my glove
one day and it was like trying to wrench the end of a spanner in
half. We simply could not move her one fraction of an inch; it was
a case of waiting till she relaxed her grip.

Once she was coming well to the lure, I got an old hareskin,
wrapped a large iron bolt in some sacking and sewed it all up inside
the skin. 'Stuffy', as this elegant affair was called, had a piece of
meat tied to him at first, but once Mrs Murdoch had learnt to come
to him, I removed the meat, and she learnt to fly at fur.

Two other difficulties now arose. Once she had hold of 'Stuffy' it
was extremely difficult to take him away. She thought she was very
clever to have caught him and she was not prepared to give him up
without a struggle. Only by holding a piece of meat in my glove
and getting her to shift onto this, was I able to remove him. Sometimes she would leave him as I approached her and come straight
at me, and it required a certain amount of dodging on my part before
I attained my object. In no time 'Stuffy' became 'Scruffy' and lost
both ears and all resemblance to a hare. By the end of the month I
had to call upon his understudy to take up duty.

The other difficulty was her weight. I weighed her on some bathroom scales and she turned just under fourteen pounds. You try

carrying fourteen pounds on your arm, held parallel to the ground, over heather and rocks and up hills. By the time you've gone a few hundred yards your arm is dropping off. Even the Holy Roman Emperor Frederick II, in his treatise on falconry, complained that eagles were too heavy.

When that fourteen pounds tries to take off, with a six-foot wing-spread, you soon become exhausted. But the onlookers don't really realize the trouble and tend to think you are unfit or a bit soft when you stop to rest so often.

We tried her first at hares and had her on a line, as I saw no reason to have her loose if she could catch one while trailing a light, nylon creance behind her. But she hadn't had enough daily exercise and the drag on the line was too great. She tried, but she puffed and blew after several vain attempts to overhaul them, and I took the creance off and had her loose.

She behaved very well, though, not being used to trees, she blundered about a bit when she tried to land in one and tended to choose little branches far too thin to support her weight. Then she would flounder about before getting onto a stronger one.

Eventually she got fed up with chasing hares which she couldn't catch; although she had several near misses, she just didn't make the grade. But if 'Stuffy Two' was produced and pulled along the ground she came out of the tree and was after him, her great feet coming forward beyond her head as she came up and grabbed him. Then I would have a battle to get him away and hood her up again.

She was a bit of an old cow in her hood. I tried solving the problem of carrying her by putting her on a stout branch held between two people, but she disliked the swaying movement and jumped off every so often, hood and all.

Then, one day, when I had her up in a tall beech tree, she spotted a rabbit running several hundred yards off. She hesitated a moment and then swung out and was off after the rabbit, obviously keen to catch it and really meaning business.

But a convenient hole spoilt her chance and when I came up she was peering down it, hackles raised and an angry look on her face. I gave her a big meal to reward her, for she had got the right idea now.

But rabbits were few and far between and mostly in thick wood-land, which was not suited to her great wing-spread.

The next day I was going to fly her in the afternoon, but when I went to hood her up and take her out, I noticed at once that she had an enormous crop of food. I knew no one would feed her unless I asked them to. It was obvious that she had caught something on her own account. I searched around her perch but could find nothing. Then I spotted a few bits of brown fur on the grass. It wasn't soft enough for a rabbit or the right colour for a hare; it was rather coarse fur. I picked her up and felt her crop to see if that would give me a clue, but I could make nothing of the mystery. I hunted deep down in the grass and finally found three sharp prickles from a hedgehog. So that was her first proud kill!

But how does an eagle eat a hedgehog? The whole darn thing had gone down her, prickles and all. A most uncomfortable thing to swallow, but quite an achievement. No wonder the old devil looked a bit smug. I wondered if all those prickles would do her some injury internally, but she was 'kewping' on her perch early next morning and was keen to fly.

The difficulty of finding a rabbit for her in the open, where she had a good chance of getting it, made me try bolting one for her with a ferret. It meant keeping her hooded till the rabbit appeared, for she would have no respect for the ferret, and I didn't want him caught by mistake. He was a very good ferret: too good really. He would catch the rabbits down the hole, and the first day was a com-plete blank as far as Mrs Murdoch was concerned, though Charlie ferret had three.

The second day started quite well. We put a rabbit up as we were walking along, I took her hood off and she was away at once. It was downhill, and the rabbit was quite a way from home, but he was a dodgy bunny and his white scut got down a hole just in time, though twice she nearly had him.

Then we tried bury after bury and not a rabbit showed up. Finally, by a croft, we found a good-looking hole, with fresh earth stamped down hard at the entrance by rabbits' feet. Charlie was taken out of his box and, after a twitch of his nose at the entrance, he shook himself and vanished.

We waited, hood loosened ready, and out shot a half-grown rabbit, Mrs Murdoch hard after him. He ran to the nearest cover, a dump of logs and scrap-iron by a chicken house. Mrs Murdoch was going too fast to stop and was brought up short by a collision with an old bicycle. I picked her up and we routed the rabbit out, and this time she took him before he could reach the hole.

With her great claspers round him he was a gone goon at once. I fed her up on her kill and took her back. For the next two weeks she had as much as she could eat. I had taught her all that I could; she knew what rabbits meant; she could fly well; and it was time she was independent.

We took her by Land-Rover to a remote glen in good eagle territory, away from human habitation and all possible harm. I took her on the glove, carried her up the hill a short way and, with a sharp knife, cut her jesses off. I unhooded her, stroked her feathers back into position where the hood had ruffed them up, and, turning her into the wind, held her up.

She was in no hurry to go. She looked around and flew a short distance onto a rock. I walked up to her, stroked her once more and offered her some food, but she was too well fed and ignored it entirely. She flew to another rock, and I walked back down the hill to the rest of the liberation party. We drank her health and to her future and sat and watched her. She made her way from rock to rock up the hill into the wind. Then she flew right across the glen and pitched in a more sheltered place on the other side, shifted twice more and then settled herself on one foot. She looked very small in that great area of country. The clouds were rolling in over the tops, and it started to drizzle as we left her on her own. I put her hood and the cut jesses in the Land-Rover. It was up to her now.

N

21 * The Taming of the Shrew

Trudy was curled up comfortably on the seat opposite me. Four hooded falcons sat patiently on their cadge, which was placed on the floor between us. The grouse-hawking season was over for the year. James, after a few years, had moved house to Sutherland, and, we having failed to find anything suitable in Scotland, had moved to Dorset. I was on my way back home there, to keep the falcons going and look after them till the next season.

The train pulled out from Inverness and the long journey began: jolting and swaying through the night, half asleep, yet too uncomfortable to sleep properly. Travelling with trained falcons is not easy; if you put them in hampers they tend to break their feathers and get all mussed up, and taking them on the cadge means keeping an eye on them to see that one does not jostle or snatch at its neighbour.

Cadge is an interesting word; the boy who carried the cadge in medieval times added to his wage by telling inquisitive onlookers the names of the falcons and what they had achieved, getting a tip for his trouble. He didn't own the birds and was probably learning to become a falconer, but doubtless he went out of his way to pick up the additional tip and he probably embellished his tale in order to get a bigger one. The word 'cadger' is said to derive from this, meaning someone who gets something for very little.

Every so often one of the falcons would scratch at its hood, for wearing one for several hours at a stretch is naturally irritating. If one of them persisted I would take her on my glove and unhood her for a while.

Trudy, a hardened traveller by now, resigned herself to sleep most of the time, though if I got up to attend to the falcons her eyes would open to watch me. Now and again she would yawn, stand up to stretch, shake herself and turn round and round before settling down again on my old duffel coat.

The train stopped at the main stations and porters trundled barrows along the platform and heaved sacks of mail or bundles of papers on board the guard's-van, while others hurled out packages in apparent disorder. A passing railway official would catch sight of the falcons, and in no time a little bunch of men would collect outside the carriage windows. Their accents told me roughly how far we had got.

One would tap on the window and ask, 'What do yer do with them, mate?' or 'Why they got them little 'ats on?' Some would look at Trudy's unusual markings and say 'That's a funny-looking dawg, mister, what sort do you call that?' Once the engine-driver was hauled down from the cab to have a look at his strange passengers.

At Crewe we had quite a long stop, and I took Trudy out for a walk along the platform, bought myself a cup of tea and gave Trudy a drink, keeping an eye on the falcons through the window. I joined the group of men watching the falcons and listened to their remarks. 'Bloody great boonch of parrots 'ere, Bert. . . .' 'Cor, I wouldn't like to 'ave them round my place. . . .' 'Ee, lad, they're not parrots, they're 'awks, tear yer eyes out they will, soon as look at yer.'

And so we rattled on southwards, down through the length of the land, the glare of blast furnaces or the silhouette of a pit-head telling the change from the hills to industry. As the first light of grey dawn filters through the dirty smoke-stained windows, the countryside starts to stir – a farmhand driving cows in for milking; paper boys on their morning rounds, jamming the papers through the letter-boxes and blowing on their cold hands before cycling on to the next house; early morning rooks, sitting on dew-beaded fence-wires, making up their minds whether to start the day poking around in the stubble, or to wait till the train has gone past in the hopes of an easy breakfast of scraps from the dining-car.

Most of the houses lie dark, but in one or two the windows light up and, as the train chuntles over the points, I spot Dad, shaving in front of a mirror, his braces hanging in loops on either side. More lights go on, and I imagine the outstretched hand, groping for the strident alarm clock, as it goes off with that ghastly, shuddering, juddering, rattling clatter that is enough to put anyone in a bad mood for the next few minutes.

The background noise of the train alters as we cross over a canal, and I can see smoke coming from the galley on a narrow-boat moored to the side. The panelled doors of the cabin are painted in the traditional castles-and-roses manner. It looks a peaceful sort of life, just chugging slowly along the waterways, but I suppose it has its snags like everything else.

As we near London and the pressure of rail traffic gets greater we go slower and slower. An electric train overtakes us, packed with City workers from the suburbs, standing swaying, bowler-hatted, briefcased and umbrella'd, reading the *Financial Times* or doing the crossword puzzle. I suppose they consider my job as nutty as a fruit cake; though, except for the fact that they are all the same way up, they look rather like a can of sardines to me, and getting about the same amount of enjoyment from life too.

I can hear the next-door passengers lugging their suitcases off the racks and getting themselves spruced up, so I put Trudy's lead on and pack up. By now I am accustomed to the stares which I receive as I wait for a taxi to carry me across London. The taxi-driver looks a bit taken aback, but I pile everything in, Trudy jumps up beside me, and we are off, with a jerk that throws the falcons off balance. I do my best to see that they don't break any feathers as they flip their wings out to help regain their positions.

We climb into another train and move out through the ever-encroaching sprawl of new houses. Familiar places flash past; the patch of brambles by the water-cress beds near Andover where Pru once caught a cock pheasant; I look to see if any rabbits are left along the big thorn hedge at Laverstock; there's the field where Greensleeves, stooping hard at a partridge, hit a wire fence. I re-live the agony of that moment, the falcon a black bundle on the ground, the partridge running out and taking wing again, myself wondering whether the falcon has broken a wing or a leg, and my relief as she slowly takes off in hopeless chase after it.

Salisbury Cathedral: jackdaws twisting and playing round the spire, the water-meadows where Medusa caught a stoat and stank of musk for days after. We are off again, the engine wheels slipping as they try to lug the long, heavy line of coaches under way. I wonder if the kestrels still nest in the old chalk-pit. There's the wood with the enormous wild cherry tree where I tried to capture a lost goshawk one night. But the gos had gone pretty wild after being out a few days, and a dead branch, cracking under my weight as I climbed up to her, startled her; the full moon gave her plenty of light as she flew out across the golden stubble field and vanished into the black wood beyond.

At the junction Bill is waiting on the platform, and the friendly porter, who keeps racing pigeons, helps me put the luggage on his barrow. It is like going back nearly a month in time. No frosts here yet, so the dahlias are still in bloom. The leaves have hardly begun to fall and are still more green than yellow. No vast open spaces here; one's horizon is limited to the hedgerow timber round the fields. Birds too are different, magpies flirting their long tails and dipping across the fields.

The stone cottage with its thatched roof looks just the same, and the children and dogs are waiting to greet me. Trudy's hackles go up as the other dogs crowd round her and snuffle before accepting her back into the family circle. I tie the falcons up to their waiting blocks and unhood them. They rouse and preen their displaced feathers back into position and are doubtless as glad as I am that the long journey is over.

Bill brings me a welcome cup of coffee, and I gulp it down amidst the tangled jumble of the children's voices, all talking at once and trying to tell me the latest news.

The falcons are fed, not too much, for in a couple of days time I will try them at rooks and see what they think of them. Then a walk round the garden: the blind hedge-pig is still quite happy, snuffling around his run and searching for slugs as an additional titbit to his saucer of bread and milk and a piece of raw meat. He is fat and well and probably thinking about hibernating soon in his nest of dead leaves and hay. Trudy goes off with Emily the dachshund and Candy the cairn. All three cross the plank bridge over the stream, but Lena, our great, woolly, long-eared deer-hound, jumps the whole affair, flailing her great tail to balance. Gibby the golden lurcher, always wary of Lena's bumptious barging, follows more sedately. One of them finds a mouse in a grass tussock and they all crowd round, getting in each other's way, rootling and snuffling into the nose-sized hole till you think they would blow the mouse out the other end.

Misti and Brownie, the two old ponies, come up to be fed, and the Chinese geese cackle as I go to see how they are. The gander lowers his head and comes running towards me, hissing, but, when I fail to show alarm at his attack, he slows up, turns round on his great orange, paddling feet, and arches his neck as he walks away, looking rather embarrassed. His wife calls to him from the stream where they spend most of their time, instead of eating the grass as they are intended to. At one time we had seven geese, but a fox killed six of them and left only the young Chinese gander, who drove the whole neighbourhood mad, honking for his lost friends. So we found Lizzie for him, a wall-flower goose from a flock of some twenty others, who, for some reason, would have nothing to do with her. Shadrach, the gander, was delighted, and the two are now inseparable.

One winter's day Trudy solved a mystery that had been puzzling us. She suddenly pointed in perfect style in one of the bedrooms and, following this up, we discovered a cache of chocolate biscuits, numbers of which had been disappearing of late. She was rewarded with some, which she adores, but was somewhat unpopular with the child concerned, who considered it unfair to employ canine detectives.

As soon as spring came I was badgered by the children to get them another grey squirrel. There were plenty about. I took a young one whose eyes had not yet opened, and in no time it was feeding out of the bottle. I think any young mammal taken at this age is very easy to tame, and this one certainly had no fear of us.

I built a wire-netting run for him outside the kitchen window, with a tunnel leading to a sleeping-box. I fixed a large twisted branch inside and, as soon as his eyes opened, he started to climb. He would lie in the sun for hours on end, his bushy tail over his back. Then, suddenly, he would start to play, rushing round his cage, jumping onto the branch and running along it like the big dipper at Blackpool. Then off it and through a hollow log I had put in for him. The baker would bring him a bun or a biscuit when he called on his rounds, and Arthur would lope up and down in his excitement, waiting for his treat.

By opening the window we could let him inside without fear of him running away, and he learnt to scratch on it when he was hungry or wanted attention. We let him in every morning at coffee-time. At first he was rather shy and at the slightest move he would rush back to his run. But in no time he had overcome his alarm and came loping in to jump from person to person, running round and round them as though they were tree-trunks. Biscuits were his passion, and he would snatch them from an unwary child and then sit up on his hind legs and hold them in his front paws, turning them round as he nibbled at them. As he grew up, his woolly coat was replaced by a sleek, greyish-red fur, and his tail grew even longer and bushier.

We were worried about the cats, but he had full command of the situation. He was nibbling a biscuit on the floor one morning, when one approached him. He sat watching it and then, when it was about a foot away, he carefully put down the biscuit, ran daintily forward, gave the cat a left and right on the ears with his front paws and, as it shot away in dismay, turned round and continued his interrupted meal, his long whiskers wobbling and his beady eyes gleaming. As a special treat he was taken out into the garden and allowed to play on the swing.

We had a visiting eagle come for a couple of months while his owner was abroad. Shub was an imperial eagle and had had a some-what varied life. His owner had rescued him from a fortune-teller in Istanbul, where he had ignominiously had his wings clipped and been tied by a piece of string round the leg. Once the price had been settled the fortune-teller dumped him on the café table and left hastily with his cash, before the new owner changed his mind.

The airway was informed of this addition to his owner's luggage for the journey back. There was a pause when the identity of the new passenger was made known, and a request to hold the line. But all was well, the voice came back after a few minutes' interval and said, 'Pan-American welcomes anything, even eagles.' So Shub came to England and, in due course, grew new feathers and regained his self-respect. He arrived in the self-same Turkish laundry basket that had been hastily purchased for him while he was still sitting on the café table in Istanbul.

We fixed up his perch in the garden and he was introduced to everyone. The children scratched his head as though he were an old parrot, and he was as tame and friendly as Ramshaw. But, like Ramshaw, once he had been with us a few days, he considered the area round his perch was his alone and would launch himself at all and sundry who came in range. As his perch was close by the stream that ran through the garden, several people, in their haste to avoid his attentions, landed in the water, though in fact I had arranged matters so that there was a clear path along it.

But with me he never tried these tricks. I could walk up and stroke him, and he never attempted to do me any harm. Poor Shub, his troubles were by no means over. When his owner returned and took him home a gang of boys stoned him one day, broke his wing and very nearly killed him.

I took one of the falcons up to Frensham Ponds to do some filming for television. Later on one of them came with me to London, and we were photographed as an advertisement for stout. I posed in various attitudes all morning, the photographer imploring always for, 'just one more chuckle'. Never having been very good at chuckling, I was not surprised that the results were never used. By some odd chance no one in the studio liked stout; bottle after bottle was opened so that it would look fresh in the glass I held, and, as each glassful subsided, it was poured down the dark-room sink. An ardent stout drinker would have had a wonderful time.

The falcons were no longer flown, but, instead, had all they could eat in order that they should moult quickly and get their new flight feathers grown in time for the next season.

One day the children found that one of the cats had pulled a pygmy shrew's nest out of the garden wall. They rescued the sole surviving youngster and carried it in, demanding that it should be housed and fed and allowed to join the menagerie.

Its Latin name, *Sorex minutus*, was very appropriate. For anything more minute of that nature one would have required a magnifying glass. It was a scrap of dark velvet fur, with a tail and four spindly legs stuck on at the right places, and a nose that was more like a

Dabbing-time

Dancing-time

Half-time

Time to go home

The falcon looks black against the sky
– her wings like a full-drawn bow

Trudy gets a firm point

trunk. Its eyes were still closed, and our hopes of rearing it successfully seemed pretty dim. However, there was no alternative but to
try.

We put it in a cage and it promptly walked straight through the
wire mesh, which was of the smallest size. So a small raffia work-
basket was hastily denuded of its more normal contents, and Sylvia
was placed in a cotton-wool nest inside. We put the basket on top
of the boiler, which was nicely warm without being hot enough to
cook her.

The valve off a baby's feeding bottle, which we had long ago found
to be ideal for squirrels and other small creatures, was put on an
aspirin bottle, and Sylvia, with amazingly little trouble, was induced
to suck up the milk-and-sugar mixture. The amount she took at one
go would hardly have moistened a postage stamp, but it mounted
up if given often enough, and she not only survived but grew almost
visibly.

In no time at all the removal of the lid of her home was the signal
for her to come rushing out, wobbling her long nose in search of her
next meal. When her eyes opened we reckoned it was about time
that she was taught to drink properly and had something more added
to her diet. Shrews being eaters of worms and insects, we tried her
on some of the hawk's meat. We cut the smallest scraps of this we
could; they probably looked like porter-house steaks to her, but she
ate them quite happily.

Drinking was an entirely different matter. Quite how a wild adult
shrew drinks, I have no idea, possibly it relies on dew or raindrops,
for we found that thirsty shrews have a problem all of their own.
Their upper jaw is very much longer than their lower one and,
as their nostrils are placed right at the end of it, if they try to
drink in normal animal fashion, their nose dips into the liquid
before their lower jaw and tongue can start to lap. All that our
shrew succeeded in doing, at first, was to blow bubbles through her
snout.

Her drinking-dish was an upturned tin-lid about two inches
across. The shrew solved her own drinking problems by wading into
the lid with all four feet, resting her upper snout on the rim at the
far side and then lapping up the milk with her lower snout. Once

replete, she would continue her journey across the lid and, on reaching dry land, would halt, shake each foot separately, sit up on her hind legs and wash her front paws and face very thoroughly and comb her whiskers with the tiny claws on her front toes.

Soon it was time for me to overhaul the gear for the coming season. Blocks and baths needed repainting; my hawking-bag wanted repairing; new hoods were needed, and old ones had to be reblocked into shape and new plumes put on. The old falcons had worn out their jesses and needed fresh ones, and new ones had to be cut for the eyasses. My climbing-ropes had to be oiled to preserve them and some of the hampers relined with sacking. I made a trip up to Scotland to get new peregrines and then had about three weeks' respite, while the eyasses were loose in the mews until they were hard down and ready to pick up.

I had just started training the first of the eyasses when two Peale's falcons arrived by air from Canada. These are like very big, dark peregrines and nest on Queen Charlotte's Island off the north-west coast. They had been presented to the Duke of Edinburgh a few weeks previously, and we were to try them out at grouse.

When I put them out on blocks I found that they were both screamers. The tiercel was not too bad, but the falcon was terrible and even screamed with her hood on. They had been handled too young, and the noise was so piercing and irritating that it was sheer misery even to carry them on the hill. So bad were they that we had to give up flying them, which was very disappointing, for they had the weight to deal with grouse very easily.

We fell back on the well-tried, home-brewed, peregrine, whose capabilities we already knew and who, as usual, did not let us down. So, a few days before the grouse season began, Trudy and I once again took the train north with a cadgeful of falcons.

22 * '. . . So Man Hath His Desires'

Back at Spinningdale, Cathy and George, who between them run the house, greet Trudy and myself and tell me all the local gossip over a cup of tea in the kitchen.

The house lies on the edge of the Dornoch Firth, in a sheltered, sun-collecting bay and northwards along the Firth the sea comes in through a narrow gut and then spreads out in a great basin, making a small salt-water loch before narrowing down again to where the river joins it. At the mouth there are sandbanks and, in rough weather, the breakers thunder in a spume of white water. All around the shores are sea birds and waders. When the tide turns and starts to ebb the water rushes out through the narrows, and it is as though someone has pulled out an enormous bath-plug. As the tide recedes great mussel-beds and sandbanks appear, and vast stretches of flat, sandy mud are left, covered with thousands upon thousands of worm-casts. On the sandbanks the seals haul themselves out, lying on their sides with their tails up at one end and heads up at the other, playing at gravy-boats. As the sun dries their sleek, wet coats, so they change colour and their spots become more obvious. They yawn and doze and hump themselves into more comfortable positions.

On the mussel-beds the gulls, oyster-catchers and curlews all search for food left behind by the tide. Redshanks flit along the water's edge, and, if you are extremely lucky, you may even see an osprey, hovering like a great, pale buzzard, searching the water below for grilse and sea-trout. If you are even luckier, you may see him catch a fish, diving in, feet foremost, his talons stretched out right in front of his head, for he catches them with his feet, which have hard, knobbly excrescences under the toes, like sharkskin, to help him hold the slippery fish.

As he rises he gains height a bit and then stalls, dropping a few feet as he shakes the water from his feathers. Then away he goes, unheeding of the gulls that mob him; and, by putting the foot that has the head of the fish in front of the other, he streamlines it, so making it easier for him to fly. Quite leisurely he makes his way into the hill or onto a distant sandbank.

It is here, at low tide, that the dabs and plaice lie in the little creeks left in the hollows of the sand. Wearing old plimsolls and shorts, and sweaters if the wind is cold, we walk out over the mud-flats to the main channel and then wade in line abreast up these creeks, each person armed with a sharp-pointed wooden stick. The sun has warmed the shallow water, and if there is no wind it is easy to see the bottom. Here, in anything from six inches to three feet of water, you may spot a dab lying. He will be covered with a fine layer of sand and only his outline is visible to the eye. The little dabs are not much bigger than half a crown, but the big ones are the size of dinner-plates, or more. They vary in colour, depending on whether they live in a sandy creek or in one that is black with old mussel shells, or gravelly with little pebbles and cockles. So they match the bed of the stream they frequent, making it extremely difficult to see them.

We wade up the creek – James, with eel-spear, looking like Father Neptune. Sooner or later someone flushes a dab or even stands on him by accident; feeling something squirm under their foot, most people instinctively jump. In either case, away the dab goes, in-credibly fast, undulating across the sand and, in shallow water, send-ing up a tiny V-shaped bow-wave as he darts off. The hunt is on.

The experienced dabster, or dab-hand, lets loose a cry of 'Dab-Ho!' or 'Dab Forrard!' and wades forward as fast as he can without splashing away the visibility. The object is to try to keep the dab in view until he goes to ground. This he does with a flurry that sends up a cloud of sand, and in this smoke-screen the dab disappears.

You are dead certain you know within inches where he is, but the dab is no fool and rarely settles in the smoke screen but does a quick turn to one side and glides unseen to a place a foot or more away.

Peering through the water, you think you see him and strike with your spear, only to find nothing. You approach closer to get a better view and, ten to one, the dab goes between your feet and vanishes in the sand-cloud that you have created. The experienced dabster jabs at it as it shoots past him, and is feet behind; for the dab is very much faster than you think. The splashing and the shouts that go on, as dabs twist and turn and blunder, thinking your feet a refuge, is all part of the fun. You are a primitive native again, hunting with poor weapons and pitting your skill against the hope of a fresh fish for breakfast. On a good day a bunch of six or seven people may catch one apiece; but if the wind is riffling the surface of water you are lucky if you get any.

The tide is on the turn and, as the creeks grow wider with the incoming flow, the sand, dried by the sun and wind, floats over the surface. It is time to make our way back across the flats, gathering cockles, mussels or winkles for the larder, then to make tracks for the saltings, where the sea pinks and white bladder-campion flower. Behind, the terns whissick as they hover over the creek you have left, diving in to catch the silvery little sand-eels that you have disturbed.

Up on the inland rock cliffs, the fulmars are sitting, making the most odd selection of grunts and coos and quarks. Close by the shore, on a small rock, is a cow seal in sole occupation. She lies facing us and, unless she is very shortsighted, must be well aware of our presence. Her coat, dried by the wind and sun, is light grey, dappled with darker spots and patches. Her large eyes look straight towards us, now wide open, now half closed.

The expression on her whiskered face is like a very contented, well-dined-and-wined alderman who has not a care in the world and has found a comfortable seat in the sun for an afternoon's zizz. Every so often she rolls on one side and scratches an urgent tickle with a front flipper – even this is done in slow motion, with the same amiable, blissful expression.

Every so often a wave, slightly braver than its fellows, slaps against the rock and breaks into a shower of spray over the seal. She sits up a little higher, hunching her back and moving her front flippers back a little, yawns, and looks down at the water as if considering whether it is warm enough for a swim yet. Other seals have already been washed off from the sandbanks farther out, and every so often one pokes his head out of the sea a few yards away from her and looks at her as if to say, 'Come on in, it's not so bad once you're there.'

Finally, as the waves grow bolder and cheekier and break over her more often, she lollops a couple of awkward paces forward, lifts her head, takes a last look round and slides into the sea with hardly a splash. The rock is empty.

Some oyster-catchers fly past, uttering their piping notes. A sheldrake, still very handsome in his courting plumage, dibbles in the seaweed along the shore's edge. Every so often a seal's head bobs up for a moment; they all seem to be playing a game of 'Periscope up – periscope down', except for two, who are having a necking party, rubbing their necks against each other, diving down and coming up to start all over again. The seals, the sea birds, the clumps of pink thrift on the rocks, the smell of the sea, the wind on one's face, all make one feel pleasantly lazy and seal-snoozy oneself.

James keeps the hawking-season clear of all filming, broadcasting or television engagements, and by the first week of August he is back at Spinningdale. The falcons are flown every day that the weather permits, but, the British climate being somewhat variable, there are days when the wind is too strong or when rain stops play. Then we take advantage of the fact that bad weather on the east coast means good weather on the west, and westwards we go.

I spent one glorious sunny day on the west coast trying to film Mij, Gavin Maxwell's tame otter.

Gavin's house is just over a mile off the road, right on the sea. Mij had free run of the place, and I spent nearly all day trying to catch this elusive, velvety, bewhiskered creature on film. He sat up on his hind legs and ate hard-boiled eggs; he played in the water with ping-pong balls and rubber ducks; he and Gavin fished the burn, Gavin turning over the stones and Mij streaking away after the eels unearthed.

He glissaded down sandbanks, rolling in the sand to dry his sleek coat. He swam under water in the sea, porpoising along. He lolloped after Gavin, stopped to investigate the wing of a gull, climbed in and out of a fish crate that had been washed ashore. He opened the eel can and helped himself to a meal, he played in the whirlpool at the bottom of the falls. I chased after him with both movie- and still-cameras; and never, the whole day, was this quicksilver animal still for more than a few moments.

He was a photographer's nightmare. It was exhausting. But he was so delightful that you simply could not get cross. Nor could you stop filming him, for every minute he was different, and every pose you felt you simply had to try to record. Finally I ran out of film.

Spinningdale is invariably full of guests whenever James is at home. They come out with the falcons, go dabbing, drive up to the Shin or Oykel Falls to see the salmon jump, or go over to the west to Suilven, Canisp, Stac Polly, those hills which, although not so high as some, look very dramatic because they rise so suddenly out of the land.

Somehow or other, Cathy is never disorganized by the sudden influx of guests that sometimes tends to bulge the walls a bit. It is not that these guests are uninvited, but merely that the master of the house has forgotten when they were coming and has asked a few more in the meantime. Do not think that this quiet, calm, soft-spoken Cathy would not say bo to a goose. When the early hours of the morning have been shattered by the blowing of bag-pipes during a party, disturbing her beauty sleep, she has been known not only to issue an edict that musical instrument players will not be fed in future, but has also retaliated by attaching cow-bells under the offender's bed.

But in George, Cathy has met her match in more than one sense. He was quietly reading the paper one evening, the day's chores being done, when I looked in.

'George, put that paper down and help me make a cup of tea,' said Cathy.

George remained firmly seated.

'George, aren't you going to help?'

He never even looked up from his reading, 'I am helping. I'm helping by keeping out of the way.'

To that sort of reply, there is no answer. But don't run away with the idea that George sits around all day. Since he joined the *ménage*, the policies (as the grounds are called in Scotland) have all been tidied up, the cars are cleaned, the log supply is never short, and in the back-end when the leaves start to fall and block up the strainer pit, stopping the flow of water to the turbines so that the lights fade out altogether, George is off into the dark, armed with a torch, to get it all going again.

By August the twelfth, the first day of the grouse season, the falcons are all trained and ready to go. By then I will have a pretty good idea which ones I think are going to turn out well. By no means all peregrines make good game hawks. Those who tend to fly round low down may do very well at rooks and crows; but to knock down an old cock grouse a falcon must be well up. A great deal depends on the dog too. A dog that false points at pipits and larks is useless; for young falcons won't wait on for long at first, and to put one on the wing and then not find any grouse does a lot of harm. Trudy, as far as I am concerned, will never be beaten as a perfect hawking-dog. She will go all day once she is fit.

The English pointers and setters rarely have the stamina to do this. People seem to be breeding faster and faster dogs that wear themselves out in an hour or so and have to be brought in to rest while another dog takes its turn. They go so quickly that, on a bad scenting day, their legs tend to overrun their noses, and the grouse are up and away before the dog can stop. But the German pointers are a good deal slower and so are able to keep up a steady pace.

Trudy will stay on a point for over half an hour if necessary. I had her out with me alone with one falcon, and I was humping a heavy movie-camera as well at the time. She came on a point a long way off, and it took me some time to get up to her. I sat the falcon on a rock and tied her to my hawking-bag while I got the camera set. Then the sun went behind some clouds, and I sat and waited. Trudy remained motionless, except for her mouth, which was slightly open, sucking up the scent.

While I waited, I spotted the grouse, crouched on an open patch of short heather only about three yards in front of her. By the time the sun came out again twenty minutes had passed. I took some shots of both dog and grouse, first on the normal lens and then on the telephoto. I put the camera away, strapped on my hawking-bag and cast the falcon off. Once she had got to her pitch and was well placed overhead, I sent Trudy in. A dog that will flush on command and go in really fast when told to is worth untold gold.

Very rarely do you know exactly where the birds are lying. They may be under the dog's nose, or sixty yards away if the wind is blowing the scent down to her. If the falcon is overhead, you can almost tread on them before they will get up, and even three or four people can run right over them. These delays may well mean that a young falcon, tired of waiting, has drifted downwind and is now badly placed. The grouse are watching her and will take advantage of this and go away in the opposite direction as fast as they can, leaving the falcon to beat upwind in a stern chase that is not much fun to watch and will probably end in disappointment for her.

Trudy flushed this grouse at the chosen moment, and the falcon had only to turn over and stoop for it to be soon in the bag.

If you want to see grouse-hawking at its best, you should wait till September or October. By then the young falcons will have gained experience, the old ones from the previous season will be really fit, and the grouse will be very strong, full-grown birds capable of flying hard and giving the falcon a run for her money.

The day starts with each falcon being given a chance of taking a bath before we go off. Most of them like bathing, especially if the sun is out, and, if they are not given a chance to do so, may well take the law into their own hands and, instead of waiting on over the dog, go off in search of a convenient pool. Then one has to wait till she is done and has dried and preened herself, an hour or more. Birds of prey rarely drink except when ill or after travelling a long time. When they do they are said to bowse – hence we get the word booze.

While the falcons are bathing, the lures must be made up and binoculars and so on put into the car. The falcons are then hooded up and each one carefully weighed to check her condition. They are then put on the cadge, and off we go to the hill.

o

Where we start depends on the direction of the wind and which piece of ground has not been disturbed lately. You can't decide this until you get there, for wind is very local amongst the hills. The hill we use has more grouse on it now than it had five years ago. It is never shot, nor is it keepered. You can run a dog on it in December, and the grouse will still lie to the point. It is not ideal, for it is really too hilly, and there are some places where it is dangerous to fly because there is so much dead ground. The falcon will be out of sight in no time and easily lost. But usually there are enough coveys sprinkled around to give each falcon three or four flights in a day.

By now Trudy has developed an eye for grouse-haunted spots and ignores the swampy, low-lying patches, where it is too wet to hold the birds. Pointers trained for shooting are taught to turn at a whistle signal, but on a moor like this, where grouse take a bit of finding, it is better to let an intelligent dog alone and not to worry if she goes over the skyline. If she doesn't show up in a few minutes, then you know she is on a point, while, if there is nothing there, she will be back, ranging and quartering till she does come on them. With a young dog that is still learning and not to be trusted to stay long on a point, discipline must be stricter and a watchful eye kept on her. The most difficult thing about Trudy is to stop her working. While we are having a brief spell to rest and eat our piece, she will continue to carry on unless firmly ordered to sit down.

Sooner or later she will come on some grouse, and I raise an arm to tell the rest of the party that she is firmly on a point. A plan of campaign is quickly settled on. The lie of the land, the wind direction and strength, whether an experienced falcon or a beginner is to be flown are all taken into consideration. We post the onlookers in the best strategic positions, where they will not only see what is going on, but will be able to follow the flight should it go into ground I cannot see from my own position. James does the placing while I get round into position as quickly as I can and put the falcon on the wing. Once she is up the grouse will stay put, but until then any loud talking or untoward noise may put them up.

I took off the falcon's leash and swivel as soon as Trudy went out. Now I give the ends of her jesses a twist, as a precaution against them catching in a tough bit of heather or on a wire fence. I pull her hood braces undone, one side of them with my hand and the other between my teeth, for you have only one free hand and everything must be done with it. As I take her hood off, I raise her up into the wind and let her take off on her own. If she is a bit slow, then I assist her with a gentle forward movement of the gloved hand she is sitting on.

Trudy is still on the point, and the rest of the party are in position. James, leaning on his stick, binoculars ready, is watching. Gale swings round and starts to gain height. She is one of the best we've had, and she takes no notice of the people below but concentrates on the dog. She wastes no time in getting up, and, when she is nicely placed, she stops beating her wings and sails easily round, her head turned down, watching.

I wait till she is facing the way in which I expect the grouse to go and then send Trudy in with a loud 'Hi, lost!' Trudy leaps into action across the heather to where her nose tells her the birds are lying hidden. Up they get, and away, never very high above the ground; Gale gives a couple of quick wing flips that send her forward and, at the same time, she turns down and is streaking towards them.

One gets up a bit late and Gale, clouting him hard as she goes past, drops him into the heather. She throws up and comes in to grab him, and I walk in with Trudy at heel. Her strong beak has broken his neck long before I get there. The rest of the party can now come up, and I take her on my fist, slip the grouse into my hawking-bag, and hood her up.

We have a brief rest while I hand her over to James and take Canisp from him; she is a young falcon who has killed a few grouse but still tends to fly too low. If we can find a point along the next piece of ground, which has a steady breeze blowing up the slope, she may be more inclined to get up and have a better chance. Also, I know that there is a covey round here which was hatched rather late and will, therefore, be easier for her, so long as she picks out one of the young birds. A falcon takes the bird that is best placed for her, and rarely changes her mind unless a bird subsequently gets up late and is obviously better placed. Even then she may ignore it, and you can sometimes see her stooping at one while a late-riser is flying towards her, following the rest of the covey.

Canisp is a long, rakish falcon, a shape that I dislike because they rarely turn out to be good game hawks. I prefer the cobby, thickset ones. Trudy finds a point almost at once, away to the flank, and I have to climb up to place myself above the grouse and give Canisp all the height I can. I cast her off and put her hood onto the wooden block attached to my belt, to stop it getting squashed in bag or pocket.

Canisp gets up quite well, with the breeze under her sails, and, although she might go higher, I prefer to put the grouse up now rather than wait, for I know that she may drift away with this breeze, and, if I show her the lure to bring her back, she may lower her pitch. So, in goes Trudy, and I shout to attract Canisp's attention as they get up. She's well placed, but the grouse double back suddenly and, instead of a good stoop, it develops into a chase. They make for a big patch of bracken and dive in just as she is getting on terms with them. She throws up and, as Trudy has been following them and is quite close, I run up and send her in again. As Canisp is still overhead, it's worth trying. One of them gets up, but, as the falcon stoops, it dives back into the bracken. Trudy is there again, pointing once more, and I try again. But Canisp has drifted off and is having to beat back against the wind, and the affair is fast becoming a rat hunt.

I leave Trudy on the point, and get upwind of her and bring Canisp in to the lure. As soon as she is past Trudy I hide the lure and, as Canisp swings round again, I send Trudy in. The grouse nearly loses his tail as Trudy puts him up, and Canisp is on him at once and grabs him in the air – not a very stylish flight and I doubt if Canisp has learnt much from it.

The rest of the party are watching in the distance, and I make my way back to them. After a rest we decide to fly Poacher. In her first season she was very good. She did not do so well in her second season, though her speed earned her quite a number of kills. This year she seems faster than ever. In her adult plumage she looks very beautiful, with her salmon-pink chest and cross-barring below. Her feet have turned a good yellow, a lot brighter than the young falcon's.

We are on the tops now, in among the peat hags, and the old peat cuttings are very wet; but where the banks run between the cuttings the heather is long, and we often find some birds here. It is not an ideal place to fly, but, with a party of people to help mark the flight, things could be a lot worse.

But the grouse aren't here today: only a golden plover, which gets up and goes away with quick beats of its wings. They really are bright gold, and their black waistcoats make a good contrast. The wild peregrines kill them, but they take a lot of catching. Looking down on the loch, we see a pair of red-throated divers fishing and sit down to look at them for a bit. They see us and swim off to the far end of the loch, and we go on again, Trudy impatient at the delay, for divers hold no interest for her.

We move on, Trudy, quartering the steep slope and finding nothing, tries out the flat by the lochan. This is blank too, until just at the end, when we get a very firm point close to the march fence. I leave the rest of the party half-way up the slope; there is no need to post markers here, whichever way the flight goes, it will be in full view. I put Poacher up and she swings low round me, flying in that clipping style that I would recognize a long way off. I want to avoid sending the grouse over the march off our ground; and I hope also that, by getting round behind them, I can make them fly away from the fence and towards the onlookers. But they don't agree, and, just as I am nearly across the flat, they get up and go the wrong way. Poacher is after them; her speed makes up for the lack of height and, as they cross the fence, she knocks one down and is trying to grab it in the long heather. The last bird of the covey is so busy looking behind him, to see what Poacher is doing, that he hits the fence and drops down too.

Poacher on the ground is too fumble-footed, and the grouse, with his quick steps, is dodging her clumsy efforts. Trudy joins in, and the grouse decides to make across the lochan, his wingtips brushing the water he flies so low. Poacher is up and after him and overtakes him just as he is passing the little island. He swings in towards the land and dives into the sallows. For one moment I think Poacher has him, and I foresee a somewhat chilly swim to get her back, but the cover is very thick and she comes into the lure and catches it neatly.

She jumps to my fist as I go in and leaves the lure on the ground for me to pick up, taking her reward from my glove. I wind up the lure line and put her hood on, leaving the braces loose because I want to investigate the bird that hit the fence-wire. If he suddenly jumps up, then I can get Poacher on the wing at once by whipping the hood off. I call Trudy up to help, but she is not interested in dead grouse, and this one is ready only for the larder when I find him. He goes into the bag, and I tighten Poacher's hood.

The next bit of ground is very swampy and full of cotton grass, bog asphodel and myrtle: fit only for frogs. Before going on we all take a rest in the heather, and I put Poacher down on a convenient rock.

It's Gale's turn again, and we go down towards the head of a big gully that runs out of the swamp and down into the burn half a mile away. It provides ideal cover for grouse, and yet they rarely use it unless very hard pressed. Once they get into it, they are generally pretty safe; for, even if you post a marker on the edge, the gully bends so much that, once he goes round the corner, the grouse is out of sight and might be anywhere on the steep slopes either side of the burn. A grouse that has put into a large area of thick cover like this and is unmarked is extremely hard to find, for he has little or no scent then. If it's known, within a few yards, where he has gone, then it is better to wait twenty minutes, and by then the scent will be strong enough for the dog. But, once in the gully, you will be very lucky to get a grouse out; even if you do, he will double back in again for sure. He is best left alone; we shall meet him again some other day, and he'll probably use the same trick then.

As we go down Trudy gets a point in a clump of rushes on the swamp edge. It is not a very likely place for a grouse, though they eat the rush seeds at times, just as partridges will, jumping up in the air and pulling the seed head down to deal with it on the ground.

I put Gale on the wing, and she is soon well up, cruising around at a good three hundred feet or more. She really is a delight to fly. Whether she kills or not, I know she will put on a good show. Trudy is sent in, and up gets a snipe, one of the few that we occasionally come across on this hill. Gale puts in a stoop, which he avoids

by a neat twiddle at the right moment, and climbs away in long
zig-zags with Gale hard on his tail, following every twist and turn.
She is so close that he dare not seek refuge in the gully but goes over
it and away, climbing all the time. The binoculars are essential now,
for they are probably five hundred feet up and a mile away, growing
rapidly smaller every second. The snipe is only a speck at this
distance, and the falcon is pretty small too. Several times I see her
try to grab him, and at least once I think she's got him; but Mr
Snipe is a very smart fellow and manages to slip out of the way.
Each time Gale tries she loses a bit of ground; but in no time she is
on his tail again, and still they climb. Gale tries another grab and
again is thrown out, and the snipe suddenly decides on different
tactics. The few feet Gale lost trying to snatch him give him a
chance suddenly to double back. Gale swings round after him, and
now the snipe is coming down in a shallow dive, making for safety
in the gully.

She is above and behind him and is wise enough not to keep on
his tail, but retains her height and flies even harder. She gets right
over him and puts in a stoop as hard as she can go; he twists away,
and she is directly below him, but she throws up beautifully and is
back in position for another stoop. Again she turns over and comes
at him. They are both quite close to us now, and we can hear the
noise of her wings as she comes down in a sizzling stoop that will
send the snipe to his happy dibbling grounds if she touches him.

But he is right over the gully now and he plummets in like a stone;
as Gale pulls out to avoid hitting the steep banks, the snipe drops
into safety, doubtless very thankful, and probably a good deal out
of puff. We leave him there and Gale comes in to my lure. For once
her beak is open from her exertions, and she is certainly due for a
rest. In fact, we decide that she has done enough and feed her up on
the old grouse she killed earlier on. As is so often the case, the best
flight of the day ended in the quarry getting away; only the hungriest
of hunters would have any regrets.

Canisp misses an easy one by raking away downwind; the grouse,
seizing the opportunity, makes off in the other direction, and she
gets nowhere near him. Poacher goes well and gives us a nice young
grouse for the larder.

We make our way down to the cars and go home, Poacher feeding up on my fist as we drive along. Trudy gets what remains of my pick-up piece of meat, and the hawking-party discuss the day's flying. The grouse that eluded us have rejoined their coveys by now and are doubtless telling the tale to their chums, describing how cleverly they eluded that silly falcon.

I put the falcons back on their blocks, unhood them and give them clean bathwater for the morning. They rouse and preen a bit and then tuck one foot up and rest, contented with their full crops and their day's outing.

Cathy and George are surrounded by a pile of silver, polishing away hard. I feed Trudy, change out of my peat-stained trousers and join James and the guests. Dan, the gardener, is mowing the lawn. In a few days' time, Prince Philip and Prince Charles are coming for a brief visit, and James and I only hope that Gale and Poacher will behave as they have done today.

Dinner is ready, and we are having some of the results of our labours: grouse from the hill, mussels from the loch, chanterelles from the birch woods. It seems a pity that more people don't have a chance to enjoy a day like this. I only wish that Unk were here now; he would have been more than enthusiastic over today's flights. I can just imagine him, after Gale had flown that snipe: 'Well, old boy, you can't expect to do much better than that. What a show!'

Glossary of Falconry Terms

Note. As this is not a technical book on falconry I have used as few technical terms as possible and explained them where first used in the text. They are also explained in the glossary, though this is not a collection of all the terms used in falconry.

Austringer – one who trains hawks, as compared with a falconer, who trains falcons. From the French *autour*.

Bate – to fly off the fist or perch either away in fright or at lure or quarry. 'These kites that bate and beat and will not be obedient . . .' *The Taming of the Shrew*, IV, ii.

Bells – small bells, usually of brass, attached to help find a lost falcon. 'Neither the king, nor he that loves him best, the proudest he that holds up Lancaster, dares stir a wing if Warwick shake his bells.' *3 Henry VI*, I, i.

Bewit – the leather strap by which the bells are attached.

Bind – to grab and hold on.

Bird of the fist – a bird trained to come to the fist only, not to the lure. Only short-winged hawks are trained in this way, not falcons.

Block – the perch used for falcons out of doors.

Blood feathers – feathers not yet fully grown, whose shafts contain blood at the top.

Bob – head movement made by falcons when especially interested in something.

Bow-perch – the semi-circular perch used for hawks out of doors, similar to the more modern ring-perch.

Bowse – to drink. Hawks rarely drink except when ill or after travelling. Booze is said to derive from this term.

Cadge – a device by which several falcons can be carried by one person. There are several designs of cadge. The cadge proper is a wooden frame on which the falcons sit hooded. It has straps which go over the cadge-boy's shoulders so that it can be carried to the field. The cadge-boy stands in the centre of the frame. When not being carried the cadge stands on short legs. The box-cadge is simply a square or oblong box, without a lid; the top edges are padded, and the falcons sit round the edge. It is smaller than the cadge proper and is very useful for car or train journeys, but not in the field. The pole-cadge is simply a long pole, padded, and with short biped legs at each end and a hand-hold at the centre. It can be used both for travelling and in the field but is easily tipped over.

Cadger – the person who carries the cadge, the cadge-boy.

Call off – to call a hawk or falcon from a perch to the lure or to the fist.

Cast – a word of many meanings. A cast of hawks is two hawks, though not necessarily a pair. To cast a hawk is to hold it for imping or to put jesses on, etc. To cast off a hawk is to gently impel it forward off the fist to get it airborne. A hawk casts its hood when it pulls the hood off by accident. To cast, of a hawk, is the action of throwing up a casting.

Casting – the pellet of undigested bones, fur or feathers that is cast by all birds of prey some hours after eating such substances. The size of the casting must depend on the quantity of such food eaten, and it has nothing to do with the size of the bird.

Cere – the waxen portion above the beak, from the Latin *cera*.

Check – to change from one quarry to another, or to hesitate because of sighting another quarry.

Condition – the hawk is in high condition when it is fat, too high when it is over-fat and not keen. In low condition the hawk is thin, and when it is too low it is too thin.

Coystril – an old name for kestrel. 'He's a coward and a coy-stril . . .' *Twelfth-Night*, I, iii. Kestrels, feeding on mice and insects, are considered to be cowardly as compared with more useful falcons.

Crab, or *crabbing* – when hawks seize each other, either in the air or on the ground.

Creance – the light line attached to the swivel of a partly trained falcon before she is allowed to fly loose.

Crop – the sack in which a falcon first stores its food.

Deck feathers – the two centre feathers of the tail.

Enter – to introduce a falcon to quarry successfully for the first time.

Eyass – a bird taken from the eyrie, from the French *niais*.

Eyrie – the place where the hawk nests.

Falcon – the female peregrine, sometimes used for females of the other species of *falconidae*, but then the species is named, i.e. gyr-falcon.

Feak – When a bird feaks she strops her beak clean.

Feed up – to give the falcon her full ration for the day. A falcon which is fed up is no longer interested in flying quarry, hence the modern sense of fed-up. 'My falcon now is sharp and passing empty, and till she stoop she must not be full-gorg'd . . .' *The Taming of the Shrew*, IV, i.

Flights, or *flight feathers* – the main feathers used in flight, the primaries.

Foot – to strike with the feet.

Fully-down, or *full summed* – when all the feathers are full grown.

Gentle – an old name for the peregrine. 'O! for a falconer's voice, to lure this tassel-gentle back again.' *Romeo and Juliet*, II, ii.

Hack – a method of rearing young hawks completely free for a few weeks till they are old enough to train.

Hack back – to hack a hawk that is no longer wanted and so ensure that it can fend for itself in the wild.

Haggard – a bird caught in mature plumage. 'Another way I have to man my haggard . . .' *The Taming of the Shrew*, IV, i.

Hard down, or *hard penned* – when the new feathers are full grown and the shafts have hardened off to a quill. Full summed or full down are alternative terms.

Hawk – a most confusing term. Strictly speaking, a hawk is a short-winged, yellow-eyed bird of prey, as opposed to the long-winged, dark-eyed falcon. But the word is often used to cover both hawks and falcons and hawking is done with either.

Hood – the leather cap put on a hawk's head to hoodwink or blindfold it. 'Hood my unmann'd blood, bating in my cheeks, with thy black mantle . . .' *Romeo and Juliet*, III, ii.

Hood-block – the wooden block on which some types of hoods are blocked, like a hat, to shape them.

Hood-shy – a hawk that dislikes being hooded, generally through a fault of the falconer, is hood-shy.

Imp – the process of repairing broken flight feathers. 'Imp out our drooping country's broken wing . . .' *Richard II*, II, i.

Intermew – to moult a trained hawk in the mews. Thus a bird in adult plumage may be either a haggard or an intermewed eyass or an intermewed passager.

Jack – the male merlin.

Jesses – leather straps round a hawk's legs. 'Though that her jesses were my dear heart-strings . . .' *Othello*, III, iii.

Leash – the leather thong used to tie a hawk to its perch.

Lure – an imitation bird or animal used to entice the hawk back. It is usually made from a pair of wings of the quarry at which the bird is to be flown and sometimes has raw meat tied to it. Attached to the lure is the lure-line, which, in turn, is tied to the lure-stick. The lure and other equipment are kept in the lure-bag. To lure is to use the lure, and a bird of the lure is trained to return to the lure rather than to the fist. 'As falcon to the lure, away she flies . . .' *Venus and Adonis*.

Make in – to approach a hawk on the ground to take it up.

Man – to tame a hawk, not to train it.

Mantle – to spread the wings and tail around the food like a cloak or mantle. Young hawks do this in the nest and they tend to continue doing so if they are handled too young. The habit is lost in the wild, after leaving the nest, and passage or haggard hawks rarely mantle.

Mark – a call used by the falconer as a request to onlookers to watch where both hawk and quarry go.

Mark down – to pin-point the spot where hawk or quarry has gone.

Mews – the place where hawks are kept and moulted. The horses on which the falconers rode were also kept in the mews, hence the Royal Mews today. 'And therefore has he closely mew'd her up, because she will not be annoy'd with suitors.' *The Taming of the Shrew*, I, i.

Musket – the male sparrow-hawk. The gun was named from this; falconets and falcons were also types of cannons. 'How now, my eyass-musket!' *The Merry Wives of Windsor*, III, iii.

Ostringer – another way of spelling austringer.

Passage hawk – a bird caught on passage or migration and still in its immature plumage.

Pennes – flight feathers – the feathers from which quill pens were made.

Pitch – has two meanings. To pitch is to land on a perch. The pitch of a falcon is the height to which she climbs before waiting on to stoop. 'How high a pitch his resolution soars!' *Richard II*, I, i.

Petty singles – the toes of a hawk.

Plume – to pluck.

Pounces – the talons of a falcon or the claws of a hawk.

Primaries – the main wing feathers, ten in each wing.

Put in – to take refuge in cover.

Put out – to flush from cover.

Put over – to empty the crop into the digestive system.

Quarry – the game flown at.

Rake away – to fly wide, or even away from the intended quarry, possibly after a different quarry.

Re-block – to reshape a hood by soaking it in water and drying it on a hood-block.

Reclaim – to retrain a hawk that has been idle for a period.

Ring-perch – a modernized form of bow-perch.

Ring up – to climb in circles.

Ringing flight – a flight that necessitates a falcon's ringing up after the quarry.

Robin – the male hobby.

Rouse – to shake the plumage into position.

Rufter hood – a type of hood used by hawk-catchers, not by falconers.

Screen-perch – the perch on which hawks are kept indoors. The screen hanging from it stops the hawk tangling itself round the perch and helps it to regain the perch if it bates off.

Slight falcon – an old name for the peregrine.

Soaring – when a hawk takes to the air and enjoys flying for the sake of flying rather than at quarry.

Stoop – to fall rapidly from a height, at quarry or lure, with wings nearly closed. The meaning is similar to that of swoop. 'And though his affections are higher mounted than ours, yet when they stoop, they stoop with the like wing.' *Henry V*, IV, i.

Swivel – two rings, connected in figure-of-eight fashion with a bolt or rivet, which prevent the leash and jesses from twisting.

Take stand – to pitch on a tree or perch and wait.

Take the lure – to catch hold of the lure.

Tiercel, tassel, tercel, tarcel – the male of the peregrine, from the French *tierce*, meaning a third. The tiercel is a third less in size than the falcon. The term is sometimes used wrongly by ornithologists to denote the male of all hawks and *falconidae*, but by no means are all male birds of prey a third less in size. 'The falcon as the tercel, for all the ducks i' the river . . .' *Troilus and Cressida*, III, ii.

Varvels – before swivels were invented a metal ring was sewn on to the end of each jess and the leash put through. The rings were flat, like washers, and often had the arms of the bird's owner or his name engraved upon them. They were sometimes made of silver or gold.

Wait on – to circle round high up over the falconer, waiting for him to flush the quarry or throw out the lure.

Weather – hawks or falcons are said to be weathering when they are sitting outside on their perches.

Yarak – an Eastern term used generally for short-winged hawks when they are keen and ready to be flown. A bird that is out of yarak is not in the right condition to be flown.

TERMS USED FOR POINTERS AND SETTERS

Backing – a dog which backs another is one which points when it sees another dog pointing although it does not necessarily scent the game itself.

False point – either a point where no birds are flushed because they have already left the place, or a point at the wrong type of game.

Flush – to put the quarry up out of cover.

Honour the point – to back another dog already pointing.

Lie to the point – when game stays in cover while the dog points.

Point, or *set* – to come to a halt at the scent of game. Pointers stand, setters sometimes sit or set. The dog's nose is generally pointing in the direction of the scent.

14th Century

14th Century

14th Century

13th Century